AUTOMATED AGENCIES

Automated Agencies is the definitive account of how automation is transforming government explanations of the law to the public. Joshua D. Blank and Leigh Osofsky draw on extensive research regarding the federal government's turn to automated legal guidance through chatbots, virtual assistants, and other online tools. Blank and Osofsky argue that automated tools offer administrative benefits for both the government and the public in terms of efficiency and ease of use, yet these automated tools may also mislead members of the public. Government agencies often exacerbate this problem by making guidance seem more personalized than it is, not recognizing how users may rely on the guidance, and not disclosing that the guidance cannot be relied upon as a legal matter. After analyzing the potential costs and benefits of the use of automated legal guidance by government agencies, *Automated Agencies* charts a path forward for policymakers by offering detailed policy recommendations.

Joshua D. Blank is Professor of Law at the University of California, Irvine School of Law. His scholarship focuses on tax administration and compliance, taxpayer privacy and tax transparency, and administrative agency communication.

Leigh Osofsky is the William D. Spry III Distinguished Professor of Law at the University of North Carolina School of Law. Her research focuses on the tax system, administrative law, and the ways that the federal government makes and communicates complex legal regimes.

Automated Agencies

THE TRANSFORMATION OF GOVERNMENT GUIDANCE

JOSHUA D. BLANK
University of California, Irvine School of Law

LEIGH OSOFSKY
University of North Carolina School of Law

CAMBRIDGE
UNIVERSITY PRESS

Shaftesbury Road, Cambridge CB2 8EA, United Kingdom

One Liberty Plaza, 20th Floor, New York, NY 10006, USA

477 Williamstown Road, Port Melbourne, VIC 3207, Australia

314–321, 3rd Floor, Plot 3, Splendor Forum, Jasola District Centre, New Delhi – 110025, India

103 Penang Road, #05–06/07, Visioncrest Commercial, Singapore 238467

Cambridge University Press is part of Cambridge University Press & Assessment, a department of the University of Cambridge.

We share the University's mission to contribute to society through the pursuit of education, learning and research at the highest international levels of excellence.

www.cambridge.org
Information on this title: www.cambridge.org/9781009347129

DOI: 10.1017/9781009347105

© Joshua D. Blank and Leigh Osofsky 2025

This publication is in copyright. Subject to statutory exception and to the provisions of relevant collective licensing agreements, no reproduction of any part may take place without the written permission of Cambridge University Press & Assessment.

When citing this work, please include a reference to the DOI 10.1017/9781009347105

First published 2025

A catalogue record for this publication is available from the British Library

Library of Congress Cataloging-in-Publication Data
NAMES: Blank, Joshua D., author. | Osofsky, Leigh, 1981– author.
TITLE: Automated agencies : the transformation of government guidance / Joshua D. Blank, University of California, Irvine; Leigh Osofsky, University of North Carolina, Chapel Hill.
DESCRIPTION: Cambridge, United Kingdom ; New York, NY : Cambridge University Press, 2025.
IDENTIFIERS: LCCN 2024052456 | ISBN 9781009347129 (hardback) | ISBN 9781009347082 (paperback) | ISBN 9781009347105 (ebook)
SUBJECTS: LCSH: Law – Automation. | Law – Data processing. | Information storage and retrieval systems – Law. | Chatbots.
CLASSIFICATION: LCC K87 .B59 2025 | DDC 353.4/274802854678–dc23/eng/20241105
LC record available at https://lccn.loc.gov/2024052456

ISBN 978-1-009-34712-9 Hardback
ISBN 978-1-009-34708-2 Paperback

Cambridge University Press & Assessment has no responsibility for the persistence or accuracy of URLs for external or third-party internet websites referred to in this publication and does not guarantee that any content on such websites is, or will remain, accurate or appropriate.

To my mother
—Josh

To Zach, Noah, and Avry
—Leigh

Contents

Acknowledgments		*page* ix
	Introduction	1
1	The Rise of Automated Customer Service	12
2	Automated Legal Guidance	26
3	Simplexity: The Law in Plain Language	57
4	Simplexity in Automated Legal Guidance	71
5	View from the Inside: Interviews with Federal Agency Officials	95
6	How Automated Legal Guidance Helps Agencies and the Public	110
7	The Hidden Costs of Automated Legal Guidance	121
8	The Democracy Deficit	144
9	How Should Automated Legal Guidance Evolve?	170
10	The Future of Agency Communications	190
	Conclusion	205
Index		209

Acknowledgments

Since we first started researching how the government uses technology to communicate the law to the public in preparation for a conference on tax law and artificial intelligence in 2019, many people have helped us expand and refine those early ideas into this book.

First, we thank our families for their love, support, and patience throughout the research, drafting, and publication process.

We would also like to acknowledge and express our gratitude to many colleagues who helped us grapple with the theoretical and policy issues in this book, including Vicki Been, Stuart Benjamin, Yariv Brauner, Martin Brinkley, Neil Buchanan, Jeff Butler, Emily Cauble, Danshera Cords, John Coyle, Kate Elengold, Alan Feld, Heather Field, Victor Fleischer, Samantha Galvin, Ari Glogower, Christopher Hanna, Daniel Hemel, Kristin Hickman, Stephanie Hoffer, Robert Jackson, Eisha Jain, Osamudia James, David Kamin, Mitchell Kane, Margaret Kwoka, Annie Lai, Sarah Lawsky, Michelle Layser, Leandra Lederman, Charlene Luke, Roberta Mann, Omri Marian, Orly Mazur, Susie Morse, Aaron Nielson, Noam Noked, Shu-Yi Oei, Nina Olson, Leopoldo Parada, Gregg Polsky, Katie Pratt, Jedediah Purdy, Tony Reese, Richard Revesz, Diane Ring, Jim Rossi, Richard Schmalbeck, Bernard Schneider, Catherine Sharkey, Ted Sims, Sloan Speck, Kathleen Thomas, Charles Tyler, David Walker, Richard Winchester, and Lawrence Zelenak; participants in the 2024 International Conference on Taxpayer Rights, Duke Law Journal's 2024 Administrative Law Symposium, the 2023 American Bar Association Tax Section May Meeting, the 2022 Critical Tax Conference, the 2021 National Tax Association Annual Meeting, the 2021 Law and Society Annual Meeting, the 2nd Annual University of California, Irvine School of Law/A. Lavar Taylor Tax Symposium, and the Indiana University Maurer School of Law/University of Leeds School of Law Tax Workshop Series; and faculty workshops at Duke Law School, New York University School of Law, the University of California, Irvine School of Law, Boston University School of Law, the University of Florida Levin College of Law, the University of Minnesota School of Law, Southern Methodist University Dedman School of Law, and Queen Mary University of London School of Law.

Acknowledgments

We are also deeply indebted to Reeve Bull, Kazia Nowacki, Alexandra Sybo, and Mark Thomson at the Administrative Conference of the United States (ACUS) for their extensive assistance in our study of automated legal guidance across the US federal government. We could not have completed our study without the generous participation of the agency officials who took the time to speak with us about agency development of automated guidance. We are very grateful for the time they took with us and the information they were able to provide to further this research. The views expressed in this book are ours alone and do not necessarily represent the views of ACUS or any of its members.

We are especially grateful to Matt Gallaway and the other members of the editing and production team at Cambridge University Press for guiding us through the publication process and for helping us revise our draft manuscript into a published book. We also thank several anonymous peer reviewers who provided invaluable suggestions and comments on early versions of our work. We are grateful to Jennifer Allison, Katrina Hauprich, and Aaron Kirschenfeld for their extremely helpful editing and research assistance. We also thank the University of California, Irvine School of Law and the University of North Carolina School of Law, which provided funding for research assistance and summer research grants.

We also express our gratitude to many law review editors who have provided invaluable research and editing suggestions, as well as substantive feedback on our research. This book includes discussion that has been adapted or excerpted from the following articles: Joshua D. Blank & Leigh Osofsky, *Simplexity: Plain Language and the Tax Law*, 66 EMORY L. J. 189 (2017); Joshua D. Blank & Leigh Osofsky, *Automated Legal Guidance*, 106 CORNELL L. REV. 179 (2020); Joshua D. Blank & Leigh Osofsky, *The Inequity of Informal Guidance*, 75 VAND. L. REV. 1093 (2022); Joshua D. Blank & Leigh Osofsky, *Automated Agencies*, 107 MINN. L. REV. 2118 (2023); and Joshua D. Blank & Leigh Osofsky, *Democratizing Administrative Law*, 73 DUKE L. J. 1615 (2024).

Finally, we thank our many students at different institutions where we have each taught, who have helped us consider whether the government's informal explanations, through automated legal guidance and other tools, align with, or diverge from, the complex web of statutes, regulations, judicial decisions, and other authorities that comprise the formal law.

Introduction

In 2022, after Jake Moffatt's grandmother died in Ontario, Mr. Moffatt booked a roundtrip flight on Air Canada to travel to Toronto for the funeral. While researching flights, Mr. Moffatt encountered a chatbot (an automated information system) on Air Canada's website. Mr. Moffatt asked the chatbot whether it was possible to obtain a bereavement fare for the trip, to which the chatbot provided this reply:

> Air Canada offers reduced _bereavement fares_ if you need to travel because of an imminent death or a death in your immediate family... If you need to travel immediately or have already travelled and would like to submit your ticket for a reduced bereavement rate, kindly do so within 90 days of the date your ticket was issued by completing our Ticket Refund Application form.

Mr. Moffatt took a screenshot of the chatbot's answer, booked the ticket, and took the flight. Later, he tried to apply for the reduced bereavement fare, just as the chatbot had instructed. Unfortunately for Mr. Moffatt, it turns out that the chatbot had "hallucinated" the possibility of receiving a retroactive bereavement rate. While the actual Air Canada policy provided for bereavement rates, it did not permit retroactive claims for them. Had Mr. Moffatt clicked the underlined words "bereavement fares" in the chatbot's answer, Mr. Moffatt would have been able to click a hyperlink that would have directed Mr. Moffatt to a more detailed, and accurate, statement of Air Canada's policy, which was located on Air Canada's website. Understandably, however, Mr. Moffatt did not think it necessary to do this. The chatbot, which had been made available by the airline on the airline's website, had provided Mr. Moffatt with a clear answer to his question: a retroactive bereavement rate was possible. Further, this answer was being provided by Air Canada itself, not by some less reliable source on the internet. Like most people would have, Mr. Moffatt accepted the answer as true and reliable.

Having been misled by the company's own chatbot, Mr. Moffatt filed a legal claim against Air Canada in the British Columbia Civil Resolution Tribunal. In the case, Air Canada argued that it could not be held liable for the information provided by its chatbot because the chatbot was responsible for its own actions. The tribunal that heard the case rejected Air Canada's argument, calling it a "remarkable submission." Mr. Moffatt, according to the tribunal's holding, relied on the chatbot to provide accurate information, and Air Canada had a duty to ensure that its chatbot was providing accurate information. Accordingly, Air Canada was liable to Mr. Moffatt for the harm that the chatbot's inaccurate information had caused him.[1]

It is easy to sympathize with Mr. Moffatt. Air Canada created and offered a chatbot on the company's own website. Through its chatbot, the airline offered customers clear and straightforward explanations to the questions they posed about their specific situations. Air Canada presumably did this to make it easier for its customers to book flights. It was reasonable for Mr. Moffatt to think that the answers the chatbot offered would be accurate. But Air Canada was not willing to be bound by the statements made by its own chatbot, instead expecting that customers would somehow know that these statements may not reflect more detailed, underlying policies. Thus, Air Canada was both inviting the public to use the chatbot as an easy way to understand the company's rules and, at the same time, disclaiming the public's ability to rely on the very explanations the chatbot offered. The airline's attempt to have it both ways does seem inherently and problematically inconsistent, or, as the tribunal judiciously put it, "remarkable."[2]

Yet, the United States federal government has done something very similar to Air Canada. Administrative agencies that are responsible for running federal government operations have increasingly turned to chatbots, virtual assistants, and other automated tools to offer guidance to the public about the law. Together, these tools can be thought of as "automated legal guidance."

This automated legal guidance takes a variety of forms. Visitors to the Internal Revenue Service's (IRS) website encounter an Interactive Tax Assistant that "provides answers to several tax law questions specific to your individual circumstances." If you enter information in response to prompts, the Interactive Tax Assistant will provide personalized answers to particular tax questions, such as whether you have to file a return, if you can claim a dependent, and whether you can take various deductions.[3] "Emma," a virtual assistant on the website of the US Citizenship and Immigration Services, will "help you find the immigration information you need." Emma explains that she will "answe[r] questions based on your own words," so that "you don't need to know 'government speak.'"[4] The US Department of Education's Federal Student Aid office, meanwhile, features Aidan, a "virtual assistant that can answer questions about federal student aid."[5]

All of these automated legal guidance tools, and many more in various emerging and developmental stages across federal government agencies, advertise that they can help the public understand and comply with legal requirements. Similar to Air Canada's chatbot, these tools promise to be an easy-to-use source of information about underlying rules.

But, as Mr. Moffatt experienced with Air Canada's chatbot, there is an unexpected catch. To make federal law accessible, the tools often flatten out complexities in the underlying legal system. Further, the federal laws that these tools try to explain to the public in a straightforward way are inordinately more complicated than Air Canada's ticketing policies. As a result, when automated legal guidance tools offer "answers," or explanations, in response to questions, they may not, in fact, be accurate representations of the underlying law. As was the case with Air Canada, moreover, federal government agencies, perhaps somewhat surprisingly, do not allow the public to rely on the answers and explanations provided by their own chatbots, virtual assistants, and other tools. Rather, federal agencies disclaim the very tools that they make available as merely offering "information about the law,"[6] rather than providing the actual federal law itself. This attempt by federal agencies to distance themselves from what their own automated legal guidance tools say is not too far from Air Canada's protestations that the chatbot offered on the airline's website was somehow responsible for its own actions.

Alarmingly, members of the public who rely on automated legal guidance tools have even less redress available to them than Mr. Moffatt did in the case of the Air Canada chatbot. Under current law, if an agency later challenges a position that a member of the public took in reliance on the agency's own automated legal guidance tools, the agency would not be legally bound by what the tool said. Further, that member of the public would have a hard time relying on the statements that tool made to avoid legal penalties. Therefore, while these tools may be making the federal law appear accessible, this might take place at the cost of misrepresenting what the law is, or how it might apply in each situation. Unfortunately, members of the public may end up relying upon these tools, unknowingly, at their peril.

Why do agencies use such tools? Why does the public turn to them? While the answers to those questions are important to understand, they still do not explain how it can be that administrative agencies' own automated legal guidance tools could be misrepresenting the underlying law. Nor do they shed light on why members of the public may be even more vulnerable if they rely on these tools than Mr. Moffatt was when he acted based on the answers he received from Air Canada's chatbot. In the end, perhaps the most critical question is as follows: What does the existence of these tools, and the rules surrounding them, tell us about the US legal system?

To address these questions, this book builds on years of research we have undertaken regarding how agencies communicate the law to the public. It explores the roots of automated legal guidance systems, explaining why agencies and the public are increasingly turning to them. It also sheds light on why such tools systematically offer easy-to-understand explanations and applications of the law that may deviate from the underlying law.

In conducting our research, we interviewed federal agency officials who are responsible for creating and managing automated legal guidance tools. Their answers to the questions we posed offer insights into what agencies think about these tools and the roles they are serving. Based on these insights, we explore not only the benefits of such tools but also their costs, and examine the ways that some of these costs tie in with broader democracy deficits in the application of administrative law to the public. At its foundation, this book explores not only automated legal guidance systems but also the deep-seated problem of having the government try to explain an extremely complex system of laws to a population that often cannot fully understand it. In writing this book, our goal is to offer a guide toward ways to best resolve this problem, especially considering technological innovation that seems to promise only more automation of the law going forward.

Understanding federal agencies' automated legal guidance systems must start with an understanding of federal government agencies' duty to explain the law to the public. For instance, the IRS is bound not only to enforce the law through tax audits but also to provide important services to the public, which include explaining the law and helping the public apply it. Indeed, federal law even requires agencies to use plain writing in their public communications. These communications make clear how federal law applies to countless situations, such as the application of labor law to various working conditions, the entitlement to public benefits such as Social Security, the reach of environmental laws in many different types of building projects, and the application of tax law to personal and business transactions.

The problem is that, in all these situations, and so many more, applicable federal law is extraordinarily complex. Further, most people cannot access and understand the sources of federal law, including statutes, regulations, case law, and administrative decisions. For example, to even begin to use the formal tax law, you must find a way to access it, either through print books in a library or through a reliable online version. After accessing the tax law, you also have to understand the relative authority of its different sources, which include (1) the Internal Revenue Code, which is the governing law; (2) the Treasury Regulations, which are a binding application of the Code; and (3) case law and administrative guidance, each of which have varying levels of authority, based on how relevant they are, what jurisdiction you are in, and other factors.[7]

Even if you know how to find and use these sources of formal tax law authority, you still must be able to search these dense texts, beginning with the Internal Revenue Code, all the way down to administrative guidance, to find the governing law and any related provisions. This is all before embarking on what is probably the hardest task – reading the extremely complicated governing tax law and determining how it applies to your specific circumstances. Most people do not have the ability to engage in this kind of difficult legal analysis themselves, even though the federal law applies to so many aspects of their daily lives.

Administrative agencies fill the gap between the ubiquitous application of federal law to the public and the inability of many to access the formal law. They do this by offering extensive "guidance" to the public, which includes statements by administrative agencies that explain or interpret the law. Because guidance is not itself supposed to be binding law, it is generally not subject to certain procedures, such as notice-and-comment rulemaking, that agencies must use to promulgate administrative regulations. Rather, its purpose is merely to *advise* the public about the law. That said, administrative law scholars have recognized that, notwithstanding its relatively informal legal status, agency guidance can be highly influential on the public. In this way, guidance can have a quasi-binding function, even while it is exempt from legal procedures that are supposed to apply to the promulgation of binding law.

In response to the use of technological innovations in the private sector, like Air Canada's website chatbot, agencies increasingly are attempting to provide guidance through the use of chatbots, virtual assistants, and the like. These tools seem to offer the government a simple and affordable way to respond to pressures on agencies to explain the law, quickly and clearly, in line with private sector standards. The rise of large language models (LLMs), built on generative or conversational artificial intelligence (AI), such as ChatGPT, has only increased pressure on federal agencies to automate their legal guidance to the public. For this reason, the federal government is already using automated legal guidance tools, like the Interactive Tax Assistant, Emma, and Aidan, to respond to tens of millions of inquiries from the public about the law every year.

As these systems are built and expanded, they have a vast capacity to influence public perceptions of law. This expansion has the potential to change the public relationship with the federal law in profound ways. In many circumstances, a precise application of the underlying law may be replaced with automated legal guidance tools' approximation of that law. Without further study and critique, the government's use of these tools may expose the public to a significant risk: People may not be able to reasonably rely on the very explanations or applications of the law that federal agencies are themselves offering to the public.

As technology makes agency guidance more widely accessible online, deviations in such guidance from the underlying law can become more influential as well. When automated legal guidance tools try to answer and explain legal questions that implicate a complex, and frequently ambiguous, underlying legal system, they often present the law as simpler than it is. In our research, we have identified this phenomenon as "simplexity."

Simplexity occurs when the government presents clear and simple explanations of law that is, in fact, ambiguous or complex. Automated legal guidance relies on simplexity because of the tension between two competing forces: (1) the inherent complexity of the law and (2) the expectation that agencies should explain the law as simply as possible in ways the public can understand. Moreover, even relative to older forms of guidance, such as printed IRS publications, the use of automated legal guidance exacerbates the existence and effects of simplexity. Agencies believe that people looking to automated tools for answers to questions about law expect explanations that are "super concise."[8] This puts even more pressure on these tools to provide easy-to-understand answers, which, in turn, causes greater deviations. Further, website visitors who receive information in this way may also be highly influenced by it, especially considering that automated legal guidance provides instantaneous, often seemingly personalized, feedback.

Imagine, for instance, that you graduated from college several months ago. You were lucky enough to land a job right when you graduated, in operations management at a large manufacturing company. You like the job, but you are not sure how much your career will progress, and whether you will be able to take on a more managerial role, without a more advanced degree. A more senior (and higher-paid) colleague told you that getting a master's degree in business administration (MBA) was critical to her own career. After looking into it, you learn that your company even offers higher pay for employees with MBAs, and the company will allow you to work while studying for the degree. You would have to pay for the MBA yourself, though, and you are not sure whether you can afford it. But if you could claim a tax deduction for the cost of the degree, you think you might be able to make it work.

To decide what to do, you first need to figure out whether you can deduct the cost of tuition for an MBA. To get an answer to this question, you visit the IRS's website, through which you access the Interactive Tax Assistant. It asks you a short series of questions, to which you provide answers, indicated in italics below.

Question 1:
Were the expenses attributable to a trade or business or employment already established at the time the education was undertaken?

Your Answer: Yes
(You answer yes because you are already working at your job before you get the MBA.)

Question 2:
Was the education necessary in order to meet the minimum educational requirements of your trade or business or your employer's trade or business?

Your Answer: No
(You answer no because you already have the job, and didn't need the MBA to get it.)

Question 3:
Was the education part of a study program that may qualify you for a new trade or business?

Your Answer: No
(You answer no because you will be staying at the same job, not going to a new one, after getting the MBA.)

Question 4:
Did your employer or a law or regulation require the education for you to keep your present salary, status, or job?

Your Answer: No
(You answer no because no one is requiring you to get the MBA.)

Question 5:
Did the education maintain or improve skills needed in your present work?

Your Answer: Yes
(You answer yes because you will be more skilled after getting the MBA, which is why you will be getting paid more after you get it.)

Question 6:
Did your employer reimburse your educational expenses under an accountable plan?

Your Answer: No
(You answer no because you will be paying for the degree yourself.)

After answering these questions, the Interactive Tax Assistant provides you a definitive response: "Your work related education expenses are deductible."[9]

While this straightforward answer can help you decide whether or not to pursue the MBA, unfortunately, the tax guidance it provides may not be correct. Not only is the underlying tax law quite complex, but it is also not settled, despite the Interactive Tax Assistant's representation of it as clear.

There is a critical question about whether you will be engaged in a "trade or business" prior to enrolling in the MBA program, which is a legal requirement for deductibility.[10] The Interactive Tax Assistant's first question does, in fact, ask about whether the expenses are "attributable to a trade or business or employment already established at the time the education was undertaken." But this seemingly simple question (to which you reasonably responded "yes" in this case) glosses over a much more complicated reality. For instance, whether a trade or business or employment is "already established" may depend on how long the taxpayer has been engaged in it prior to beginning the educational program. This is not determinable by reading the statute alone, however. In the case of *Link* v. *Commissioner*, the Tax Court decided that a taxpayer who graduated from college and was employed for three months as a market research analyst was not "established in a trade or business prior to enrolling in the MBA program," and, therefore, his MBA expenses were not deductible.[11] This case suggests that you may not, in fact, be able to deduct the cost of the MBA, as it might be determined that you do not have a "trade or business" prior to entering the MBA program.

This is further complicated by the fact that cases in this area have reached different results that are sometimes difficult to reconcile.[12] As the *Link* court itself stressed, no case in this area "is dispositive of the issue in this case, as a legal or factual precedent."[13] While the Interactive Tax Assistant gave you fast and seemingly clear guidance about the deductibility of the cost of getting an MBA, its advice may not, in fact, be accurate in your particular circumstances. If you pay for the MBA and claim a corresponding deduction, you may ultimately face disallowance of the deduction on audit, and even the possibility of a penalty.

This example illustrates one of the many ways automated legal guidance can get things wrong. Members of the public may receive what appears to be tailored, clear guidance that, although it may be easy to follow, possibly also glosses over more complex, and binding, points of law. Moreover, this use of simplicity is not unique to the IRS's Interactive Tax Assistant, but rather is inherent to federal agencies' use of automated legal guidance, as we also discovered when we analyzed the advice provided by the US Citizenship and Immigration Services' virtual assistant, Emma, and the Federal Student Aid's virtual assistant, Aidan.

Worse yet, this book will show how the simplicity inherent in automated legal guidance can be particularly costly to people who are already vulnerable. In Chapter 8, for instance, we will explore the example of a chronically ill individual who hires a home health aide because she is not able to take care of her daily needs such as bathing, cooking, basic house cleaning, and administering daily medication. While a close examination of the relevant statute and legislative history reveals there is a good case that this individual can claim a tax deduction for the home health aide expense, the IRS's automated legal guidance system says otherwise. Indeed, in our research, we found that, even if this individual correctly answered all the questions asked by the Interactive Tax Assistant, the tool would inform the taxpayer, "The Household Help Expenses are not a deductible expense. Your Household Help Expenses are not a qualified medical expense."[14] As we will explain, this statement likely reflects the IRS's decision that the automated legal guidance system should offer responses that are correct for most taxpayers, even at the cost of offering incorrect responses for some. This decision has the benefit of offering answers that seem simple, straightforward, and easy to understand. But it also may cause some people, like the chronically ill individual in this case, to lose out on valuable tax deductions. As in this example, federal agencies' use of automated legal guidance systems can thus have significant, distributive costs. Moreover, the fact that automated legal guidance can make the law seem so simple and straightforward can mask these thorny distributive questions, thereby shielding them from critique.

In addition to these case studies, this book also offers a fuller picture of the federal government's adoption of automated legal guidance by describing interviews we conducted with federal agency officials who developed or worked closely with the Interactive Tax Assistant, Emma, and Aidan. Under the auspices of the Administrative Conference of the United States (ACUS), an independent federal agency that convenes expert public- and private-sector representatives to recommend improvements to administrative process and procedure, we conducted these interviews as part of a study of federal agencies' use of automated legal guidance in 2021 and 2022. These interviews yielded three significant findings:

1. Agency officials believed that legal guidance offered by automated tools must be extremely simplified, in part because users are unwilling or unable to read complex legal rules and regulations.
2. At the same time, agency officials, because they did not think that users could or should rely on information from automated tools as a source of law, were not concerned about how that information deviated from the underlying formal law. These officials held this belief despite the widespread use of such tools, which often have no disclaimer regarding the risks of relying on them.
3. There is also little to no outside review of the use or reliability of such tools by federal agencies.

To be sure, despite its simplexity-related drawbacks, automated legal guidance has some important benefits. In some ways, the vignette about the deductibility of the MBA illustrates the real dilemma federal agencies face in advising people about the law and the useful role that automation can play in responding to it. There are no easy answers to whether you can deduct the costs of the MBA, and merely telling taxpayers that the law is very complex and, frankly, not clear, is not particularly helpful. Automated legal guidance seems to offer the government a way to skirt some of these difficulties by offering a clear answer to a specific question, even when the formal law falls short of being optimally informative. Automated legal guidance also is a useful way to reveal agencies' views, or interpretations, of the formal law. By making agency positions regarding unsettled legal issues more transparent, it can also help ensure that agencies administer the law consistently.

However, the use of automated legal guidance also comes with important costs. Critically, we show how, precisely because of its perceived strengths, especially when compared to the often messy, or ambiguous, formal law, automated legal guidance can obscure what the binding legal provisions actually are. Additionally, when it deviates from the formal law, automated legal guidance can undermine essential features of democracy: the public's ability to inform itself about what the laws truly are and hold the government accountable for the legal provisions it enacts. Paradoxically, these deviations can also diminish the public's understanding of and respect for the law's complexity, in part by explaining it in such an unrealistic and simple way.

In the end, these and other features of automated legal guidance create underappreciated inequities. As a practical matter, individuals who lack access to legal counsel will tend to follow the guidance that government chatbots, virtual assistants, and other automated tools provide, even if doing so is contrary to their own financial and other interests. By contrast, where the formal law is ambiguous, wealthy individuals and businesses that have access to sophisticated advisors are far less likely to follow guidance that is favorable to the government position. Further, during audits, challenges, and litigation, federal agencies are not bound to take positions that are consistent with statements expressed by virtual assistants, chatbots, and other online tools. Finally, the informal nature of automated legal guidance means that it is of limited use in supporting defenses against penalties for noncompliance. Individuals who can access formal law with the assistance of counsel, however, may use both statements from formal law and the advice of counsel to establish penalty defenses.

Our legal system relies on principles and provisions of administrative law to help ensure that administrative agencies treat members of the public fairly. However, administrative law fails to respond to some of the problems of automated legal guidance. This is due to administrative law's broader inattention to the ways that agencies influence the public through informal explanations of the law. As we explore, the administrative law regime centers and privileges sophisticated parties and focuses on the ways agencies create binding law to govern those parties. This leaves the many ways that agencies influence the public with explanations of the law largely unconsidered, which, perversely, creates a legal system that provides the most protections for those with the most resources. While it would be a mistake to bog down basic explanations of the law to the public with exhaustive procedural formulation requirements, it is also important to acknowledge the ways that these explanations can affect people's beliefs about rights and duties in ways that do not always align with the law.

By providing a careful, and sometimes critical, look at automated legal guidance, our goal in this book is not to convince readers that the government should reject automation in how it offers explanations of the law to people. In addition to the fact that automated legal guidance has benefits for both the government and the public at large, as well as potential costs, the fact is that automation is changing the way we all relate to information about the world, whether we like it or not. In light of these realities, our goal is to offer a clear-eyed assessment of automated legal guidance, in hopes of improving it.

To this end, we argue that agencies should adopt multiple policy interventions. We begin by offering detailed policy recommendations for federal agencies that have introduced, or may introduce, chatbots, virtual assistants, and other automated tools to communicate the law to the public. Our recommendations are organized into five general categories: (1) transparency; (2) reliance; (3) disclaimers; (4) process; and (5) accessibility, inclusion, and equity. We then describe how policymakers should increase participation by the members of the public in the process of designing automated legal guidance tools and should also give users the ability to formally challenge agencies when they deviate from the formal law. Finally, we consider how policymakers and government officials should prepare for a future in which technology evolves such that agencies shift from deploying automated legal guidance tools on their websites to automating individuals' compliance actions.

With these recommendations, together with their underlying analysis, we hope that this book can help set a solid foundation for the transformation of government guidance that is happening now, and that will take place in the future. In our complex world, we expect the public to be able to understand and apply complex law, even if the reality is that most people cannot do so. The combination of this reality, with the rise of automation, means that automated legal guidance will continue to play an important, and increasing, role in our legal landscape. This book provides guidance about how to make this landscape as transparent, legitimate, and equitable as possible.

NOTES

1. *Moffatt v. Air Canada*, 2024 BCCRT 149 (Can.).
2. *Id.* at para. 27.
3. *Interactive Tax Assistant (ITA)*, IRS, https://www.irs.gov/help/ita [https://perma.cc/Y88Y-JS4C] (last updated Jan. 16, 2024).
4. *Meet Emma, Our Virtual Assistant*, U.S. CITIZENSHIP & IMMIGR. SERVS., https://www.uscis.gov/tools/meet-emma-our-virtual-assistant [https://perma.cc/42DP-J5XM] (last updated Apr. 13, 2018).

5. *Meet Aidan*, FED. STUDENT AID, https://studentaid.gov/h/aidan [https://perma.cc/FA4L-4YUK (uploaded archive)].
6. *See* Chapter 5, "Agency Interviews."
7. For a good primer on the types, and uses, of tax law authorities, *see* GAIL LEVIN RICHMOND & KEVIN M. YAMAMOTO, FEDERAL TAX RESEARCH: GUIDE TO MATERIALS AND TECHNIQUES (11th ed. 2021).
8. *See* Chapter 5, "Agency Interviews."
9. *Are My Work-Related Education Expenses Deductible?*, IRS, https://www.irs.gov/help/ita/are-my-work-related-education-expenses-deductible [https://perma.cc/CK7L-554K (uploaded archive)] (click "Begin"; then click "Continue"; then select a tax year; then provide the answers indicated in the text to get this response from the Interactive Tax Assistant) (last updated Jan. 16, 2024).
10. The Internal Revenue Code section only allows deductions for ordinary and necessary expenses "in carrying on any trade or business." I.R.C. § 162(a).
11. 90 T.C. 460, 464 (1988).
12. *See, e.g., Reisine* v. *Comm'r*, 29 T.C.M. (CCH) 1429 (1970) (finding that taxpayer who was employed as an engineer for a year prior to leaving to obtain an advanced degree in engineering was not sufficiently established as an engineer prior to leaving so as to support deductibility of the advanced degree); *Ruehmann* v. *Comm'r*, 30 T.C.M. (CCH) 675 (1971) (finding that taxpayer who was employed as a lawyer for several months prior to obtaining an advanced law degree was engaged in the trade or business of practicing law prior to obtaining the advanced degree).
13. *Link*, 90 T.C. at 464. One factual difference between our hypothetical employee and the taxpayer in *Link* was that, in *Link*, the taxpayer stopped working while getting the MBA (except in the capacity as a research assistant at the MBA school). *Id.* at 462. The *Link* Court noted this factor in its decision, *id.* at 464, although it is unclear how much this difference should affect the outcome, especially since the legal question appears to be whether the taxpayer was established in a trade or business *prior* to entering the MBA program.
14. *See* Chapter 8, "The Democracy Deficit."

1

The Rise of Automated Customer Service

Not all that long ago, if you wanted to complete a consumer transaction, you had to interact with a human being. You might have waited in line to pay for what you wanted to purchase or to speak with someone on the phone. You might even have had to send a letter or other correspondence by mail and wait for a reply. In a relatively short time, technology has fundamentally altered this landscape and, with it, consumer expectations. Major technological developments have made increasingly sophisticated automation of customer service not only possible but also practically essential.

This chapter describes this evolution and its impact on consumer expectations. There are two major benefits to this development. The first is that consumers can now reasonably expect round-the-clock, rapid, personalized customer service through a variety of easy-to-access portals that are often accessible through their mobile phones and other electronic devices. The second is that companies can use automation to meet these expectations while keeping costs low. This fundamental change in how consumers interact with the world has set the stage for a transformation of how the government interacts with the public as well.

A NEW WORLD OF CONSUMER EXPERIENCE

Imagine that you were growing up in 1965, and your mother had some checks to cash as well as other bank business to conduct. If you accompanied her to the bank, you would have waited in line to meet with a teller. Your mother would have spoken to the teller about what she wanted to do, filled out a deposit form, endorsed the checks, and deposited them. To conduct her other bank business, your mother (and you) might have had to wait more time to meet with yet another bank official. Your mother would have had to explain this additional business and probably fill out more forms. Then, the bank official would have written some information on other papers or in an official-looking book and done whatever other tasks were necessary to complete the transaction. This might have even required the bank teller to confer with colleagues. Many minutes, and perhaps even up to an hour later, your mother would finally have walked out of the bank with cash and deposit or other slips recording the business conducted, and you would be unwrapping a bright yellow lollipop. But before you received this sweet, sticky reward, you likely had to endure some boredom during the errand.

What if, instead, you were growing up in 2025? If your mother has some checks to cash, and some other business to conduct with her bank, there probably is no need for her to drag you along on a boring trip to the bank. She will most likely access her bank account on her phone (perhaps through an app and some form of facial or fingerprint authentication), upload images of the checks she wants to cash, click on some buttons to conduct her other bank business, and then put the phone back down. In fact, she might not even have to go through the bother of cashing the checks at all, because the payments she gets are more likely to be automated, using a direct, electronic deposit to her bank account, or one of the many available digital payment applications, such as Zelle, Venmo, or PayPal. The whole business, to the extent she even needs to conduct it, will likely take a few minutes, at most, or even perhaps a matter of seconds. She will not need to leave the house, and, in almost all cases, she will not even have to speak to a human being. As for you, you won't have to leave whatever entertainment or activity you were engaged in, and you won't even know about the lollipop you are missing out on.

These descriptions of banking activities illustrate a more general transformation: The consumer experience has become heavily digitized and now primarily involves self-service through technology.[1] This means that human interaction is a much less frequent aspect of the regular customer service experience. At the extreme, technology may even detect what consumers want or need before the consumers themselves know they want or need it.[2] Technology has replaced not only the humans with whom consumers interact in their transactions but also, to some extent, even consumers' own agency in the consumer process.

AUTOMATION AND ARTIFICIAL INTELLIGENCE

How did such a rapid transformation in consumer experience occur over such a relatively short period of time? A big part of the story is the rapid development of technology that enabled automation, which involves the operation of machines or computers without human intervention.[3] These machines can then replace what used to be human functions.

The technology of automation has improved substantially over recent decades, allowing machines to perform more complex tasks. For example, the creation of automatic teller machines (ATMs) in the 1960s was one of the first, and most critical, steps in removing humans from consumers' banking business.[4] Automatic teller machines represent a triumph of automation. They transformed over time from clunky objects that served a relatively limited function to sleek machines that could not only withstand the elements but also perform a wide variety of key banking services, including dispensing cash, taking deposits, and notifying customers of their account balances. They do it all through user-friendly electronic interfaces, thereby eliminating the need for many human interactions.[5]

Automation technology is far from monolithic, and some automated interactions are more sophisticated than others. While the ATM is a technological feat, its most central feature – dispensing cash in response to a customer's prompt – is not what we would describe as particularly "intelligent." Rather, it is a series of predictable responses to a set of stimuli.[6] While certain forms of automation can eliminate some human role in customer service, the most significant advances require what we would think of as "artificial intelligence" (AI). Unlike basic automation, AI involves using machines (hence, the word "artificial") to address complex problems in a varying world (hence, the word "intelligence").[7]

While progress has not always been steady,[8] AI has made extraordinary advances over time, as has the technology available to automate transactions with consumers. One of the most important of these advances was the development of machine learning,[9] a sophisticated method of making predictions from data that enables decision-making under conditions of uncertainty.[10] A key feature of machine learning is that it is capable of learning from data, rather than only responding to programming or explicit instructions.[11]

Machine learning has spawned even more advanced developments, including deep learning, which interprets patterns in data through the use of multilayer neural networks, in ways that mimic the human brain's neural architecture.[12] Deep learning has produced remarkable successes across different areas, including image recognition, reconstructing brain circuits, and advanced processing of natural language, including sentiment analysis and question answering.[13] Most recently, generative AI, which uses foundation models to process extremely large amounts of data and perform particularly complex tasks, such as generating new content, has taken this technology even further.[14]

These advances have intensified changes in how consumers interact with the world around them. Rather than just receiving money from an ATM instead of a human teller, banking customers can expect a slew of other automated banking services that, in addition to being both personalized and intelligent, span the physical and digital worlds across multiple contexts and devices. For instance, a banking customer's bank app may make recommendations for stores to visit based on spending patterns, provide personalized offers based on health and sleep habits, and provide periodic assessments regarding whether savings and spending goals are met.[15] Automation innovations currently employed in the banking industry include, among others, "smile-to-pay facial scanning to initiate transaction"; "microexpression analysis with virtual loan officers"; "biometrics (voice, video, print) to authenticate and authorize"; "machine learning to detect fraud patterns"; "conversational bots for basic servicing requests"; "humanoid robots in branches to serve customers"; "machine vision and natural language processing to scan and process documents"; and "real-time transaction analysis for risk monitoring."[16] Each step of the way, the development of these technologies helped craft the digitized consumer experience, which allows customers to conduct complex banking business while minimizing human interaction.

WIDESPREAD APPLICATION IN CUSTOMER SERVICE INDUSTRY

Widespread Application

While the banking industry exemplifies the impact of automation on the consumer experience, this trend applies widely across the customer service industry. For instance, travel companies have long relied on AI to replace human customer service agents in travel planning functions, such as flight and hotel booking. Expedia, a travel technology company, boasts that it uses AI and machine learning "to deliver personalized and relevant trip options out of 1.26 quadrillion variables like hotel location, room type, date ranges, price points and much more" and to "compare today's flight price with historical price trends and track price fluctuations, so travelers can confidently decide when to book and earn rewards."[17] Expedia also promises that "[f]or unexpected trip changes, travelers can resolve issues quickly using Expedia's AI-powered Virtual agent available 24/7."[18] The development of more sophisticated AI has expanded the possibilities further. It is now possible to imagine a traveler describing the type of trip that interests them to an automated agent and having the automated agent produce an itinerary, complete with all the reservations.

Customer service is one of the industries with the highest rate of AI adoption.[19] Any number of customer service transactions now use automation for a range of tasks, from simple online shopping to more complicated interactions. By using vast volumes of data, including that indicating a particular customer's habits and preferences, automated customer service tools offer personalized recommendations for even complex questions. A company's ability to capitalize on this type of technology matters. Industry analysts have suggested that the use of AI to create personalized consumer experiences has "unequivocally become the basis for competitive advantage."[20] Moreover, automated customer service accomplishes this instantly while minimizing informational demands on consumers.[21]

Examples of ways that automation is offering personalized services abound. For instance, Stitch Fix, an online styling company, promises to provide each customer with clothing that is "personalized" and "picked just for you."[22] As the company acknowledges and openly describes, it uses a dizzying array of AI algorithms to accomplish this, to such a degree that it claims that "data science is woven into the fabric of Stitch Fix."[23]

On the customer-facing side alone, Stitch Fix uses mixed-effects modeling to learn and track customers' preferences over time, drawing on data such as clothes the customer has kept, items elsewhere on the internet that the customer "liked," and written feedback from the customer that the company uses natural language processing to interpret before feeding it into a machine learning system.[24] In this way, and with so many other similar technologies, such as those behind Netflix's and Amazon's recommendation systems, automation is taking seemingly intuitive decisions about what people "like" and replacing them with data and technology.

Companies are not only automating decision-making for relatively trivial tasks (such as selecting your next Netflix show) but also automating tasks that seem particularly complex and potentially impactful. For instance, Wealthfront, a company that has automated personal investing, promises "smarter investing, brilliantly personalized" through technology.[25] The company asks you to answer just a few questions, after which point its automated software will "build you a personalized portfolio of low-cost index funds from up to 17 global asset classes."[26] The software boasts that it will handle all sorts of tasks that will allow you to enjoy long-term wealth.[27] In this regard, Wealthfront and the many companies like it[28] are offering to eliminate a laborious set of decisions that would require significant information, attention, and time from consumers.

Companies are also making and executing personalized choices for consumers by using AI to integrate data about customers with data about varying environmental conditions. For instance, Starbucks collects extensive data about customers through its rewards app and mobile programs and integrates it with information about daily weather conditions, day of the week, and the like.[29] Through this integration, and with the use of sophisticated AI, Starbucks is able to target consumers with food and beverages they are likely to want, perhaps even before they realize they might want it.[30] Moreover, Starbucks also uses AI to enable customers to place their orders by means of a voice command or a message to a virtual barista.[31]

Chatbots, Virtual Assistants, and Related Tools

While automation has taken many forms in the customer service industry, one important customer-facing tool is the use of chatbots, virtual assistants, and similar technology, which can field and respond to customer inquiries. As with Starbucks's virtual barista, these tools can mimic an interaction with a human customer service agent while still being powered by sophisticated AI. These tools have a variety of important advantages, including that they are "always on," enabling them to respond to customer inquiries twenty-four hours a day, seven days a week.[32]

Advances in natural language processing allow customers to submit their questions in the form of their natural speech, rather than by answering lengthy questionnaires. Further, advances in machine and deep learning enable the chatbots, virtual assistants, and similar technology to perform a variety of functions, such as making account changes, in addition to responding to questions.[33] The chatbots may even appear to adopt human affect, thereby further increasing customer satisfaction and freeing human employees to perform other tasks.[34] For these reasons, it has increasingly become the case that customers not only accept interactions with chatbots and virtual assistants but often actually prefer them.[35]

The use of these tools has proliferated. Companies across the spectrum – from big tech companies such as Amazon, Microsoft, and Google, to a slew of smaller companies and startups – employ chatbots as a central part of their customer service.[36] This is in part because of the increased availability of data and technology to enable their use and in part because of necessity (for instance, because of the need for greater automation during the pandemic). The more companies have used these tools, the more they have become usable, with their question–answer accuracy ratings shooting up precipitously over just a few years.[37]

Generative AI

Generative AI, one of the most important recent developments in automation, has introduced an entire new realm of possibilities. A 2023 Stanford University AI Index Steering Committee Report described how "ChatGPT, Stable Diffusion, Whisper, and DALL-E 2, are capable of an increasingly broad range of tasks, from text manipulation and analysis, to image generation, to unprecedentedly good speech recognition."[38] As a result of these developments, Silicon Valley has been "gripped" with excitement about generative AI's potential, yielding massive investments in the development of the technology.[39] Ebullient estimates suggest that generative AI may save 60 to 70 percent of workers' time and result in the automation of half of all work between 2030 and 2060.[40]

Customer service is essentially a pattern-matching problem that requires finding the right solution to a given prompt. Generative AI, which excels at this task and can also mimic a human interaction, is particularly well suited to revolutionize customer service.[41] A study of over 5,000 customer service agents found that generative AI increased productivity by 14 percent on average, with the highest gains accruing to novel and low-skilled workers.[42] McKinsey & Company estimates that, while "roughly half of customer contacts made by banking, telecommunications, and utilities companies in North America are already handled by machines," generative AI, by improving automated interactions with customers, could reduce human-serviced contacts by up to 50 percent more.[43]

These automated contacts may even yield improvements for customers relative to the current customer service possibilities. Not only can generative AI offer immediate, personalized responses, but it can also access a customer's data more quickly to offer tailored answers and suggestions. Generative AI can even provide dynamic recommendations, such as virtual "try-ons" of products, all with seemingly human-like engagement.[44] The CEO of Ada, a company that has automated billions of customer service transactions, has described that the new technology is making him feel "a little bit like a kid in a candy shop right now, just given how quickly everything's developing ...."[45]

These developments amplify the existing uses of AI in customer service experiences, and companies seem very willing to implement them. For instance, in April 2023, Expedia launched an in-app planning experience powered by ChatGPT.[46] As a result, not only can customers leverage AI and machine learning technology to quickly evaluate a multitude of options, but they can also do so through open-ended conversations.[47] Stitch Fix, by using generative AI for tasks such as creating ad headlines and product descriptions, can offer consumers automated, but personalized, descriptions of possible clothing options to consider, such as, "A smart choice for everyday wear, this crew neck T-shirt is a versatile addition to your wardrobe, pairing well with jeans, leggings and shorts."[48] Wealthfront has also suggested that generative AI will "facilitate even greater ease of use, personalization, and lower costs in financial services that the consumer will ultimately benefit from."[49] As Wealthfront has declared, "The days of needing to meet in person with an adviser will become obsolete."[50]

Benefits for Consumers

The instantaneous and personalized nature of automated customer service can provide consumers with what may appear to be quicker, and better, responses to inquiries, saving them time and energy. While the child who doesn't have to accompany his mother to the bank may get more play time at home, the mother saves herself the hassle and inconvenience of a trip to the bank as well.

Further, these savings apply across the consumer spectrum. For instance, onboarding new customers and processing new loan applications, which, in the past, took multiple time-intensive steps involving different levels of mandated review, has now, through the use of various forms of automation, become a real-time decision.[51] Whereas a human representative evaluating a credit increase request may have needed a significant amount of a customer's time and personal information, an automated system can process and respond to the request in a matter of seconds, by applying algorithmic risk analysis to data available through a variety of digital sources.[52] This time saved can translate into dollars for consumers. The consumer can thus get the credit increase faster, which will not only increase purchasing power, but could also potentially stave off negative financial consequences.

Benefits for Companies

Automating customer service functions also offers potential benefits to companies by providing them ways to produce more revenue at less cost.[53] One estimate by McKinsey & Company suggests that, in the global banking industry alone, "AI technologies could potentially deliver up to $1 trillion of additional value each year."[54]

This value will come from "increased personalization of services to customers (and employees); lower costs through efficiencies generated by higher automation, reduced errors rates, and better resource utilization," as well as "new and previously unrealized opportunities based on an improved ability to process and generate insights from vast troves of data."[55]

Automated customer service does this, in part, by reducing the need for employees to perform tasks that are relatively labor-intensive for humans while offering enhanced products for consumers.[56] Indeed, McKinsey warns that banks that fail to become what they call "AI first" (making AI core to strategy and operations) will be overtaken by competitors and deserted by customers.[57] Across industries, experts believe that, increasingly, "competitive advantage will derive from the ability to capture, analyze, and utilize personalized customer data at scale and from the use of AI to understand, shape, customize, and optimize the customer journey."[58]

Potential Issues

To be sure, there are well-known risks and concerns about developments in automation. At the extreme, a large group of signatories, including many artificial intelligence luminaries, warned in an open letter that "AI systems with human-competitive intelligence can pose profound risks to society and humanity...."[59] More concretely, generative AI has been known to "hallucinate," or fabricate, information. This can result from either relying on data that is not, itself, accurate, or putting together truthful data in ways that are ultimately inaccurate.[60] Like other forms of artificial intelligence, generative AI can also reflect biases in underlying data, such as a preference for individuals of a certain race.[61]

Opacity in how the systems are making decisions can render any lack of truthfulness or bias more problematic. If automated decisions are based in discriminatory factors, which are not fully intelligible to humans, discrimination may become both perpetuated and hidden.[62] In the context of the dissemination of information and ideas, AI that is both persuasive and untruthful can threaten democracy and institutions.[63] Automation also raises concerns related to worker displacement, data privacy, and the potential creation of anti-competitive environments.[64]

More theoretically, automation of basic human decision-making may rob us of important experiences. Some research suggests that, when facing anxiety-inducing decisions (like making investment choices in a bad market environment), consumers may feel more satisfied if they have the option to speak with a human, even if they don't actually use that option.[65] Even in situations that are not anxiety-inducing, when automation starts making decisions for us, we may lose the serendipitous outcomes that come from potential variations in human decision-making. In other words, as convenient as it is to have Stitch Fix pick your clothes for you, one only needs to receive the same style shirt so many times (because it is what the algorithm predicts you will like), or the same pattern as one of your co-workers (because the two of you apparently fit a similar algorithmic mold), to feel like you might be missing some of the uniqueness that comes from making your own sartorial choices. There is even research to suggest that nontransparent automation of customer service operations may cause customers to fail to appreciate the work being done for them, resulting in decreased loyalty to a company over time.[66]

At the extreme, an oversaturation of automation may even reduce our capacity to make decisions. As one example, legal scholars have worried that, to the extent that machine learning appears to outperform doctors in diagnosis, there may be a variety of deleterious effects on the medical profession, including the reduced incentive for doctors to independently develop diagnostic skills.[67] Finally, and perhaps most alarmingly, increased automation may threaten to fray human bonds. For a society that, according to some, is beset with a loneliness epidemic,[68] being able to conduct all your bank business on your phone, without having to interact with any other human beings, may not be such a great thing after all, for either the customers or employees.[69] The loss of a bank lollipop may turn out to be more than just a lollipop. Automation may also undermine, if not eliminate, casual encounters between people that may be critical for human well-being.[70]

Consumer Expectations

Notwithstanding these concerns, the widespread application of automation in customer service appears to be here to stay, due in no small part to how it has transformed consumer expectations. Customers have become accustomed to conducting digitized, personalized transactions quickly and easily, and they expect to be able to do so in the future.[71] According to banking industry commentators, for example, "Remote banking, shortened transaction processing times, and increased security are all customer expectations stemming from the introduction of hyperautomation technologies in the industry."[72]

This shift in expectations can be seen across consumer transactions, regardless of the industry. Practically, it is almost impossible to imagine customers reverting to a time in which they had to stand in line to conduct almost every aspect of their consumer business by interacting with another human being. Instead, customers expect real-time, personalized, excellent customer service such as automated banking reminders, personalized clothes recommendations, sophisticated investment advice, and so much more, delivered by technology, with little customer effort required.[73]

At its best, automated customer service provides all of this through a "seamless, positive, and distinctive experience that will only improve over time," especially as automation technology improves, and existing technology gathers and integrates more and more data about the consumer.[74] The widespread automation of customer service that exists today has thus become an integral part of our daily affairs, and it appears to be here to stay.

NOTES

1. *See, e.g.*, Pavel Orlov, *Customer Experience and Digital Transformation: Challenges and Opportunities*, FORBES (Oct. 28, 2022, 7:45 AM), https://www.forbes.com/sites/forbestechcouncil/2022/10/28/customer-experience-and-digital-transformation-challenges-and-opportunities [https://perma.cc/ND5Y-VUGE] (describing customers' self-service expectations and companies' use of technology to meet such expectations).
2. *See, e.g.*, Christian Terwiesch & Nicolaj Siggelkow, *Designing a Seamless Digital Experience for Customers*, HARV. BUS. REV. (Dec. 2, 2021), https://hbr.org/2021/12/designing-a-seamless-digital-experience-for-customers [https://perma.cc/L86Z-3FDH (uploaded archive)] (describing this possibility as one along a spectrum of expected, seamless digital experiences).
3. *See, e.g.*, Daron Acemoglu & Pascual Restrepo, *Artificial Intelligence, Automation, and Work*, in THE ECONOMICS OF ARTIFICIAL INTELLIGENCE: AN AGENDA, 197, 200 (Ajay Agrawal et al. eds., 2019) (describing automation as "using machines and computers to substitute for human labor in a widening range of tasks and industrial processes"); *Automation*, CAMBRIDGE DICTIONARY, https://dictionary.cambridge.org/us/dictionary/english/automation [https://perma.cc/KYE5-P76Z] (defining "automation" as "the use of machines and computers that can operate without needing human control").
4. *See, e.g.*, Bernardo Bátiz-Lazo, *A Brief History of the ATM*, ATLANTIC (Mar. 26, 2015), https://www.theatlantic.com/technology/archive/2015/03/a-brief-history-of-the-atm/388547/ [https://perma.cc/VLM3-SMYN (private, uploaded archive)] (describing history of developments of ATMs).
5. *Id.*
6. *See, e.g.*, Rupert Jones, *Who Invented the Cash Machine? I Did – and All I Earned Was £10*, GUARDIAN (Apr. 29, 2016, 7:09 AM), https://www.theguardian.com/money/2016/apr/29/who-invented-cash-machine-james-goodfellow-first-atm-pin [https://perma.cc/YNA4-XBAP] (describing how cash dispensing aspect of ATMs is basically a modern iteration of an early, card-punching system).
7. *See, e.g.*, John McCarthy, *What Is AI? Basic Questions*, PROJECT JMC, http://jmc.stanford.edu/artificial-intelligence/what-is-ai/index.html [https://perma.cc/QLK3-URFA] (describing artificial intelligence as the "science and engineering of making intelligent machines" and intelligence as "the ability to achieve goals in the world"); *see also, e.g.*, Shane Legg & Marcus Hutter, *A Collection of Definitions of Intelligence*, in ADVANCES IN ARTIFICIAL GENERAL INTELLIGENCE: CONCEPTS, ARCHITECTURES AND ALGORITHMS 17, 21–22 (providing definitions of intelligence in AI researcher definitions); Christopher Manning, *Artificial Intelligence Definitions*, STANFORD INSTITUTE FOR HUMAN-CENTERED ARTIFICIAL INTELLIGENCE, https://hai.stanford.edu/sites/default/files/2023-03/AI-Key-Terms-Glossary-Definition.pdf [https://perma.cc/D5GW-GNRY] (last updated Apr. 2022) (emphasizing the need to operate in an "uncertain, ever-varying world"); *cf., e.g.*, Om Malik, *The Hype – and Hope – of Artificial Intelligence*, NEW YORKER (Aug. 26, 2016), http://www.newyorker.com/business/currency/the-hype-and-hope-of-artificial-intelligence [https://perma.cc/42GY-HFTV (uploaded archive)] ("The only thing [interviewed experts] all seem to agree on is that artificial intelligence is a set of technologies that try to imitate or augment human intelligence.").
8. *See, e.g.*, Gil Press, *A Very Short History of Artificial Intelligence (AI)*, FORBES (Dec. 30, 2016, 9:09 AM), https://www.forbes.com/sites/gilpress/2016/12/30/a-very-short-history-of-artificial-intelligence-ai/?sh=5d1d138a6fba [https://perma.cc/3GL4-EAKQ] (describing major advancements in artificial intelligence over time); *see also, e.g.*, Melanie Mitchell,

Why AI Is Harder Than We Think 4 (Apr. 28, 2021) (unpublished manuscript), https://arxiv.org/pdf/2104.12871.pdf [https://perma.cc/DQ9Y-SJN6] (discussing the role of perception in human thinking and ways this role has stymied development of artificial intelligence).

9. THE WHITE HOUSE, THE IMPACT OF ARTIFICIAL INTELLIGENCE ON THE FUTURE OF WORKFORCES IN THE EUROPEAN UNION AND THE UNITED STATES OF AMERICA 4–5 (2022), https://www.whitehouse.gov/wp-content/uploads/2022/12/TTC-EC-CEA-AI-Report-12052022-1.pdf [https://perma.cc/A2SR-YL9Y].
10. KEVIN P. MURPHY, MACHINE LEARNING: A PROBABILISTIC PERSPECTIVE 1 (2012); David Lehr & Paul Ohm, *Playing with the Data: What Legal Scholars Should Learn about Machine Learning*, 51 U.C. DAVIS L. REV. 653, 671 (2017).
11. Erik Brynjolfsson et al., *Generative AI at Work* 1–2 (Nat'l Bureau of Econ. Rsch., Working Paper No. 31161, 2023).
12. *See, e.g.*, Laith Alzubaidi et al., *Review of Deep Learning: Concepts, CNN Architectures, Challenges, Applications, Future Directions*, 8 J. BIG DATA, no. 53, 2021 (describing deep learning).
13. Yann LeCun et al., *Deep Learning*, 521 NATURE 436, 436 (2015).
14. MICHAEL CHUI ET AL., MCKINSEY DIGITAL, THE ECONOMIC POTENTIAL OF GENERATIVE AI: THE NEXT PRODUCTIVITY FRONTIER 5 (2023), https://www.mckinsey.com/capabilities/mckinsey-digital/our-insights/the-economic-potential-of-generative-ai-the-next-productivity-frontier [https://perma.cc/29T2-HG6W].
15. Suparna Biswas et al., *AI-Bank of the Future: Can Banks Meet the AI Challenge?*, MCKINSEY & CO. (Sept. 19, 2020), https://www.mckinsey.com/industries/financial-services/our-insights/ai-bank-of-the-future-can-banks-meet-the-ai-challenge [https://perma.cc/YWZ7-D98G].
16. *Id.*
17. *ChatGPT Wrote This Press Release – No, It Didn't, But It Can Now Assist with Travel Planning in the Expedia App*, EXPEDIA GROUP (Apr. 4, 2023), https://www.expediagroup.com/investors/news-and-events/financial-releases/news/news-details/2023/Chatgpt-Wrote-This-Press-Release--No-It-Didnt-But-It-Can-Now-Assist-With-Travel-Planning-In-The-Expedia-App/default.aspx [https://perma.cc/P2VX-BE5J].
18. *Id.*
19. Brynjolfsson et al., *supra* note 11, at 1.
20. David C. Edelman & Mark Abraham, *Customer Experience in the Age of AI*, HARV. BUS. REV., Mar.–Apr. 2022, at 116, 118.
21. *See, e.g.*, COGNIGY, https://www.cognigy.com/ [https://perma.cc/LX2C-CWTX] (for a leader in enterprise conversational AI offering "turbocharged" and "personalized" conversational AI).
22. STITCH FIX, https://www.stitchfix.com/ [https://perma.cc/B6ZU-8FQU].
23. *Algorithms Tour*, STITCH FIX: MULTITHREADED, https://algorithms-tour.stitchfix.com/ [https://perma.cc/9ETU-6YNP].
24. *Algorithms Tour: Recommendation Systems*, STITCH FIX: MULTITHREADED, https://algorithms-tour.stitchfix.com/#recommendation-systems [https://perma.cc/G34M-NWJH]. All of this is in addition to artificial intelligence used to manage inventory, select certain stylists for certain customers, and perform many other functions. *Algorithms Tour*, *supra* note 23.
25. WEALTHFRONT, https://www.wealthfront.com/investing [https://perma.cc/5FDR-UNTF].
26. *Id.*
27. *Id.*

28. *See, e.g.*, *14 Best Wealthfront Alternatives*, IMPACT INV., https://theimpactinvestor.com/wealthfront-alternatives/ [https://perma.cc/GT5Z-KMZ8] (last updated Nov. 6, 2023) (offering a slew of companies performing similar services).
29. Madeleine Johnson, *Starbucks' Digital Flywheel Program Will Use Artificial Intelligence*, ZACKS (July 31, 2017), https://www.zacks.com/stock/news/270022/starbucks-digital-flywheel-program-will-use-artificial-intelligence [https://perma.cc/U4UF-2ZE2]; Barnard Marr, *Starbucks: Using Big Data, Analytics and Artificial Intelligence to Boost Performance*, FORBES (May 28, 2018, 2:39 AM), https://www.forbes.com/sites/bernardmarr/2018/05/28/starbucks-using-big-data-analytics-and-artificial-intelligence-to-boost-performance/?sh=1c29967d65cd [https://perma.cc/3CGB-7PM6 (uploaded archive)].
30. Johnson, *supra* note 29; Marr, *supra* note 29.
31. Marr, *supra* note 29.
32. Jania Okwechime, Deloitte, *How Artificial Intelligence Is Transforming the Financial Services Industry*, RISK ADVISORY INSIGHTS, https://www.deloitte.com/content/dam/assets-zone1/ng/en/docs/services/risk-advisory/2023/ng-how-artificial-Intelligence-is-Transforming-the-Financial-Services-Industry.pdf [https://perma.cc/4ZNE-TW24].
33. *Id.*
34. Gregory H. Bergmann, *How AI and Low-Code Can Transform the Banking Sector*, ECON. TIMES, https://economictimes.indiatimes.com/news/how-to/how-ai-and-low-code-can-transform-the-banking-sector/articleshow/94830591.cms [https://perma.cc/2KSP-EHFL] (last updated Oct. 13, 2022, 1:21 PM).
35. Avinash Chandra Das et al., *The Next Frontier of Customer Engagement: AI Enabled Customer Service*, MCKINSEY & CO. (Mar. 27, 2023), https://www.mckinsey.com/capabilities/operations/our-insights/the-next-frontier-of-customer-engagement-ai-enabled-customer-service#/ [https://perma.cc/T4DU-KKY4].
36. Steve Lohr, *Ending the Chatbot's "Spiral of Misery,"* N.Y. TIMES (Mar. 3, 2022), https://www.nytimes.com/2022/03/03/technology/ai-chatbot.html [https://perma.cc/NJ6Y-TGH9].
37. *Id.*
38. NESTOR MASLEJ ET AL., AI INDEX STEERING COMMITTEE, STANFORD INSTITUTE FOR HUMAN-CENTERED AI, THE AI INDEX 2023 ANNUAL REPORT (2023), https://aiindex.stanford.edu/wp-content/uploads/2023/04/HAI_AI-Index-Report_2023.pdf [https://perma.cc/EEE5-TPP6].
39. Yiwen Lu, *As Businesses Clamor for Workplace A.I., Tech Companies Rush to Provide It*, N.Y. TIMES (July 5, 2023), https://www.nytimes.com/2023/07/05/technology/business-ai-technology.html [https://perma.cc/8X4T-AHAE].
40. Yiwen Lu, *Generative A.I. Can Add $4.4 Trillion in Value to Global Economy, Study Says*, N.Y. TIMES (June 14, 2023), https://www.nytimes.com/2023/06/14/technology/generative-ai-global-economy.html [https://perma.cc/MFT4-XL5H].
41. Brynjolfsson et al., *supra* note 11, at 7; Chui et al., *supra* note 14, at 15.
42. Brynjolfsson et al., *supra* note 11, at 9.
43. Chui et al., *supra* note 14, at 15.
44. *Id.*
45. Rashi Shrivastava, *ChatGPT Is Coming to a Customer Service Chatbot Near You*, FORBES (Jan. 9, 2023, 8:00 AM), www.forbes.com/sites/rashishrivastava/2023/01/09/chatgpt-is-coming-to-a-customer-service-chatbot-near-you [https://perma.cc/TF7N-9PAN].
46. *ChatGPT Wrote This Press Release*, *supra* note 17.
47. *Id.*

48. Tianlin Duan, *A New Era of Creativity: Expert-in-the-Loop Generative AI at Stitch Fix*, STITCH FIX: MULTITHREADED (Mar. 6, 2023), https://multithreaded.stitchfix.com/blog/2023/03/06/expert-in-the-loop-generative-ai-at-stitch-fix/ [https://perma.cc/J7FN-AU5B].
49. Blake Schmidt & Amanda Albright, *AI Is Coming for Wealth Management. Here's What That Means*, BLOOMBERG (Apr. 24, 2023), https://www.wealthmanagement.com/technology/ai-coming-wealth-management-here-s-what-means [https://perma.cc/6T2M-MMKG].
50. *Id.*
51. Bergmann, *supra* note 34.
52. Violet Chung et al., *Reimagining Customer Engagement for the AI Bank of the Future*, MCKINSEY & CO. (Oct. 13, 2020), https://www.mckinsey.com/industries/financial-services/our-insights/reimagining-customer-engagement-for-the-ai-bank-of-the-future [https://perma.cc/4WZF-DVT4].
53. *See, e.g.*, Renny Thomas, *Introduction: Building the AI Bank of the Future*, MCKINSEY & CO. (May 18, 2021), https://www.mckinsey.com/industries/financial-services/our-insights/introduction-building-the-ai-bank-of-the-future [https://perma.cc/XKS6-UJ5Q] ("[T]he advancement of artificial-intelligence (AI) technologies within financial services offers banks the potential to increase revenue at lower cost by engaging and serving customers in radically new ways, using a new business model we call 'the AI bank of the future.'").
54. Biswas et al., *supra* note 15.
55. *Id.*
56. John Ashley, *How AI Is Powering Modern Banking Transformation*, FORBES (July 26, 2021, 11:00 AM), https://www.forbes.com/sites/vmware/2021/07/26/how-ai-is-powering-modern-banking-transformation [https://perma.cc/R2BY-EZAC].
57. Biswas et al., *supra* note 15.
58. Edelman & Abraham, *supra* note 20, at 120.
59. *Pause Giant AI Experiments: An Open Letter*, FUTURE OF LIFE INSTITUTE (Mar. 22, 2023), https://futureoflife.org/open-letter/pause-giant-ai-experiments/ [https://perma.cc/83E3-9CU7].
60. Karen Weise & Cade Metz, *When A.I. Chatbots Hallucinate*, N.Y. TIMES, https://www.nytimes.com/2023/05/01/business/ai-chatbots-hallucination.html [https://perma.cc/5B6V-JCE8] (last updated May 9, 2023).
61. *See, e.g.*, Olga Akselrod, *How Artificial Intelligence Can Deepen Racial and Economic Inequities*, ACLU (July 13, 2021), https://www.aclu.org/news/privacy-technology/how-artificial-intelligence-can-deepen-racial-and-economic-inequities [https://perma.cc/4X3T-7DH6] (discussing the problem of artificial intelligence compounding discriminatory bias).
62. *See, e.g.*, FRANK PASQUALE, THE BLACK BOX SOCIETY: THE SECRET ALGORITHMS THAT CONTROL MONEY AND INFORMATION 38 (2015) (discussing the problem with hidden algorithmic discrimination).
63. *See, e.g.*, David Klepper & Ali Swenson, *AI-generated Disinformation Poses Threat of Misleading Voters in 2024 Election*, PBS: NEWSHOUR (May 14, 2023, 7:52 PM), https://www.pbs.org/newshour/politics/ai-generated-disinformation-poses-threat-of-misleading-voters-in-2024-election [https://perma.cc/88PY-LKSV (uploaded archive)] (discussing the problem of disinformation in the context of elections).
64. THE WHITE HOUSE, *supra* note 9, at 4–5.
65. Michelle A. Shell & Ryan W. Buell, *Why Anxious Customers Prefer Human Customer Service*, HARV. BUS. REV. (Apr. 15, 2019), https://hbr.org/2019/04/why-anxious-customers-prefer-human-customer-service [https://perma.cc/6UTH-463N (uploaded archive)].

66. *See, e.g.*, Ryan W. Buell, *Operational Transparency*, HARV. BUS. REV. Mar.–Apr. 2019, at 102, 102–13 (describing research about this phenomenon and recommending operational transparency as a response).
67. A. Michael Froomkin et al., *When AIs Outperform Doctors: Confronting the Challenges of a Tort-Induced Over-Reliance on Machine Learning*, 61 ARIZ. L. REV. 33, 70–72 (2019).
68. *New Surgeon General Raises Alarm About the Devastating Impact of the Epidemic of Loneliness and Isolation in the United States*, U.S. DEP'T OF HEALTH & HUM. SERVS. (May 3, 2023), https://www.hhs.gov/about/news/2023/05/03/new-surgeon-general-advisory-raises-alarm-about-devastating-impact-epidemic-loneliness-isolation-united-states.html [https://perma.cc/YXN9-5EWV].
69. *See, e.g.*, Ryan W. Buell, *The Parts of Customer Service That Should Never Be Automated*, HARV. BUS. REV. (Feb. 19, 2018), https://hbr.org/2018/02/the-parts-of-customer-service-that-should-never-be-automated [https://perma.cc/L3KJ-QYGC (uploaded archive)] (describing that one reason automated customer service may not seem to fill customer need in certain circumstances is because "humans are inherently social creatures who get emotional value from seeing and interacting with one another"); Buell, *supra* note 66, at 105 ("Employees also suffer when they are cut off from the business's front lines, as they lose the motivation and enjoyment that comes from making a difference in people's lives and are denied the opportunities to learn and improve that arise from interaction with customers.").
70. *See generally, e.g.*, Hanne K. Collins et al., *Relational Diversity in Social Portfolios Predicts Well-Being*, 119 PROCEEDINGS OF THE NATIONAL ACADEMY OF SCIENCES, no. 43, 2022 (exploring the importance of weak ties to human well-being); Karen L. Fingerman, *Consequential Strangers and Peripheral Ties: The Importance of Unimportant Relationships*, 1 J. FAM. THEORY & REV. 69 (2009) (same); Gillian M. Sandstrom, *Is Efficiency Overrated? Minimal Social Interactions Lead to Belonging and Positive Affect*, 5 SOC. PSYCH. & PERSONALITY SCI. 437 (2013) (same).
71. Thomas, *supra* note 53.
72. Bergmann, *supra* note 34.
73. Chandra Das et al., *supra* note 35.
74. Edelman & Abraham, *supra* note 20, at 120.

2

Automated Legal Guidance

As described in Chapter 1, in today's world, when individuals engage in daily transactions online, such as banking, making travel plans, choosing clothes, scheduling home appliance service repairs, or making investment decisions, they almost always encounter automated agents and other forms of customer service technology. Consumers are used to automated customer service, which they expect to be fast, personalized, and accurate.

Now imagine these same people performing tasks that require them to engage with the federal government. For instance, assume that the mother from Chapter 1 has just finished her banking transactions on her phone and that these are the next items on her to-do list:

1. She needs to complete an application for disability insurance benefits.
2. She needs answers to her questions about how her current unemployment situation will affect her student loan obligations.
3. She needs someone to explain whether and how she should enter the benefits she will be receiving on her tax return.

How might she fulfill these tasks or answer any questions she might have about how federal law applies to her circumstances?

At one point in time, she may have gotten in her car and driven to a local government office to ask questions. But it is unlikely that she will do this now. Even if there were an office near her, and she had the means and desire to get there, many federal employees may themselves be working remotely.[1]

She could try calling the government offices that would likely have the answers to these questions: (1) the Social Security Administration (SSA), (2) Federal Student Aid (FSA), and (3) the Internal Revenue Service (IRS). If she does this, it's likely, if not practically guaranteed, that she will find herself with long wait times, and potentially little by way of useful help at the end of it.[2]

Moreover, even if she could reach a government employee on the phone, as a result of the trends highlighted in Chapter 1, many people simply do not have the inclination or patience to seek help from human customer service agents. Indeed, industry analysis has affirmed that people "want the same convenient, personalized experience from government services as they do when planning a trip or ordering supplies online."[3] According to one innovation and technology think tank, "When customers can do practically everything from their laptops or smartphones, digital technology disproportionally contributes to greater customer satisfaction in service delivery – especially following a pandemic that saw digital transformation accelerate across all industries."[4]

So, what is this busy individual to do? Additionally, and just as importantly, how has the federal government responded to the new world of technology and the accompanying expectations it has created? This chapter explores how the federal government, and, specifically, its administrative agencies such as the SSA, FSA, and IRS (referred to as "agencies" throughout), have digitized and automated their interactions with the public.

The government has made a conscious effort to mimic the types of automation that exist in the private sector. While this effort has been far from perfect, it does mean that the mother from Chapter 1 can expect that, after she conducts her banking tasks, she can keep clicking on her phone to fill out myriad government forms, or to get answers to many questions about the law.

FEDERAL GOVERNMENT CUSTOMER SERVICE

At first, it might be strange to think of public interactions with the government as similar to customer service experiences in the private sector. Many interactions between the government and the public hardly seem to involve customer service, at least in the way that people generally understand it. Take, for instance, a Department of Labor (DOL) investigation of an employer, an immigration officer detaining an undocumented individual, or the Department of Justice prosecuting a tax fraud case. Because each of these is an exercise of the coercive power of the state, they can be quite frightening or even dangerous, and people do all they can to avoid them. Indeed, these sorts of interactions seem nothing like ordering a pumpkin spice latte at Starbucks from a virtual barista, choosing what items to put in your Amazon cart based on the website's automated recommendations, or finding the lowest flight prices and best times for your next trip through the use of Google Flights' algorithms.

However, a more holistic picture of the federal government reveals that, while it certainly exercises coercive power, it also serves the public in many ways. Consider the roads we use when we drive to work or school in the morning, the safe food we consume, the rules that require our employers to ensure our health and safety, and the financial rules that protect our earnings. In these ways, the government serves the public throughout day-to-day life, and this service often takes the form of a direct, customer-facing approach. As the Government Accountability Office (GAO) has described, "Federal agency personnel interact with the public in a vast number of ways: providing medical and insurance benefits to veterans, informing and educating visitors within national parks and forests, and helping people understand their student loan obligations."[5]

For this reason, the federal government has a formal definition of "customer."

> A customer is any individual, business, or organization (such as a grantee or state, local, or tribal entity) that interacts with an agency or program, either directly or through a federally funded program administered by a contractor, nonprofit, or other federal entity.

Based on this definition of what a customer is, the government has also defined "customer experience."

> Customer experience is the public's perceptions of and overall satisfaction with interactions with an agency, product, or service.[6]

Applying these definitions, the federal government and its agencies have an enormous number of customers, as these examples make clear:

In October 2023, 87,289,666 individuals were enrolled in Medicaid and the Children's Health Insurance Program (CHIP), which is administered by the U.S. Department of Health and Human Services' (HHS) Centers for Medicare and Medicaid Services (CMS).[7]

In fiscal year 2022, the IRS processed more than 262.8 million tax returns and other forms and assisted more than 58.2 million taxpayers who called or visited an IRS office.[8]

The US Department of Veterans Affairs (VA) employs around 400,000 people to provide veterans with benefits, health care, and cemetery services.[9]

The Veterans Health Administration is the largest integrated health care system in the nation, providing care to more than 9 million veterans in over 1,300 health facilities.[10]

Federal Student Aid, part of the Department of Education, is the nation's largest provider of federal student aid,[11] serving nearly 43 million individuals – one in six adult Americans – with federal student loan debt.[12]

These are only a small fraction of the services that the over 430 federal agencies provide.[13] This makes the US federal government, through its agencies, one of the most far-reaching service providers in the world.

Indeed, members of Congress and presidents going back several administrations have explicitly and broadly embraced the customer service role that federal agencies play, and how it should match private industry's highest standards. As the Office of Management and Budget (OMB) stated in 2023, "A customer's experience interacting with the Federal government directly contributes to their trust in government itself."[14] That said, this idea is not new: The federal government has, in fact, been expressing this commitment for more than three decades. For example, in the Government Performance and Results Act (GPRA) of 1993, Congress pledged to "improve Federal program effectiveness and public accountability by promoting a new focus on results, service quality, and customer satisfaction."[15] Also in 1993, President Clinton declared, in Executive Order 12862, that "putting people first means ensuring that the Federal Government provides the highest quality service possible to the American people."[16] This Executive Order established that the standard for federal government services would be the "best in business," which was defined as providing "the highest quality of service delivered to customers by private organizations providing a comparable or analogous service."[17]

In the GPRA Modernization Act of 2010, Congress affirmed the importance of customer service by putting measures in place to assess agency performance and improvement.[18] One such measure required the OMB to work with agencies to develop priority goals.[19] Improving agency customer service was subsequently identified as one of the top cross-agency priorities, with the OMB explaining that agencies should "[i]ncrease citizen satisfaction and promote positive experiences with the federal government by making it faster and easier for individuals and businesses to complete transactions and receive quality services."[20] However, more than twenty years later, Congress continues to propose new legislation to try to improve the federal government's customer service standards.[21]

In emphasizing the importance of customer service, the government, including each of the most recent three presidential administrations, has explicitly referred to and benchmarked the private sector model. In 2011, President Obama issued Executive Order 13571, which built on Executive Order 12862 by requiring government managers to "learn from what is working in the private sector and apply these best practices to deliver services better, faster, and at lower cost."[22] In his 2018 Management Agenda, President Trump pledged to "[p]rovide a modern, streamlined, and responsive customer experience across government, comparable to leading private-sector organizations."[23] In 2021, President Biden's Executive Order 14058 stated that "[e]very interaction between the Federal Government and the public ... should be seen as an opportunity for the Government to save an individual's time (and thus reduce 'time taxes') and to deliver the level of service that the public expects and deserves."[24]

DIGITIZATION OF FEDERAL GOVERNMENT SERVICE

Falling Short

It's all well and good for the federal government to proclaim that it should have top-quality customer service, on par with the private sector. The reality, however, has not always lived up to expectations, as numerous examples illustrate. In fiscal year 2020, the United States Postal Service (USPS) received 10.7 million residential customer complaints, 69 percent of which were attributable to packages not being delivered by the expected delivery day or time.[25] In 2023, many travelers missed long-anticipated postpandemic trips due to the State Department's inability to handle the heavy traffic of passport renewal requests.[26] Constituents who called their representatives for help getting their passports renewed faced long wait times, often followed by dropped calls or the receipt of incorrect information.[27] Even those who were eventually able to travel successfully were not spared many weeks of daily mail checks and anxious fretting about whether they would be able to take that long overdue trip after the pandemic.

Inadequate funding for agencies is certainly part of the problem. For instance, due to decades of insufficient appropriations, the IRS has struggled with meeting even the most basic customer service needs. In 2022, at the height of this problem, the National Taxpayer Advocate observed that taxpayers' access to telephone support had "gone from bad to worse."[28] The seriousness of this problem is evident by the agency's statistics from fiscal year 2021, during which "the IRS received a record 282 million calls, but only 32 million of those calls were answered" by customer service representatives.[29] Moreover, "[i]n the first half of 2021 alone, fewer than 15,000 employees were available to handle more than 240 million calls – one person for every 16,000 calls."[30] Further, while the IRS reported "average hold times of 23 minutes," practitioners and taxpayers were often kept on hold for much longer, in addition to being deeply dissatisfied with the service that they ultimately received.[31]

Other federal agencies have experienced similar challenges, due in part to similar resource constraints. As one example, although the SSA workload has increased significantly in recent years as the population has aged, the agency's ability to serve the public has been hampered by a large number of retirements.[32] This, according to the GAO, has negatively impacted the SSA's provision of customer support services, both in offices and over the phone.[33]

The SSA is not alone in this struggle. In 2014, the GAO reviewed the customer service standards across a number of agencies, including US Customs and Border Protection (CBP), the US Forest Service, FSA, the National Park Service (NPS), and two services in the Veterans Benefits Administration (VBA) – disability compensation and Veterans' Group Life Insurance (VGLI). The goal of this assessment was to determine the extent to which these agencies were meeting federal mandates for customer service standards.[34] While the GAO found that all five agencies had some type of customer service standards in place, the agencies failed, in varying ways, to establish the appropriate performance targets, goals, and measures sufficient to ensure that the agencies would effectively meet these standards.[35] As a result, the GAO concluded that the agencies risked failing to meet their customers' needs.[36]

Digitization as a Way to Improve

Mindful of these failures, and with the private sector as a benchmarking model, the federal government has sought to digitize its customer service offerings by using computers and the internet to perform customer service tasks. The goal of these efforts has been to close the gap between the promise of high-quality government customer service and a reality that has often fallen short. On top of potentially providing a way for agencies to cut customer service costs, the government has also promoted digitization as a way to meet consumer expectations.

Calls to Digitize

Digitization of the government's customer service has not happened fortuitously. Rather, it has been the result of a direct, targeted effort. For instance, Executive Order 13571 issued by President Obama in 2011 stated that agencies must match the private sector's best customer service practices by expanding "increasingly popular lower-cost, self-service options accessed by the internet or mobile phone."[37] Agencies were thus tasked to identify "ways to use innovative technologies to accomplish ... customer service activities ... thereby lowering costs, decreasing service delivery times, and improving the customer experience."[38]

In 2018, Congress passed the 21st Century Integrated Digital Experience Act (21st Century IDEA).[39] This law requires all executive branch agencies to improve customer interaction by modernizing their websites and digitizing customer services and experiences.[40] According to Representative Ro Khanna, a California Democrat who sponsored the bill, "[g]overnment exists to serve citizens, and this bill ensures government leverages available technology to provide the cohesive, user-friendly online service that people around this country expect and deserve."[41]

The government synopsis of the Act, which is available on the Digital.gov website, underscores the importance of the changes made by the Act as follows: "Digitally is now the default way the public wants to interact with the government. More than ever, digital experiences are central to federal agencies' mission delivery. And of course, the public expects their digital interactions with the government to be on par with their favorite consumer websites and mobile apps."[42]

Similarly, according to President Biden's 2021 Executive Order 14058, the "Federal Government's management of its customer experience and service delivery should be driven fundamentally by the voice of the customer through human-centered design methodologies; empirical customer research; an understanding of behavioral science and user testing, especially for digital services...."[43] The OMB subsequently issued a circular in support of this, which stated that "[a]gencies should ensure, to the greatest extent practicable, that all services and tasks are made available through digital channels [including websites, mobile apps, email, text messaging, and social media], using industry leading practices and human-centered design."[44]

By embracing digitization of its customer service offerings, the federal government is explicitly aiming to put its service on par with automation efforts in the private sector. The reason justifying this shift is clear. Just as people expect to be able to plan a trip, order groceries, or even engage in complex banking through a few simple clicks on a laptop from the comfort of their own couches, they also expect similar service when interacting with the government.

Agency Responses to Calls to Digitize
Agencies have responded in far-reaching ways to the federal government's embrace of automating its customer service infrastructure. For instance, the IRS has expanded online filing options and now allows taxpayers to respond to all sorts of correspondence from the IRS online.[45] According to the National Taxpayer Advocate, "chat and voice bots ideally can more quickly connect with taxpayers to complete tasks such as checking the status of a return or establishing an installment agreement," and, as a result, the IRS has "deployed voice and chat bots with basic functionality, including accepting one-time payments, and plans to implement robotics with more sophisticated capacities including setting up streamlined installment agreements...."[46]

By August 2023, the IRS reported that it had nine taxpayer-facing voicebots and ten chatbots, all of which helped taxpayers with a "wide range of issues, including securing account transcripts, getting answers to questions about balances due and getting help from the Taxpayer Advocate Service."[47] In that same report, the IRS also offered data related to the use of these bots that reflected not only their ability to handle heavy traffic but also their significant added value, claiming that: "[m]ore than 13 million taxpayers [had] successfully called in and gotten information through voicebots," and "[n]early 24,000 payment plans [had] been established via voicebots[,]" which represented "a total of over $152 million in projected revenue since going live in 2022 – eclipsing the project costs of $13 million...."[48]

Other agencies are also in various stages of digitizing their customer service experience. The SSA, for example, is continuing to streamline its digital offerings: As of 2021, it is allowing customers to conduct more business securely through the "my Social Security" portal, fill out and upload more forms digitally, receive many more publications linked through online transactions, and much more.[49]

Another agency that has devoted significant effort to its digital service is the VA. Its new chatbot is designed to offer "seamless and secure access to VA's online resources," thereby "resulting in a timely, on-demand service," twenty-four hours a day, seven days a week.[50] "Our new artificial intelligence chatbot is one step toward reimagining the customer support experience at VA," explained Charles Worthington, the VA's Chief Technology Officer.[51] Shortly after the VA launched its new chatbot, more than 36,000 people had asked the bot at least one question, covering a wide variety of topics, including education, claims, general benefit eligibility, and health care.[52] The VA has pledged that the chatbot's artificial intelligence capabilities will continue to expand, allowing it to offer more automated information and benefits services to veterans.[53]

The Launch of HealthCare.gov
An infrastructure dedicated to supporting the expansion of digital, and automated, customer service by federal agencies has buoyed these developments and others like them. In 2014, following the disastrous initial launch of the government's HealthCare.gov online health insurance portal, President Obama launched the United States Digital Service (USDS). The USDS works to "improve and simplify the digital experience that people and businesses have with their government" by raising the government's digital services to private sector levels, in particular by collaborating with agencies to develop and deploy high-quality, customer-facing digital services.[54] The USDS's self-stated motivation is simple yet powerful: "Accessing government services should be as easy as ordering a book online."[55]

Since its launch, the USDS has supported numerous transformative projects, including:

- the digital modernization of the VA's website and user experience to connect veterans efficiently and effectively with the information and services they need,[56]
- digitizing the immigration process thereby enabling a faster, more transparent, and personalized journey through the immigration system,[57]
- building an online vaccine finder tool and readying it for immense traffic during the release of COVID-19 vaccines,[58] and
- launching a website to help people understand and access the expanded Earned Income Tax Credit and Child Tax Credit enacted by the 2021 American Rescue Plan.[59]

The General Services Administration (GSA) also houses efforts to support and transform the government's technical capacity. Like the USDS, the GSA's 18F team was created in the wake of the launch of HealthCare.gov to "collaborate with other agencies to fix technical problems, build products, and improve public service through technology."[60]

18F is itself an outgrowth of, and related to, other GSA initiatives to digitize government effectively, including the Presidential Innovation Fellows program (whose participants work with agencies to create "stronger public services using data science, design, engineering, product, and systems thinking").[61] The GSA's Technology Transformation Services (TTS) is the umbrella organization that houses 18F, the Presidential Innovation Fellows, and other groups "to design and deliver a digital government with and for the American people."[62] The GSA has also encouraged the federal government's adoption of chatbots and similar technology to provide customer service through the GSA's Artificial Intelligence Center of Excellence.[63]

*****

As these illustrations show, the government has fully embraced digitizing its far-reaching customer service function and, with such digitization, the automation trends from the private sector that were explored in Chapter 1. This means that the mother who has questions about her tax return, is filling out her disability benefits form, or must make decisions about her student loan obligations can keep clicking on her phone after she finishes her banking transactions to conduct her business with the government. The days of having to wait a frustratingly long time to speak to a human being who works for a government agency on the phone or having to drag a child along to a local government office to get answers appear to be mostly over.

GOVERNMENT'S ROLE AND CHALLENGES IN EXPLAINING THE LAW

In some ways, the mother's banking tasks and her government business may seem indistinguishable – she is filling out forms and engaging in transactions. As a result, extension of private sector automation trends to the government may seem unremarkable. If you want to know where your Amazon package is, you can track it online. You may even get to see a picture of it on your doorstep when it arrives (or on your neighbor's doorstep if it has been waylaid), all without ever having to talk to a human being. So, too, it might practically be taken for granted that if you have questions about your federal student loan balance, your tax payment schedule, or any detail about your interactions with the government, you should also be able to get answers to them in an automated fashion.

Some aspects of the federal government's customer service offerings are, however, unique, making them different from those of a private sector service provider.[64] For example, the government is required to interpret a complex legal regime, and then explain it to the public. In some ways, this creates special challenges for automation that will be explored in more detail in Chapter 3. For now, let's focus on the government's underlying responsibility: providing the public with an explanation of the law.

Explaining the Law to the Public

To serve the public, the government is often required to explain the law and its application. Agencies fulfill this responsibility by providing extensive guidance to the public about the applicable legal framework.

Indeed, this term, "guidance," is even a special legal term (or "term of art"). "Guidance" refers to the government's informal explanations of its view of the law. As will be explored in greater detail in Chapters 7 and 8, formal administrative law rules that require agencies to follow certain practices and procedures to explain the law do not apply to guidance. Instead, because guidance is not supposed to be binding on the public, agencies can convey it more casually. That said, because guidance tends to be an important way in which agencies communicate, administrative law experts refer to it as "the bread and butter of agency practice."[65]

In line with this characterization, agencies across the federal government offer extensive guidance to the public about their legal regimes. In the case of one agency, the Securities and Exchange Commission (SEC), this responsibility is carried out by its Office of Investor Education and Advocacy. This office performs two significant duties in this area: (1) educating "investors about investment-related topics, including the functions of the SEC" and (2) warning "investors about the latest investment frauds and scams."[66] This office's website includes links that allow members of the public to file complaints, ask questions, and request public documents,[67] and actually requests that investors search for answers to their questions on its *Fast Answers – Key Topics* page before trying to contact the agency by email or phone.[68]

Other agencies have adopted a similarly web-friendly presence. The DOL has a very user-friendly website that provides information about the law and how it applies to workers. This includes, for example, information about workers' rights to pump breast milk at work,[69] how a DOL rule would ensure fair compensation for construction workers,[70] and the application of the Family and Medical Leave Act.[71]

Another federal agency, the IRS, has also built a rich, user-friendly website that offers extensive information about the tax law and tax obligations to taxpayers, presented in a highly service-oriented way. The very top of the IRS website's homepage displays the heading "How can we help you?," followed by a list of services the IRS provides, including a link to click to "Get answers to your tax questions."[72]

In many cases, offering this public guidance comes from more than just the agencies' informal role in helping people understand the law; it is also a mandated part of the agencies' mission. The IRS, through its stated mission, exemplifies this value particularly well: ***Provide America's taxpayers top quality service by helping them understand and meet their tax responsibilities and enforce the law with integrity and fairness to all.***"[73] Notably, this mission statement places helping taxpayers understand the law before the agency's enforcement of it. This IRS mission arose out of the IRS Restructuring and Reform Act of 1998,[74] which required that the agency "review and restate its mission to place a greater emphasis on serving the public and meeting taxpayers' needs."[75]

Indeed, a Taxpayer Bill of Rights clearly heralds the centrality of the IRS's role in explaining the law. The first two of such rights are the "right to be informed" and the "right to quality service."[76] Being informed, in this context, means that taxpayers "have the right to know what they need to do to comply with the tax laws," and "are entitled to clear explanations of the law and IRS procedures in all tax forms, instructions, publications, notices, and correspondence."[77] Quality service within the context of these rights means that "[t]axpayers have the right to receive prompt, courteous, and professional assistance in their dealings with the IRS, to be spoken to in a way they can easily understand, to receive clear and easily understandable communications from the IRS, and to speak to a supervisor about inadequate service."[78] These rights, alongside the IRS's general customer service mission and the legislative requirements behind it, illustrate the ways that this agency, like many others in the federal government, is responsible for delivering clear explanations of the law to the public.

Constraints Agencies Face

Agencies face significant constraints in meeting their responsibility to provide clear explanations of the law to the public. Such obstacles include the complexity of the law itself, the comprehension and attention limitations of the public, and the limitations of human customer service agents. Taken together, this set of hurdles creates significant difficulties for agencies to perform the essential, and mandated, service of explaining the law to the public.

Complexity of the Law

The first constraint that agencies face is that the underlying federal law is often far from clear. Statutes passed by Congress set the foundation and parameters of the law that agencies carry out.[79] Federal statutes are often extraordinarily complex.[80] Because they attempt to address increasingly difficult issues in the world and must anticipate ways that people may attempt to abuse their provisions, statutes are, by necessity, often extremely lengthy. For instance, the numerous challenges the tax law attempts to address include the need for people to save for retirement, the provision of health care, and disaster relief, among many others.[81] At the same time, to reduce their tax liability, crafty taxpayers and their advisors stand ready to exploit unintentionally ambiguous provisions in the law. Thus, to be able to respond to these potential abuses, the tax law must be even more complicated.[82]

Hyper-partisanship and other congressional dynamics have compounded this problem. Because it is increasingly difficult to pass legislation, Congress must use procedures that tend to provide little structure for Congress to engage in careful consideration of the text of legislation.[83] This can make statutes even more difficult to understand, as shown by some of the confusion created by the hastily passed Patient Protection and Affordable Care Act of 2010, or the federal tax legislation enacted in 2017 (which has no official legislative title but which was informally referred to as the "Tax Cuts and Jobs Act of 2017").[84] Worse, the drafters of the law often fail to consider that the actual text of statutes matters very much, because of a belief that few ordinary people will access and read this text. This creates something of a self-fulfilling prophecy: The law is often so complex that the drafters do not think members of the general public will be able to read it, so drafters craft statutes in ways that are nonintuitive and difficult to read.[85] This results in inordinately complex statutory regimes across the law, from immigration law (which the US Court of Appeals for the Second Circuit compared to "King Minos's labyrinth"[86]), to environmental statutes that, according to one legal scholar, "maintain an almost overwhelming degree of complexity,"[87] to Medicare statutes with such "tremendous" complexity that the US Court of Appeals for the District of Columbia Circuit declared that agencies should be due more deference when interpreting them.[88]

As complex as they are, federal statutes are only the beginning of a much more comprehensive, and often convoluted, legal regime. Federal statutes empower agencies to promulgate regulations to carry out the statutory mandates, and these regulations often surpass both the length of and complexity of statutes many times over.[89] In the end, even the voluminous statutes and regulations leave many questions unanswered. Agencies are forced to fill these substantial gaps with other types of guidance, which vary in terms of reliability and comprehensibility.

All of that said, agencies do not get the last word on what the law is. The courts are tasked with interpreting statutes and, in doing so, give varying amounts of deference to the regulations and guidance that agencies create.[90] Because of the hierarchical nature of the judiciary, court decisions have differing levels of binding and precedential value for a given issue in a particular instance.

As a result, and as we saw in the introduction to this book, how the law regulating even routine aspects of daily life applies to a given situation can depend on a mass of rules that is not only difficult to read but also frustratingly challenging to piece together.

Comprehension and Attention Limitations
In attempting to explain the law to the public, agencies not only have difficulty with the source material, but they also must deal with the comprehension and attention limitations of their audience. Recent research by the Department of Education has found that roughly half of adults (or 130 million people) in the United States lack literacy proficiency,[91] which means that about 50 percent of an agency's target audience cannot reliably infer sophisticated meaning and complex ideas from written sources.[92] This is a significant problem: The US Code (the compilation of federal statutes by subject matter), for example, has been classified by researchers to be "difficult," based on a number of empirical levels of readability.[93] Regarding certain areas of law in particular, such as tax law, immigration law, and labor law, each of which applies to large swaths of the population, the mismatch between reading comprehension abilities and the complexity of the underlying law presents a serious communication problem.

On top of this comprehension challenge, attentional limitations among members of the public can also make it difficult for agencies to provide sufficiently simple and clear explanations of the law. As we saw in Chapter 1, automated customer service tools may make people's lives easier. The mother who can conduct her banking tasks from her phone no longer has to go to the bank, and she can spend the valuable resource of her additional time elsewhere.

While this time savings is probably a good thing, mass automation may be affecting individuals' capacity to make complex decisions, which is a significant drawback. Research on the impact of digital media on traditional and complex decision-making reflects this concern. Studies have found that teenagers' increased use of digital media (such as social media, video games, texting, and the internet more generally) has diminished their time and attention for more traditional sources of information (such as books and print newspapers).[94] Of course, it is not only teenagers who have been impacted by this shift. Eighty-five percent of adults interact with digital materials daily, with 31 percent of adults reporting that they are online "almost constantly."[95]

While we should be careful not to romanticize the "good old days" of reading a newspaper by the fireplace and avoid undervaluing the benefits of new forms of communicating information, it is safe to say that new digital media, such as social media and YouTube videos, are changing not only our levels of, but also our capacity for, engagement with more complex sources of information. Research suggests that, while there may be some benefits to an increased use of digital sources, such use can also impair cognitive performance, in particular by undermining the ability to focus on a complex task.[96]

What impact does this have on the many federal agencies tasked with helping the public understand the law? The result of this trend is a mismatch between an extremely complex legal system, on the one hand, and the public's expectations that getting answers to even the most complex questions should require little sustained attention on the part of the information seeker.

Limitations of Human Customer Service Agents

It is possible to envision how agencies could use human beings to bridge the gap between the complex underlying law and the public's desire to have easy-to-access and easy-to-digest explanations of how that law applies to them. Indeed, this is something lawyers can do. If you go to a lawyer with a complicated immigration law question, the lawyer is unlikely to hand you a stack of legal texts for you to interpret in response (at least as long as the lawyer wants to gain clients). Instead, the lawyer will listen to your legal question, find and consult the relevant legal sources, and then provide you with an answer you can understand, while also asking you if you have any additional questions. Indeed, client experience surveys have suggested that "a lawyer's ability to discuss the case in an understandable way" is extremely important to people seeking legal counsel.[97] For this reason, lawyers are advised to "keep it simple but real."[98]

However, providing this level of human assistance is not feasible for agencies. As an initial matter, there are significant ethical questions about the level of detail that agency employees can provide without running afoul of prohibitions against nonlawyers dispensing legal advice.[99] Even putting these concerns aside, agency employees would need significant training to be able to sort through complex legal provisions to provide accurate answers to specific questions about the law. For the same reasons that legal complexity is overwhelming to the public, it is also overwhelming to human customer service representatives, even when they have some general knowledge about the law.

Internal Revenue Service phone assistors, for instance, may be trained to handle specific inquiries (such as when a tax return has to be filed), but this does not mean that they are prepared to answer questions that raise unusual exceptions to the general rule or that raise different issues altogether. This is especially true in light of the fact that, as of 2021, customer service agents at the IRS were paid wages that were on par with those paid to minimum wage earners.[100] Indeed, for this reason, even before the introduction and expansion of automation technology, the IRS worked to limit and standardize the types of questions its agents could answer and the responses they were allowed to provide.[101]

AUTOMATED LEGAL GUIDANCE

Not surprisingly, in light of the general digitization and automation of government services explored in this chapter, the government has turned to similar approaches as a solution to the challenges it faces in explaining the law to the public. The government has embraced varying formats and levels of sophistication in its efforts to automate the legal guidance it provides to the public.

General Automation of Explaining the Law

The government uses a variety of digitization and automation approaches to meet its challenges in explaining the law to the public. One of the options it has embraced is using apps to convey information. For instance, Medicare's "What's Covered" app delivers "accurate cost and coverage information right on your mobile device," allowing users to "quickly see whether Medicare covers their service."[102]

The government also uses social media to broadly disseminate information digitally. The Transportation Security Administration (TSA), for example, uses "AskTSA," a messaging tool that answers questions about travel restrictions and requirements it receives through Facebook Messenger and X (formerly Twitter).[103] The broad availability of AskTSA, as well as its accessible, straightforward answers, attempts to reach a wide swath of the public and make it easy for the public to get helpful information.

Agencies also use automated tools on their websites to share information with the public at large. For instance, the US Department of Agriculture (USDA) has developed "AskUSDA," which is essentially an internet search tool.[104] Users can type questions, at which point the website will bring up "knowledge articles" that offer relevant responses.

In many cases, these tools provide a mix of nonlegal and legal information. For instance, AskUSDA provides answers to general food safety questions, such as how long spiral-cut hams can be kept in the refrigerator[105] and for how many months chicken can be frozen.[106] But users can also find detailed legal explanations in response to other queries. A user who types "Can I bring produce back to the United States?" in the AskUSDA question box, for example, receives several law-related results, including "Where can I find regulatory and permit information for importing plants or plant products into the United States?" and "What are the regulations for importing rice into the United States?"[107]

Interestingly, one of AskUSDA's results in response to a question about produce is a link to a knowledge article titled, "Can I bring back South African Biltong (beef jerky) into the United States of America for personal consumption?"[108] As this response explains, the USDA "establishes agricultural import regulations to prevent the introduction of potentially devastating animal and plant pests and diseases into the United States."[109] This is followed by citations to and summaries of the regulations that apply to cured and dried meat from South Africa.[110] By presenting this information in this way, the agency is making more explicit, and visible, the legal regime that serves as the backdrop for the answer to the user's question.

In many, if not most, cases, however, the digitization and automation tools downplay the legal nature of the information being offered. Consider, for instance, Medicare's "What's Covered" app. Medicare law is extremely complex. Medicare expenses are determined by an expansive legal framework: The Medicare Act (found in Title XVIII of the Social Security Act) establishes the program and directs the Secretary of Health and Human Services to administer it, which includes issuing regulations regarding what claims are covered under the program.[111] The statutory regime also dictates the exact way that the Secretary shall annually notify Medicare enrollees of the benefits available to them under the program, as well as other details, such as limitations on benefits, limitations on payments, limitations on long-term care services, and rights to request itemized statements of Medicare items and services.[112] Yet, this legal context is invisible to users of Medicare's "What's Covered" app, which simply promises that people will be able to "quickly see whether Medicare covers a specific medical item or service."[113]

Likewise, the TSA travel rules are rooted in a robust legal regime. A statute charges and empowers TSA to "provide for the screening of all passengers and property ... that will be carried aboard a passenger aircraft operated by an air carrier or foreign air carrier in air transportation or intrastate air transportation."[114] Pursuant to this authority, TSA has promulgated extensive regulations regarding air transportation,[115] which, at least in theory, are subject to a broader legal regime, including constitutional backstops.[116] The government's use of apps (like "What's Covered"), social media (like "AskTSA"), and other forms of digitization and automation sit in the shadow of these extensive legal frameworks but do not draw any attention to the legal backdrop. Users of the tools would thus have little to no idea that the information derives from a legal regime.

This shielding of the broader legal framework from users makes sense, in light of both the private sector benchmark for the government's automation efforts and the challenges the government faces in explaining the law to the public. As explored in Chapter 1, the private sector has managed to make daily life decisions (like where to invest, what outfit to buy next, and where to travel) as simple as possible. With the government purposely trying to use these private sector standards as benchmarks for its own customer service, it is understandable that the government would attempt to downplay background legal frameworks that would make interacting with the government seem difficult. Indeed, the combination of the complexity of the underlying law and the comprehension and attentional limitations of the public in responding to it only encourages the government to simplify matters as much as possible, thereby obscuring the background legal regime.

An illuminating example of this approach is a USDS project that involves creating a website to help people understand and access the expanded tax credits enacted by the 2021 American Rescue Plan.[117] "We launched the site," the USDS explains, "to address the many needs we heard from user research, including that the site should be accessible, easy-to-read, and provide resources to find free tax filing services."[118] Moreover, "[a]s a result of user tests that included people with different levels of English proficiency and accessibility needs," the USDS has worked to ensure that "the site is mobile-friendly, available in Spanish, and reads at an eighth-grade level." Why is it so important that this site meet these qualifications? As USDS points out, "clarity and accessibility reduce the need for people to seek information via other overburdened channels, such as IRS hotlines."[119] In other words, USDS not only sought to digitize and automate the government's informational function, but it also tried to do so in a way that made important legal requirements that impact a lot of people easy to understand. This means foregrounding, and simplifying, basic information and backgrounding legal nuances and complexities.

CHATBOTS, VIRTUAL ASSISTANTS, AND SIMILAR TECHNOLOGY

As part of this general project of automating explanations of the law and making these explanations easier for the public to understand and apply, the government has begun using more sophisticated technology, including chatbots, virtual assistants, and similar tools. Just as more advanced and all-encompassing technology in the private sector has greater potential to transform consumer experiences, so too does the use of more advanced technology in government guidance have greater potential to transform the public's engagement with the law.

These chatbots and similar tools take what used to be less accessible forms of government guidance, such as printed publications and notices, and transfer them to a digital format. However, providing easier and more convenient access to this information is only one of the government's goals for this initiative. On top of this digitization effort (with some accompanying simplification of the law), chatbots may be able to personalize answers to a user's particular circumstances. This additional capability can help the government's automation efforts become significantly more useful to the public, thus resulting in a more far-reaching effect. Once generated, and as they improve over time, chatbots and similar tools face small marginal costs to engage in additional interactions. As a result, unlike customer service representatives, who are necessarily limited in their capacity to engage with customers, automated guidance tools like these may have extraordinarily broad potential reach in terms of the extent to which they can influence the public.

FSA's "Aidan"

One example of these developments is FSA's virtual assistant, "Aidan." FSA, as part of the US Department of Education, is the largest student loan provider in the country.[120] In this capacity, the agency handles numerous tasks to help more than 10 million people a year pay for a college education.[121]

Among these many tasks, FSA is responsible for providing students and their families guidance "about the availability of the federal student aid programs and the process for applying for and receiving aid from those programs."[122] The agency also carries out many behind-the-scenes roles, such as developing the Free Application for Federal Student Aid (FAFSA) form, processing nearly 18 million of these forms per year, disbursing all federal student aid funds, and monitoring the program participants.[123]

All of this means that FSA has to develop and disseminate a large volume of regulatory guidance. To assist with this task, the agency developed Aidan, a virtual assistant that relies on artificial intelligence and natural language processing to answer common questions about federal student aid.[124] Aidan, which is represented by a clickable green owl icon, is currently available on FSA's website and its mobile app. Among Aidan's benefits is that it is constantly learning and acquiring new skills through continued interactions with users.[125] FSA keeps records of conversations with Aidan, which are used to help Aidan improve its quality and develop new skills.[126]

Aidan answers a wide variety of questions that reflect the diversity of tasks with which FSA is charged. Like other forms of government automation, many of the questions that Aidan answers are traditional, nonlegal, customer service type of questions, such as "What is my account balance?" or "Who is my [loan] servicer?"[127] However, in light of FSA's responsibility to provide the public with information about the federal student loan process, many of the questions Aidan answers are also more substantive and legal. For example, asking Aidan "How can I discharge my student loan?" results not only in a substantive answer but also a linked article on the topic and a list of related questions that Aidan can answer.[128] The substantive answer that Aidan provides reads as follows: "Your loan can be discharged only under specific circumstances, such as a school's closure, false certification of your eligibility to receive a loan, or failure to pay a required loan refund, or because of total and permanent disability, bankruptcy, or death." This answer, together with its linked article, and the related questions, follow from, and are the subject of, extensive federal law on this subject.[129]

In designing Aidan, the government chose to base it on similar tools used by nongovernment businesses. When introducing Aidan, former Secretary of Education Betsy DeVos explained that "[s]implicity is commonplace in the private sector" and that FSA needed to completely modernize the way that it interacted with students.[130] Aidan, she said, would play a big role in this revamping because, "[if students] have questions ... they'll be able to ask Aidan."[131] The result would be that government financial aid services would have to be "on par with world-class financial firms."[132]

Likewise, in a panel discussion about Aidan, a representative from FSA offered this explanation:

> Our financial aid programs are complex, we know it. We have a lot of content on our site ... and we have to figure out ways ... to digest that content ... to make it easy for folks to understand given their experiences with private industry, which is ... nine out of ten times very simple and straightforward.[133]

In this way, Aidan is the digital personification of the government's concerted, and widespread, efforts to automate its interactions with the public. This includes, especially, its provision of legal guidance. Chatbots such as Aidan represent a new, and more advanced, frontier in these efforts.

USCIS's "Emma"

Another example of these more advanced efforts is Emma, which was developed by United States Citizenship and Immigration Services (USCIS). USCIS is a federal agency within the Department of Homeland Security (DHS) that "administers the nation's lawful immigration system."[134] Specifically, since 2003, this agency has been responsible for the "service functions" of the US immigration system, whereas other agencies within DHS (Immigration and Customs Enforcement [ICE] and Customs and Border Protection [CBP]) have been tasked with immigration enforcement and border security.[135]

United States Citizenship and Immigration Services has an enormous service-oriented workload, which is handled by upwards of 19,000 government employees in more than 200 offices around the world.[136] In fiscal year 2022, USCIS estimated that, on an average day, the agency performs the following tasks:

- "Adjudicate[s] more than 32,500 requests for various immigration benefits."
- "Process[es] 3,700 applications to sponsor relatives and future spouses."
- "Analyze[s] nearly 550 tips, leads, cases, and detections for potential fraud, public safety, and national security concerns."

- "Process[es] refugee applications around the world in support of the refugee admissions ceiling."
- "Receive[s] 55,000 phone calls to [the] toll-free phone line and more than 150,000 inquiries and service requests via online accounts and digital self-help tools."[137]

Of particular interest in terms of USCIS's role in guidance-giving, the agency receives approximately 1.2 million visitor sessions each day to its website.[138] As this statistic makes clear, these digital interactions with the public are a critical part of USCIS's fulfillment of its service mission. This is consistent with the agency's 2019–2021 strategic plan, a major platform of which was to create a "robust digital environment" that "[p]rovides access to 'the right data at the right time' to support decision-making processes."[139] It is also consistent with the agency's 2023–2026 strategic plan, which includes a promise to "enable people to easily find needed information, and increase satisfaction with their USCIS interactive experience" by creating "broader dissemination of information, especially in harder-to-reach communities, about USCIS' services to the public."[140]

Within this context, in December 2015, USCIS launched a computer-generated virtual assistant that answers users' questions about US immigration. USCIS created Emma to offer users an alternative means of accessing information about the immigration process in general and their immigration status in particular.[141] One hope was that Emma would alleviate the burden on USCIS call centers, which were, at the time, receiving over 1 million calls a month.[142] As USCIS described on Emma's launch, this tool "was developed in response to a growing interest in self-help tools and to enhance our applicant services." As the agency explained at the time, its "call centers currently receive many questions concerning general information requests that can be provided through the Web. Now Emma will help provide that information."[143]

Named after Emma Lazarus, the nineteenth-century poet and essayist whose words are inscribed on the base of the Statue of Liberty, USCIS has suggested that Emma also stands ready to serve immigrants by providing them accessible information about the immigration process.[144] As the agency explains, Emma answers questions based on users' own words; and people who use the service do not need to know "government speak."[145]

In addition to being able to "[p]rovide immediate responses to your questions about all of [USCIS's] services," Emma can "[g]uide you through [USCIS's] website" and "[f]ind information based on the questions and search terms you use."[146] Importantly, Emma can type answers in either English or Spanish, and she can speak answers as well (although currently only in English).[147] Users can find Emma quite easily: not only does an "Ask Emma" button pop up on USCIS web pages[148] but the agency has also widely advertised the service, including on social media platforms such as Facebook and X (formerly Twitter).[149]

United States Citizenship and Immigration Services has reported that Emma has numerous indicia of success. In 2020, the agency reported that Emma was one of the most widely used chatbots in the US government, having successfully responded to in excess of 35 million inquiries from more than 11 million users.[150] As the agency explains, Emma is a "very 'highly trafficked' and 'very useful tool for many of our applicants and the general public,' which USCIS rel[ies] on very heavily."[151] However, user volume is not the only measure of Emma's success: According to USCIS, by 2020, the service had a "success rate" of 93 percent in English and 90 percent in Spanish, having brought down the tool's "I don't know" responses significantly during the five years since its launch.[152] The agency explained that Emma learns over time: first the tool trains with adjudicators and case managers, and then with the public, all of which has enabled it to continue to build its skills.[153] USCIS has further described that Emma "ha[s] a wonderful team of product owners, including subject matter experts, who take the analysis from her powerful AI pool and use that to make decisions on how to best refine her knowledgebase," describing this refinement process as what is generally understood as "human in the loop practice."[154]

However, USCIS has acknowledged that, in some ways, Emma has not met all of the agency's goals. In particular, Emma did not substantially reduce call volumes to the call center.[155] Rather, Emma seemed to just provide another means of accessing the type of information that users could (and were) seeking through telephone calls. As a result, it is not clear that Emma has managed to allow USCIS case workers to be redeployed to more complex questions and away from more standard inquiries. To meet this goal, the agency has suggested that it may have to use authentication tools to provide users with more personalized responses.[156]

In line with the vision that Emma will provide relatable and accessible information for the public, and will not use "government speak," the service tries to offer straightforward, understandable answers to a wide variety of questions. In large part, the tool does this by acting as a concierge of sorts, directing users to the right place on the website to get answers to their queries. In so doing, Emma, like Aidan, operates as a natural language "sorting" model of automated legal guidance. Users can type their questions in their own words, and, through natural language artificial intelligence, Emma attempts to sort through information to offer users the information that is most responsive to their inquiry.

What is an example of how this works? Assume a user types "Where is my visa?" into Emma's query box. In this case, Emma will respond, "USCIS offers many different types of visa categories. Please tell me the specific type of visa or visa category you're interested in learning more about or select from the links below...."[157] If, from the visa choices that Emma offers, the user clicks on "K Visa (Fiancé Visa)," Emma will open up a webpage titled "Green Card for Fiancé(e) of U.S. Citizen."[158] This webpage contains extensive information for the user, displayed in easy-to-read pop-out text (with tabs), including information about eligibility for adjustment of status, bars to adjustment, grounds of inadmissibility, how to apply, what to submit (K-1 nonimmigrant applicants), conditional approval, family members, and employment authorization and advance parole documents.[159] It also contains a tab titled "legal reference," which links users to the applicable statutory, regulatory, and USCIS policy manual provisions.

The IRS's Interactive Tax Assistant (ITA)

A different example of a well-developed agency tool designed to respond to questions about the law is the IRS's Interactive Tax Assistant (ITA). The IRS has developed and improved this tool over the course of many years, enabling ITA to answer millions of taxpayer questions.

In 2008, the IRS created its first iteration of an online customer service interface, the "Interactive Tax Law Assistant" (ITLA). This was a new online system that the agency's human customer service representatives, known as IRS assistors, would use when addressing taxpayer inquiries over the phone.[160] The primary motivation for creating this new internal system was to address inconsistent, even conflicting, responses that had been given in the past, when IRS agents would answer taxpayer questions by consulting printed IRS publications.[161] Under this new system, IRS agents would respond to taxpayer inquiries it received through the agency's telephone hotline by asking the taxpayer a series of questions that appeared on ITLA and then, after inputting the taxpayers' responses, by reading ITLA's answer to the taxpayer's original question.[162] The IRS concluded that ITLA significantly improved agents' responses to taxpayer inquiries in terms of consistency, accuracy, and speed.[163]

Two years later, in 2010, the IRS announced its creation of an external version of its internal ITLA system, which taxpayers could access directly through the IRS website: the "Interactive Tax Assistant."[164] According to the agency, ITA is a "tool that provides answers to several tax law questions specific to your individual circumstances."[165] More specifically, this resource "can determine ... if the type of income you have is taxable, if you're eligible to claim a credit, [and] if you can deduct expenses [on your tax return]."[166]

The Interactive Tax Assistant begins a customer service session by asking the taxpayer to select a category of questions, such as "Can I deduct my medical and dental expenses?" and then poses a series of questions for the taxpayer to answer.[167] Once the taxpayer has entered their responses, ITA presents a screen titled "Answers" (which offers, for example, a response indicating that a specific type of business expense is "not a deductible expense.").[168] The answers provided are tailored to "individual circumstances" and include friendly and accessible language, such as second-person pronouns (*e.g.*, "you" and "your").[169]

Over the decade leading up to increased IRS funding through the Inflation Reduction Act, IRS budget cuts, together with other circumstances such as the

COVID-19 pandemic, had significantly reduced taxpayer access to IRS human customer service representatives.[170] In response, the IRS emphasized that ITA was the resource that taxpayers should turn to for personalized tax guidance. For example, at the close of 2021, the IRS tweeted, "Have a tax law question? Our #IRS Interactive Tax Assistant has answers," followed by a link to ITA.[171]

Five years after the launch of ITA, the IRS reported that the service had responded to 660,430 requests for answers to tax law questions, a 168 percent increase over 2014.[172] During 2020, ITA received over 5 million visits according to IRS officials.[173] Part of this traffic was attributable to office closures during the pandemic, but, in a more typical year, ITA still receives over 2.5 million visits from taxpayers.[174]

The Interactive Tax Assistant differs from similar services offered by other federal agencies. For example, unlike Aidan and Emma, ITA does not interpret users' natural language and direct them to information. Rather, in what might be thought of as a "decision tree" model, ITA exerts more control over the information that users can enter and offers more definitiveness in its responses, which take the form of "answers" to users' tax situations.

As of May 2024, ITA contained over sixty separate topics, such as "Is the Distribution from My Roth Account Taxable?"; "Do I Need to File a Tax Return?"; and "How Do I Claim My Gambling Winnings and/or Losses?"[175] The IRS tries to include topics that are simple enough to address without the need for lengthy legal analysis or extensive follow-up inquiries.[176]

Limits on Sophistication of Automation

There is clear variation in the sophistication of the government's automation of legal guidance. The spectrum runs from mere digitization on the one hand, without much technological innovation beyond that, to advanced chatbots that process natural language queries on the other. It is important to note, however, that while the digital legal guidance tools offered by some government agencies feature sophisticated current automation functionality, even they fall short of the highest-level technological options that are currently available.

For instance, FSA boasts that Aidan uses "advanced technology – artificial intelligence and natural language processing – to answer your most common questions."[177] The fact that you can type your questions into Aidan in plain language English and have Aidan answer them does, indeed, represent a sophisticated use of artificial intelligence. Although it may seem relatively straightforward, to perform this function, Aidan must use sophisticated artificial intelligence technology to take plain language English, which may express the same thought in a variety of ways and make it understandable to an automated system, to produce a reliable result.

As an illustration of how natural language processing may work with a simple example, Aidan has to decide that the following inquiries mean the same thing: (1) "Do I owe any additional amounts on my student loan?" and (2) "Please tell me if there is anything more I have to pay on my student loan." Then Aidan has to figure out what they are asking and, finally, provide the right response to the question asked. Further, Aidan learns how to do this better over time.[178] When Aidan provides an answer that is responsive to the question asked, or when Aidan fails to do so, Aidan develops a better understanding of natural language. This is no small technological feat.

However, consider what Aidan does not do. At least at present, Aidan does not generate spontaneous text to answer questions. In this way, Aidan falls short of some of the most sophisticated, generative AI currently available. Instead, Aidan is limited to preprogrammed answers, which it matches with the questions asked, based on its understanding of those questions.[179]

Aidan also does not anticipate needs and respond to them prior to being prompted. For instance, Aidan is not spontaneously messaging people with information about the federal loan process that people might need. In this way, Aidan is unlike Amazon, Netflix, or other retailers, which can inform you about products you might like based on your existing purchases, choices, or internet searches.

Further, while Aidan and other similar automated government customer service interfaces can and do answer a wide variety of legal questions, these answers still leave members of the public with many decisions to make on their own. People who learn from chatbots or apps about tax credits, or about the rules for when a student loan can be discharged, must still apply those explanations to their own situations and make decisions about how to proceed.

As a result, the mother from Chapter 1, and many other people, can pick up their phones to conduct business with the federal government. However, depending on what they are trying to do, this experience may not feel exactly like ordering clothes from Stitch Fix. In this way, agencies are straddling two distinct territories: the automation of the private sector on the one hand, and the vast complexity of federal law that applies to daily transactions on the other. Agencies are managing this balance through an increasingly vast set of automated legal guidance tools. At this critical juncture, automated legal guidance is poised to fundamentally alter the public's relationship with the law.

NOTES

1. *See, e.g.*, U.S. GOV'T ACCOUNTABILITY OFF, GAO-23-106200, FEDERAL REAL PROPERTY: PRELIMINARY RESULTS SHOW FEDERAL BUILDINGS REMAIN UNDERUTILIZED DUE TO LONGSTANDING CHALLENGES AND INCREASED TELEWORK (2023), https://www.gao.gov/assets/gao-23-106200.pdf [https://perma.cc/4VZW-7QUK] (finding very low usage of office space by federal agencies).
2. *See, e.g.*, OFF. OF THE INSPECTOR GEN., SOC. SEC. ADMIN., A-05-22-51149, AUDIT REPORT: THE SOCIAL SECURITY ADMINISTRATION'S TELEPHONE SERVICE DISRUPTIONS (2023), https://oig.ssa.gov/assets/uploads/a-05-22-51149.pdf [https://perma.cc/TD8Q-FQZD] (cataloguing issues).

3. IBM, DIGITAL TRANSFORMATION: REINVENTING THE BUSINESS OF GOVERNMENT 5 (2018), https://media.erepublic.com/document/industry-marketing-government-solutionproduct-guide-35014535usen-20180612.pdf [https://perma.cc/BWR9-N3DX].
4. ERIC EGAN, INFO. TECH. & INNOVATION FOUND., WITH CUSTOMER SERVICE AT A NEW LOW, FEDERAL AGENCIES STILL FAIL TO MEASURE IT WELL OR PROVIDE ENOUGH DIGITAL SERVICES 2 (2022), https://www2.itif.org/2022-federal-hisp-digital-cx.pdf [https://perma.cc/5FVE-SDZT].
5. U.S. GOV'T ACCOUNTABILITY OFF., GAO-15-84, MANAGING FOR RESULTS: SELECTED AGENCIES NEED TO TAKE ADDITIONAL EFFORTS TO IMPROVE CUSTOMER SERVICE 1 (2014), https://www.gao.gov/assets/gao-15-84.pdf [https://perma.cc/25PK-2JGC] [hereinafter U.S. GOV'T ACCOUNTABILITY OFF., GAO-15-84].
6. Exec. Order No. 14,058, 86 Fed. Reg. 71357, 71358–59 (Dec. 13, 2021).
7. *October 2023 Medicaid & CHIP Enrollment Data Highlights*, Medicaid.gov, https://www.medicaid.gov/medicaid/program-information/medicaid-and-chip-enrollment-data/report-highlights/index.html [https://perma.cc/VM74-DSQ7] (last updated Jan. 31, 2024).
8. IRS, PUB. 55–B, INTERNAL REVENUE SERVICE DATA BOOK, 2022, at 2, 21 (2023).
9. *U.S. Department of Veterans Affairs Structure*, U.S. DEP'T VETERANS AFFS., OFF. RURAL HEALTH, https://www.ruralhealth.va.gov/aboutus/structure.asp [https://perma.cc/9PTY-PNN8] (last updated Aug. 24, 2023).
10. *Veterans Health Administration*, U.S. DEP'T VETERANS AFFS., https://www.va.gov/health/aboutvha.asp [https://perma.cc/7ADU-FJCH] (last updated Nov. 8, 2023).
11. *About Us*, FED. STUDENT AID, U.S. DEP'T EDUC., https://studentaid.gov/about [https://perma.cc/C6RX-J4CB (uploaded archive)].
12. DAVID P. SMOLE & RITA R. ZOTA, CONG. RSCH. SERV., IF10158, A SNAPSHOT OF FEDERAL STUDENT LOAN DEBT (2022), https://crsreports.congress.gov/product/pdf/IF/IF10158/4 [https://perma.cc/CVF4-FBQR].
13. *Agencies*, FED. REG., https://www.federalregister.gov/agencies [https://perma.cc/F8Q4-R3BU].
14. OFF. OF MGMT. & BUDGET, EXEC. OFF. OF THE PRESIDENT, OMB CIRCULAR NO. A-11, PREPARATION, SUBMISSION, AND EXECUTION OF THE BUDGET 280–82 (2023), https://www.whitehouse.gov/wp-content/uploads/2018/06/a11.pdf [https://perma.cc/ZY33-PXFJ].
15. Government Performance and Results Act of 1993, Pub. L. No. 103-62, § 2(a)(3), 107 Stat. 285, 285 (codified at 31 U.S.C. §§ 1101, 1115).
16. Exec. Order No. 12,862, 58 Fed. Reg. 48257, 48257 (Sept. 11, 1993).
17. *Id.*
18. GPRA Modernization Act of 2010, Pub. L. No. 111-352, 124 Stat. 3866 (2011) (codified in scattered sections of 31 U.S.C.).
19. *Id.* sec. 3, § 1115(a), 124 Stat. at 3868 (codified at 31 U.S.C. § 1115(a)).
20. U.S. GOV'T ACCOUNTABILITY OFF., GAO-16-509, MANAGING FOR RESULTS: OMB IMPROVED IMPLEMENTATION OF CROSS-AGENCY PRIORITY GOALS, BUT COULD BE MORE TRANSPARENT ABOUT MEASURING PROGRESS 40 (2016), https://www.gao.gov/assets/gao-16-509.pdf [https://perma.cc/8XKG-X9UV].
21. *See, e.g.*, Federal Agency Customer Experience Act of 2021, S. 671, 117th Cong. (2021) (as passed by Senate, June 22, 2022).
22. Exec. Order No. 13,571, 76 Fed. Reg. 24339, 24339 (Apr. 27, 2011).
23. OFF. OF MNGMT. & BUDGET, EXEC. OFF. OF THE PRESIDENT, PRESIDENT'S MANAGEMENT AGENDA 28 (2018), https://trumpwhitehouse.archives.gov/wp-content/uploads/2018/03/The-President%E2%80%99s-Management-Agenda.pdf [https://perma.cc/AW77-QZ6P].

24. Exec. Order No. 14,058, 86 Fed. Reg. 71357, 71357 (Dec. 13, 2021).
25. U.S. Gov't Accountability Off., GAO 21–465, US Postal Service: Customer Complaints Process 10 (2021), https://www.gao.gov/assets/gao-21-465.pdf [https://perma.cc/LU2L-LEPS].
26. Michael Crowley, *A Backlog of Passport Applications Foils Summer Plans and Puts Heat on the State Department*, N.Y. Times, Aug. 17, 2023, at A10.
27. *Id.*
28. *Hello, Is Anyone There? Taxpayers and Practitioners Continue to Experience Frustration Over Lack of Adequate Phone Service*, Taxpayer Advoc. Serv.: NTA Blog, https://www.taxpayeradvocate.irs.gov/news/nta-blog-hello-is-anyone-there-taxpayers-and-practitioners-continue-to-experience-frustration-over-lack-of-adequate-phone-service/ [https://perma.cc/T7NQ-GFS8] (last updated Feb. 6, 2023) [hereinafter *Hello, Is Anyone There?*].
29. *Id.*
30. *Id.*
31. *Id.*
32. U.S. Gov't Accountability Off., GAO-18-432T, Social Security Administration: Continuing Leadership Focus Needed to Modernize How SSA Does Business 1 (2018), https://www.gao.gov/assets/gao-18-432t.pdf [https://perma.cc/Y4JZ-F795].
33. *Id.*
34. U.S. Gov't Accountability Off., GAO-15-84, *supra* note 5, at 2–3.
35. *Id.* at 11–14.
36. *Id.* at 13.
37. Exec. Order No. 13,571, 37 Fed. Reg. 24339, 24339 (Apr. 27, 2011).
38. *Id.* at 24340.
39. 21st Century Integrated Digital Experience Act, Pub. L. No. 115-336, 132 Stat. 5025 (2018) (codified at 44 U.S.C. § 3501).
40. *Id.*
41. Press Release, Ro Khanna, Congressman, House of Representatives, Rep. Khanna on the Passage of the 21st Century Integrated Digital Experience Act (IDEA) (Nov. 29, 2018), https://khanna.house.gov/media/press-releases/release-rep-khanna-passage-21st-century-integrated-digital-experience-act-idea [https://perma.cc/JWZ3-P8T6].
42. *21st Century Integrated Digital Experience Act*, Digital.gov, https://digital.gov/resources/21st-century-integrated-digital-experience-act/ [https://perma.cc/JW92-7B4R] (last updated Feb. 5, 2024, 1:48 PM).
43. Exec. Order No. 14,058, 86 Fed. Reg. 71357, 71357–58 (Dec. 13, 2021).
44. Off. of Mgmt. & Budget, Exec. Off. of the President, *supra* note 14, at 280–83.
45. IRS News Release IR-2023-148 (Aug. 16, 2023), https://www.irs.gov/newsroom/inflation-reduction-act-1-year-report-card-irs-delivers-dramatically-improved-2023-filing-season-service-modernizes-technology-pursues-high-income-individuals-evading-taxes [https://perma.cc/QD9D-D7Q8].
46. *Hello, Is Anyone There?*, *supra* note 28.
47. IRS News Release IR-2023-148, *supra* note 45.
48. *Id.*
49. Sean Brune, *Progress to Implement the 21st Century Integrated Digital Experience Act (21st Century IDEA): 2021 Annual Report*, Soc. Sec. Admin., https://www.ssa.gov/digitalstrategy/idea-report.html [https://perma.cc/3LK8-63LM].
50. Reggie Humphries & IT Strategic Communication Team, *Got a VA Question? Use the New Virtual Chatbot 24/7*, VA News (Sept. 7, 2022), https://news.va.gov/108361/got-question-use-new-virtual-chatbot-24-7/ [https://perma.cc/YSU5-MR84].

51. *Id.*
52. *Id.*
53. *Id.*
54. *FACT SHEET: Improving and Simplifying Digital Services*, THE WHITE HOUSE (Aug. 11, 2014), https://obamawhitehouse.archives.gov/the-press-office/2014/08/11/fact-sheet-improving-and-simplifying-digital-services [https://perma.cc/4M2N-XXLN].
55. *Our Mission: The USDS Origin Story*, U.S. DIGIT. SERV., https://www.usds.gov/mission [https://perma.cc/3MR4-2MBY].
56. *Simplifying Veteran-Facing Services through VA.gov*, U.S. DIGIT. SERV., https://www.usds.gov/projects/va-dot-gov [https://perma.cc/VU6V-V5P2].
57. *Modernizing Our Immigration System*, U.S. DIGIT. SERV., https://www.usds.gov/projects/n-400 [https://perma.cc/T5JF-UG54].
58. *Critical Code: Building COVID-19 Vaccine Finder Tools*, U.S. DIGIT. SERV., https://www.usds.gov/projects/vaccines-dot-gov [https://perma.cc/6ZXE-ZJ9W].
59. *Optimizing Benefits for Families*, U.S. DIGIT. SERV., https://www.usds.gov/projects/childcare-tax-credit [https://perma.cc/E54X-5X42].
60. *About 18F*, 18F, https://18f.gsa.gov/about [https://perma.cc/B2WR-8N3W].
61. PRESIDENTIAL INNOVATION FELLOWS, https://presidentialinnovationfellows.gov/ [https://perma.cc/Z9J5-NMZX].
62. *Technology Transformation Services*, U.S. GEN. SERVS. ADMIN., https://www.gsa.gov/about-us/organization/federal-acquisition-service/technology-transformation-services [https://perma.cc/E4DB-5XUA].
63. Kathleen Walch, *How the Federal Government's AI Center of Excellence Is Impacting Government-Wide Adoption of AI*, FORBES (Aug. 8, 2020, 1:00 AM), https://www.forbes.com/sites/cognitiveworld/2020/08/08/how-the-federal-governments-ai-center-of-excellence-is-impacting-government-wide-adoption-of-ai [https://perma.cc/KC77-694N (uploaded archive)].
64. The government is certainly different than customer service providers in other ways in that there are also parts of the government that are not dedicated to service at all. There has been excellent study of how and why we may be concerned about automation in some of the government's enforcement and other capacities. *See, e.g.*, Cary Coglianese & David Lehr, *Regulating by Robot: Administrative Decision Making in the Machine-Learning Era*, 105 GEO. L. J. 1147 (2017) (exploring the use of machine learning for rulemaking); Danielle Keats Citron, *Technological Due Process*, 85 WASH. U. L. REV. 1249, 1267–77 (2008) (exploring automated benefits and entitlements determinations); Aziz Z. Huq, *Racial Equity in Algorithmic Criminal Justice*, 68 DUKE L. J. 1043 (2019) (exploring role of algorithms in the criminal justice process, and impact on racial equity). Readers interested in the state of automation across the government as a whole should also see a 2020 Administrative Conference of the United States report on the matter, DAVID FREEMAN ENGSTROM, DANIEL E. HO, CATHERINE M. SHARKEY & MARIANO-FLORENTINO CUÉLLAR, ADMIN. CONF. OF THE U.S., GOVERNMENT BY ALGORITHM: ARTIFICIAL INTELLIGENCE IN FEDERAL ADMINISTRATIVE AGENCIES 6–8 (2020), https://law.stanford.edu/wp-content/uploads/2020/02/ACUS-AI-Report.pdf [https://perma.cc/RN54-GAKW].
65. Nicholas R. Parrillo, *Federal Agency Guidance and the Power to Bind: An Empirical Study of Agencies and Industries*, 36 YALE J. ON REG. 165, 168 (2019).
66. *We Inform and Protect Investors*, U.S. SEC. & EXCH. COMM'N, https://www.sec.gov/ [https://perma.cc/8LQ3-LY93].
67. *Office of Investor Education and Advocacy*, U.S. SEC. & EXCH. COMM'N, https://www.sec.gov/page/oieasectionlanding [https://perma.cc/WJQ5-Z79M].

68. *Fast Answers – Key Topics*, U.S. SEC. & EXCH. COMM'N, https://www.sec.gov/fast-answers [https://perma.cc/8R2B-2686].
69. Jessica Looman, *Expanding Protections for Millions of Workers to Pump at Work*, U.S. DEP'T OF LAB. BLOG (Aug. 1, 2023), https://blog.dol.gov/2023/08/01/expanding-protections-for-millions-of-workers-to-pump-at-work [https://perma.cc/TST4-6MKX].
70. Jessica Looman, *How Our New Rule Will Help Construction Workers*, U.S. DEP'T OF LAB. BLOG (Aug. 8, 2023), https://blog.dol.gov/2023/08/08/how-our-new-rule-will-help-construction-workers [https://perma.cc/DZ2H-5U67].
71. *Family and Medical Leave (FMLA)*, U.S. DEP'T OF LAB., https://www.dol.gov/general/topic/benefits-leave/fmla [https://perma.cc/B9VR-DWDP].
72. IRS, https://www.irs.gov/ [https://perma.cc/PJG9-4JZN].
73. *The Agency, Its Mission, and Statutory Authority*, IRS, https://www.irs.gov/about-irs/the-agency-its-mission-and-statutory-authority [https://perma.cc/L7FP-PCRP] (last updated Nov. 15, 2023).
74. *See* IRS News Release IR-98-59 (Sept. 24, 1998), https://www.irs.gov/pub/irs-news/ir-98-59.pdf [https://perma.cc/XT3W-CHUS].
75. Internal Revenue Service Restructuring and Reform Act of 1998, Pub. L. No. 105-206, § 1002, 112 Stat. 685, 690 (codified at I.R.C. § 7801).
76. IRS News Release IR-2014-72 (June 10, 2014), https://www.irs.gov/pub/irs-news/IR-14-072.pdf [https://perma.cc/KBC7-HGWG].
77. *Taxpayer Bill of Rights*, IRS, https://www.irs.gov/taxpayer-bill-of-rights [https://perma.cc/WSA2-BVMG] (last updated May 1, 2023).
78. *Id.*
79. *See* U.S. CONST. art. I, § 1 ("All legislative Powers herein granted shall be vested in a Congress of the United States, which shall consist of a Senate and House of Representatives."); U.S. CONST. art. VI, para. 2 ("This Constitution, and the Laws of the United States which shall be made in Pursuance thereof; and all Treaties made, or which shall be made, under the Authority of the United States, shall be the supreme Law of the Land."); *see also, e.g.*, Jason Webb Yackee & Susan Webb Yackee, *From Legislation to Regulation: An Empirical Examination of Agency Responsiveness to Congressional Delegations of Regulatory Authority*, 68 ADMIN. L. REV. 395, 397 (2016) (detailing relationship between Congress's legislative power and agencies' authority).
80. *See, e.g.*, Peter H. Schuck, *Legal Complexity: Some Causes, Consequences, and Cures*, 42 DUKE L. J. 1, 2 (1992) (explaining how any attempt to examine legal complexity is "fraught with difficulties").
81. *See, e.g.*, Kristin E. Hickman, *Administering the Tax System We Have*, 63 DUKE L. J. 1717, 1717 (2014) ("Congress increasingly relies on the Internal Revenue Service to administer government programs that have little to do with raising revenue and much more to do with distributing government benefits to the economically disadvantaged, subsidizing approved activities, and regulating outright certain economic sectors like nonprofits, pensions, and health care.").
82. TAXPAYER ADVOC. SERV., NATIONAL TAXPAYER ADVOCATE 2005 ANNUAL REPORT TO CONGRESS, at V (vol. 1, 2005), https://www.taxpayeradvocate.irs.gov/wp-content/uploads/2020/08/section_1.pdf [https://perma.cc/2GKE-4Z23 (uploaded archive)] (describing how "complexity begets more complexity" in part because of the cycle of taxpayers exploiting loopholes leading to anti-abuse legislation, which makes the tax law yet more complex).

83. For a notable discussion of this phenomenon, see generally, e.g., BARBARA L. SINCLAIR, UNORTHODOX LAWMAKING: NEW LEGISLATIVE PROCESSES IN THE U.S. CONGRESS (2016); see also, e.g., Abbe R. Gluck, *Imperfect Statutes, Imperfect Courts: Understanding Congress's Plan in the Era of Unorthodox Lawmaking*, 129 HARV. L. REV. 62 (2015) (exploring in the context of legal interpretation).
84. See, e.g., Leigh Osofsky, *Agency Legislative Fixes*, 105 IOWA L. REV. 2107, 2109 (2020) (exploring this phenomenon and the resulting dilemma for agencies).
85. See, e.g., Shu-Yi Oei & Leigh Z. Osofsky, *Constituencies and Control in Statutory Drafting: Interviews with Government Tax Counsels*, 104 IOWA L. REV. 1291, 1295 (2019) (exploring through interview with drafters of the tax law).
86. *Lok v. Immigr. & Naturalization Serv.*, 548 F.2d 37, 38 (2d Cir. 1977).
87. Blake Hudson, *Relative Administrability, Conservatives, and Environmental Regulatory Reform*, 68 FLA. L. REV. 1661, 1674 (2016).
88. *Methodist Hosp. of Sacramento v. Shalala*, 38 F.3d 1225, 1229 (D.C. Cir. 1994).
89. Ronald A. Cass, *Staying Agency Rules: Constitutional Structure and Rule of Law in the Administrative State*, 69 ADMIN L. REV. 225, 228 (2017).
90. See, e.g., Richard J. Pierce, Jr., *Statutory Construction in the Administrative State*, in RICHARD J. PIERCE, ADMINISTRATIVE LAW, 93, 93–98 (3d ed. 2020) (for a brief, and then-current, summary of this ever-evolving issue).
91. See JONATHAN ROTHWELL, GALLUP, ASSESSING THE ECONOMIC GAINS OF ERADICATING ILLITERACY NATIONALLY AND REGIONALLY IN THE UNITED STATES 3 (2020), https://www.barbarabush.org/wp-content/uploads/2020/09/BBFoundation_GainsFromEradicatingIlliteracy_9_8.pdf [https://perma.cc/8UQX-KN6J].
92. *Id.* at 6.
93. Robert P. Strauss & Skye Toor, *The Readability of the US Federal Income Tax System: Some First Results*, 107 PROCEEDINGS: ANN. CONF. ON TAX'N & MINUTES ANN. MEETING NAT'L TAX ASS'N, at 1, 13 (2014).
94. Jean M. Twenge et al., *Trends in Adolescents' Media Use, 1976–2016: The Rise of Digital Media, the Decline of TV, and the (Near) Demise of Print*, 8 PSYCH. POPULAR MEDIA CULTURE 329, 329 (2019).
95. Andrew Perrin & Sara Atske, *About Three-in-Ten U.S. Adults Say They Are "Almost Constantly" Online*, PEW RSCH. CTR. (Mar. 26, 2021), https://www.pewresearch.org/short-reads/2021/03/26/about-three-in-ten-u-s-adults-say-they-are-almost-constantly-online/ [https://perma.cc/V8S4-5E59].
96. See, e.g., Gary W. Small et al., *Brain Health Consequences of Digital Technology Use*, 22 DIALOGUES CLINICAL NEUROSCI. 179 (2022) (broadly reviewing studies regarding effects of media exposure).
97. *Why You Should Forego the Legalese When Communicating with Clients*, THOMSON REUTERS: LEGAL (Jan. 14, 2020), https://legal.thomsonreuters.com/blog/why-you-should-forgo-the-legalese-when-communicating-with-clients/ [https://perma.cc/PSM3-H79B].
98. *Id.*
99. See, e.g., Caroline Shipman, *Unauthorized Practice of Law Claims against LegalZoom – Who Do These Lawsuits Protect, and Is the Rule Outdated?*, 32 GEO. J. LEGAL ETHICS 939 (2019) (exploring unauthorized practice of law issues and applying them in the context of technology change in the form of LegalZoom).
100. *Hello, Is Anyone There?*, *supra* note 28.
101. See, e.g., TREASURY INSPECTOR GEN. FOR TAX ADMIN., 2011-40-043, THE INTERACTIVE TAX LAW ASSISTANT HELPS ASSISTORS PROVIDE ACCURATE ANSWERS TO TAXPAYER INQUIRIES

1 (Apr. 20, 2011), [https://perma.cc/P9R5-9JT5 (uploaded archive)] (describing standardization efforts) [hereinafter TREASURY INSPECTOR GEN. FOR TAX ADMIN., INTERACTIVE].
102. *Get Medicare's New What's Covered App!*, MEDICARE (Jan. 2019), https://www.medicare.gov/sites/default/files/2019-01/12035-whats-covered-app.pdf [https://perma.cc/UDH3-PR6L].
103. *Have a Question? Now You Can Ask TSA on Facebook*, U.S. DEP'T OF HOMELAND SEC. (July 7, 2016, 10:40 AM), https://www.dhs.gov/blog/2016/07/07/have-question-now-you-can-ask-tsa-facebook [https://perma.cc/W2P3-APND].
104. *Have a Question? Ask USDA*, U.S. DEP'T OF AGRIC.: ASKUSDA, https://ask.usda.gov/s/ [https://perma.cc/TRB4-STX8 (uploaded archive)].
105. *How Long Can You Keep Spiral Cut Hams in the Refrigerator?*, U.S. DEP'T OF AGRIC.: ASKUSDA, https://ask.usda.gov/s/article/How-long-can-you-keep-spiral-cut-hams-in-the-refrigerator [https://perma.cc/D3MH-BTSB (uploaded archive)].
106. *How Long Can You Freeze Chicken?*, U.S. DEP'T OF AGRIC.: ASKUSDA, https://ask.usda.gov/s/article/How-long-can-you-freeze-chicken [https://perma.cc/L3EQ-3K6X (uploaded archive)].
107. *Search Results for "Can I bring produce back to the United States?,"* U.S. DEP'T OF AGRIC.: ASKUSDA, https://ask.usda.gov/s/ (type "Can I bring produce back to the United States?"; then run search) [https://perma.cc/P5DF-RP47 (uploaded archive)].
108. *Can I Bring Back South African Biltong (Beef Jerky) into the United States of America for Personal Consumption?*, U.S. DEP'T OF AGRIC.: ASKUSDA, https://ask.usda.gov/s/article/Can-I-bring-back-South-African-Biltong-beef-jerky-into-the-United-States-of-America-for-personal-con [https://perma.cc/UML6-N49M (uploaded archive)].
109. *Id.*
110. *Id.*
111. *Heckler v. Ringer*, 466 U.S. 602, 605 (1984).
112. 42 U.S.C. § 1395b-2.
113. *New App Displays What Original Medicare Covers*, CTRS. FOR MEDICARE & MEDICAID (Feb. 2019), https://www.cms.gov/newsroom/press-releases/new-app-displays-what-original-medicare-covers [https://perma.cc/W5SG-Z4JK].
114. 49 U.S.C. § 44901(a).
115. *See, e.g.*, 49 C.F.R. § 1540.107 (2024) (explaining what type of screening passengers must submit to).
116. *See, e.g.*, Daniel S. Harawa, *The Post-TSA Airport: A Constitution Free Zone?*, 41 PEPP. L. REV. 1 (2013) (exploring the relationship between TSA authority and constitutional rights).
117. *Optimizing Benefits for Families*, *supra* note 59.
118. *Id.*
119. *Id.*
120. *About Us*, FED. STUDENT AID, https://studentaid.gov/about [https://perma.cc/DA7Z-J7BD (uploaded archive)].
121. *Id.*
122. *Id.*
123. *Id.*
124. *Meet Aidan*, FED. STUDENT AID, https://studentaid.gov/h/aidan [https://perma.cc/32X7-VKPZ (uploaded archive)].
125. *Id.*
126. *Id.*
127. *Id.*
128. *Id.* (type "How can I discharge my student loan?"; then click send) [https://perma.cc/X4DP-FXQ3 (uploaded archive)].

129. *See, e.g.*, Doug Rendleman & Scott Weingart, *Collection of Student Loans: A Critical Examination*, 20 WASH. & LEE J. CIV. RTS. & SOC. JUST. 215, 262–88 (2014).
130. U.S. Dep't of Ed., *Secretary Betsy DeVos Full Remarks at 2019 Federal Student Aid Conference*, YOUTUBE, at 01:59 (Dec. 5, 2019), https://www.youtube.com/watch?v=gLo2rNJXRyo.
131. *Id.* at 04:30.
132. *Id.* at 12:14.
133. Digitalgov, *How Chatbots Can Improve Customer Experience*, YOUTUBE, at 54:32 (Mar. 3, 2021), https://www.youtube.com/watch?v=UoRkoeuqKWw.
134. *Mission and Core Values*, U.S. CITIZENSHIP & IMMIGR. SERVS., https://www.uscis.gov/about-us/mission-and-core-values [https://perma.cc/S8Z5-ARGE] (last updated Feb. 5, 2024).
135. *Our History*, U.S. CITIZENSHIP & IMMIGR. SERVS., https://www.uscis.gov/about-us/our-history [https://perma.cc/S9CB-GSDK].
136. *A Day in the Life of USCIS*, U.S. CITIZENSHIP & IMMIGR. SERVS., https://www.uscis.gov/about-us/a-day-in-the-life-of-uscis [https://perma.cc/D4FZ-46KZ] (last updated Dec. 11, 2022).
137. *Id.*
138. *Id.*
139. U.S. CITIZENSHIP & IMMIGR. SERVS., 2019–2021 STRATEGIC PLAN 15, https://www.uscis.gov/sites/default/files/document/reports/USCIS_Strategic_Plan_2019-2021.pdf [https://perma.cc/YK48-PWT9].
140. U.S. CITIZENSHIP & IMMIGR. SERVS., FYs 2023–2026 STRATEGIC PLAN 13, https://www.uscis.gov/sites/default/files/document/reports/StrategicPlanFY23.pdf [https://perma.cc/H8WE-FB2F].
141. Aaron Boyd, *USCIS Virtual Assistant to Offer More "Human" Digital Experience*, FED. TIMES (Nov. 16, 2015), https://www.federaltimes.com/it-networks/2015/11/16/uscis-virtual-assistant-to-offer-more-human-digital-experience [https://perma.cc/FW8E-UJ6A].
142. *Id.*
143. *USCIS Launches Virtual Assistant – Emma Gives Customers Another Option for Finding Answers*, U.S. CITIZENSHIP & IMMIGR. SERVS. (Dec. 5, 2015), https://www.uscis.gov/archive/uscis-launches-virtual-assistant-emma-gives-customers-another-option-for-finding-answers [https://perma.cc/867E-B4UM].
144. *Meet Emma, Our Virtual Assistant*, U.S. CITIZENSHIP & IMMIGR. SERVS., https://www.uscis.gov/tools/meet-emma-our-virtual-assistant [https://perma.cc/PL4Y-RA4B] (last updated Apr. 13, 2018).
145. *Id.*
146. *Id.*
147. *Id.*
148. U.S. CITIZENSHIP & IMMIGR. SERVS., https://www.uscis.gov [https://perma.cc/UH4V-FAXM].
149. *See, e.g.*, U.S. CITIZENSHIP & IMMIGR. SERVS., FACEBOOK (Oct. 31, 2016), https://www.facebook.com/uscis/photos/emma-is-our-virtual-assistant/1322280934449790/?paipv=0&eav=AfZcmhLAEa6opvKCN5buJG4orcLj-O27FxoJP3TCnuVwqW5gnZLfoPZyVrt9WVhzZRc&_rdr [https://perma.cc/Y2WA-23MH (uploaded archive)].
150. Kathleen Walch & Ronald Schmelzer, AI Today Podcast, #125: *Emma – Immigration Chatbot: Interview with Courtney Winship, US Citizenship & Immigration Service (USCIS)*, COGNILYTICA, at 02:46 (Jan. 22, 2020), https://www.cognilytica.com/2020/01/22/ai-today-podcast-125-emma-immigration-chatbot-interview-with-courtney-winship-us-citizenship-and-immigration-service-uscis.

151. Id. at 03:01.
152. Id. at 02:56, 03:29.
153. Id. at 03:59.
154. Tom Temin, Federal Drive, *Vashon Citizen: USCIS' New Virtual Assistant Emma Gets Service Award*, FED. NEWS NETWORK, at 01:48 (May 31, 2018), https://federalnewsnetwork.com/tom-temin-federal-drive/2018/05/vashon-citizen-uscis-new-virtual-assistant-emma-gets-service-award.
155. Walch & Schmelzer, *supra* note 150, at 07:40.
156. Id.
157. U.S. CITIZENSHIP & IMMIGR. SERVS., https://www.uscis.gov (click "Ask Emma"; then type "Where is my visa?"; then click send) [https://perma.cc/A2V7-ZC6H (uploaded archive)].
158. Id. (click "K Visa [Fiance Visa]") [https://perma.cc/7P2U-74C3 (uploaded archive)].
159. *Green Card for Fiancé(e) of U.S. Citizen*, U.S. CITIZENSHIP & IMMIGR. SERVS., https://www.uscis.gov/green-card/green-card-eligibility/green-card-for-fiancee-of-us-citizen [https://perma.cc/4Y8W-3KCM] (last updated Feb. 8, 2018).
160. TREASURY INSPECTOR GEN. FOR TAX ADMIN., INTERACTIVE, *supra* note 101, at 1, 24.
161. Id. at 4–5.
162. Id. at 1.
163. *See* TREASURY INSPECTOR GEN. FOR TAX ADMIN., 2015-40-032, INTERIM RESULTS OF THE 2015 FILING SEASON 14 (Mar. 31, 2015), https://www.tigta.gov/sites/default/files/reports/2022-02/201540032fr.pdf [https://perma.cc/BKD9-RQVR] [hereinafter TREASURY INSPECTOR GEN. FOR TAX ADMIN., INTERIM RESULTS].
164. *See Interactive Tax Assistant* (ITA), IRS, https://www.irs.gov/help/ita [https://perma.cc/JQ8K-TQEP] (last updated Jan. 16, 2024).
165. Id.
166. Id.
167. Id.
168. Id.
169. Id.
170. *See, e.g.*, David Hood, Allyson Versprille & Kaustuv Basu, *Customer Service at the IRS Is So Bad, Even Tax Pros Are Fed Up*, BLOOMBERG: BUSINESSWEEK (Jan. 4, 2022, 4:00 AM), https://www.bloomberg.com/news/articles/2022-01-04/irs-customer-service-is-so-bad-even-tax-preparation-professionals-are-fed-up [https://perma.cc/3R8G-3ADF (private, uploaded archive)].
171. IRSnews (@IRSnews), TWITTER (Dec. 26, 2021, 1:01 PM), https://twitter.com/IRSnews/status/1475164767929212930 [https://perma.cc/ZX76-V3ML].
172. TREASURY INSPECTOR GEN. FOR TAX ADMIN., INTERIM RESULTS, *supra* note 163, at 14.
173. We obtained this information through interviews with agency officials. *See* Chapter 5 for detailed discussion of these interviews.
174. Id.
175. Id.
176. Id.
177. *Meet Aidan*, *supra* note 124.
178. Id.
179. We obtained this information through interviews with agency officials. *See* Chapter 5 for detailed discussion of these interviews.

3

Simplexity

The Law in Plain Language

Whether you are trying to find out the due date for your federal income tax return or how to apply for forgiveness of federal student debt, when you use the government's automated legal guidance tools, you are interacting indirectly with a complex web of legal authorities. As Chapter 2 detailed, the federal government has embraced automated legal guidance tools to help the public navigate this web.

This raises several questions:

- How do automated legal guidance tools translate a complex web of legal authorities for the public?
- Do the federal government's automated legal guidance tools provide answers that match the language of statutes and regulations? If not, which details do automated legal guidance tools include and exclude?
- What about exceptions to rules? Which legal exceptions do automated legal guidance tools include, and which do they omit?
- Finally, how definitive are the government's answers to the public in automated legal guidance when the law in question is ambiguous or uncertain?

Propelled by innovations in automation, the federal government is increasingly trying to make the law more easily accessible to the public. However, the formal law, which consists of statutes, regulations, and judicial decisions, is not easily accessible. Rather, it is extremely complex, often ambiguous, and difficult to understand. This leaves the federal government in a difficult position. How can it make the federal law seem simple and easy to use when, in fact, it is extraordinarily complicated?

We have conducted extensive research on this topic and have identified a central tool that the government uses to make the law seem simple, even when it is not. When government officials attempt to explain the law to the public in plain language, they consistently use a communication approach that we describe as "simplexity." Simplexity is different than simplification, which would involve reform of the underlying law.[1] Instead, simplexity occurs when the government presents clear and simple explanations of law that is, in fact, ambiguous or complex.

Outside of the law, simplexity is a concept that has emerged in recent years in diverse fields, including chemistry[2] and biology,[3] cognitive psychology,[4] literary analysis,[5] and even computer-animated feature films.[6] In communications with members of the general public, government officials frequently use simplexity to transform complex, often ambiguous legal provisions into what seem to be, at least on their surface, simple statements. These statements exhibit key features, including: (1) they present contested law as clear rules, (2) they add administrative gloss to the law, and (3) fail to fully explain the law, including possible exceptions. Sometimes these deviations from the formal law are favorable to the interests of individuals; at other times, they benefit the government's positions. In either case, simplexity offers a powerful platform from which the government can shape people's perceptions and understanding of the law.

The government's simplified explanations of the law have particular importance to ordinary members of the public.[7] Many, if not most, people lack access to legal counsel who can analyze the sources of law that underlie these summaries, and the complexity of many regulatory regimes exacerbates this dynamic.[8] The result is that, for most members of the public, the guidance that they obtain directly from government agencies fundamentally influences their behavior and the ways in which they view and respond to the law.[9]

This chapter reports and describes our findings regarding the widespread use of simplexity in agencies' communications with the public. It begins by re-visiting the duty of federal government agencies to explain the law. This is followed by a detailed introduction of the concept of simplexity, together with an explanation of how simplexity is unlike related concepts, such as complexity and simplicity. It concludes by offering several examples of how federal agencies have used simplexity to explain the law in static, written publications.

As Chapter 4 will discuss, the federal government is expanding its use of automated legal guidance, which means that the power of simplexity to shape public behavior will only grow. As such, it is necessary to have a foundational understanding of what the government's law-explaining duty is and how this relates to simplexity's role in fulfilling it.

THE DUTY TO EXPLAIN THE LAW

Federal law is extremely complex. In response to this complexity, federal agencies face statutory mandates to assist individuals in meeting their legal compliance obligations.

Some federal agencies are required by statute to provide customer service to members of the public. For example, as Chapter 2 described, the IRS bears an affirmative duty to assist both individuals and businesses in meeting their tax calculation and payment obligations. The agency must do this by explaining the tax law to taxpayers in plain language that is clear and easy to understand.

Following the Internal Revenue Service Restructuring and Reform Act of 1998,[10] the IRS officially revised its mission statement to include a commitment to providing taxpayers with "top quality service."[11] It subsequently adopted a Taxpayer Bill of Rights, which was later added to the Internal Revenue Code itself, providing that taxpayers have the "right to be informed."[12] The IRS has interpreted this right to include access to clear descriptions not only of the formal tax law but also all IRS forms and procedures.[13]

The IRS is but one example of a federal agency that has moved toward offering clearer and simpler explanations of laws and legal principles. Much of the movement in this area throughout the federal government has been in response to a 2010 statute that required agencies to simplify how they communicate.

The Plain Writing Act of 2010

In addition to customer service mandates that apply to specific agencies, all federal agencies are required by statute to use plain language when providing certain information to members of the public. Under the Plain Writing Act of 2010, federal agencies must use plain writing when providing the public with explanations and instructions.[14] To qualify as "plain writing," agencies must use writing that is "clear, concise, well-organized, and follows other best practices appropriate to the subject or field and intended audience."[15] The purpose of this statute is to "improve the effectiveness and accountability of Federal agencies to the public by promoting clear Government communication that the public can understand and use."[16] Or, as one of the bill's original sponsors, then-U.S. Representative Bruce Braley, put it, the statute's plain writing requirements will "increase government accountability and save Americans time and money" by eliminating "federal gobbledygook."[17]

The plain writing requirement applies to any "covered document," which includes any documents that are necessary for obtaining a federal government benefit or service, for filing taxes, for getting information about any federal government benefits or services, or for learning how to comply with a requirement that the federal government administers or enforces.[18] These documents include any letter, publication, form, notice, or instruction – whether they are in paper or electronic form.

In addition to the mandate that federal agencies communicate with the public using plain writing, the Plain Writing Act also requires the head of each federal agency to designate at least one senior official to oversee implementation of its requirements, to provide plain writing training to agency employees, and to establish a process for overseeing the ongoing compliance of the agency with the plain writing requirements.[19] The statute also requires each agency to create and maintain a plain writing section of the agency's website that includes an option for the public to provide feedback regarding the understandability of the agency's communications.[20] Additionally, each year, every federal agency must publish an annual compliance report that describes how the agency has complied with the agency's statutory plain writing requirements.[21] While the statute imposes many requirements on agencies, it clearly states that there shall be no judicial review of any agency's compliance or noncompliance with the statute.[22]

Since the enactment of the Plain Writing Act, agency officials have publicly committed to complying with its requirements to communicate with individuals in clear and understandable terms in their guidance, notices, and forms.[23] In addition, an informal working group of federal agency employees who support the use of clear communication in government writing have established the Plain Language Action and Information Network (PLAIN).[24] The PLAIN website maintains a repository of examples of plain writing initiatives, as well as success stories from different federal agencies.[25] For example, IRS officials have indicated that they strive to "communicate in clear, easily understandable language on all of [its] forms, publications, documents and notices."[26] Similarly, the Centers for Disease Control, the Federal Aviation Agency, and the Department of Defense have each developed online training sessions on plain writing techniques for their employees, as well as for external government users.[27] In addition, since 2010, federal agencies have regularly complied with the statutory requirement to publish annual plain writing compliance reports.[28]

Government officials, scholars, and other commentators have lauded the federal government's adoption of plain writing in public communications. Following enactment of the Plain Writing Act, Cass Sunstein, in his capacity as administrator of the US Office for Management and Budget's (OMB) Office of Information and Regulatory Affairs (OIRA), commented that the plain writing mandates "will not only save money but also facilitate two-way communication between agencies and the public and make it is [sic] far easier for people to understand what they are being asked to do."[29]

Government watchdog organizations have also praised the statute: they believe that communication in plain writing is essential to democracy and note that "[a] government by the people and for the people should also be understood by the people."[30] However, there is also some recognition of the initiative's apparent shortcomings. While many have praised the shift to plain writing, the authors of a 2017 Administrative Conference of the United States (ACUS) report on plain language in regulatory drafting have cautioned that agencies should also inform members of the public and other stakeholders that their simplified explanations of regulations are not substitutes for the formal regulations.[31]

Plain Writing Approaches Used by Federal Agencies

To satisfy their duty to explain the law, federal agencies have adopted several communication approaches in their interactions with the public. These methods have been developed based not only on guidance implementing the Plain Writing Act

(Plain Language Guidelines) issued by OIRA within the Office of Management and Budget but also from the policies of individual agencies.[32] Four approaches have seen wide adoption: (1) tailoring expectations, (2) eliminating complexity, (3) evaluating public impact, and (4) adopting special guidelines for internet materials.

Tailoring Explanations
Agency officials acknowledge that in their public communications, they often adjust their language depending on whether the potential readers are laypeople or experts in the relevant fields.[33] For example, regarding publications intended for the general public, the IRS states that the "plain language [it] use[s] for this group is clear, simple and meaningful" because "this group does not have a need to understand technical regulatory language."[34] On the other hand, when addressing tax professionals, such as tax accountants, tax return preparers, and tax lawyers, the IRS includes more specialized terminology that people with training and experience in the field can reasonably be expected to understand.[35]

Eliminating Complexity
As part of their efforts to help members of the public understand the law and to comply with the requirements of the Plain Writing Act, agencies often attempt to avoid using technical or legalistic terminology. According to the *Plain Language Guidelines*, agencies should "translate complicated provisions into more manageable language"[36] by avoiding complex details and discussions in these documents. For example, the guidelines state that agencies should avoid emphasizing exceptions to the law because

> [w]hen you start a sentence with an introductory phrase or clause beginning with "except," you almost certainly force the reader to re-read your sentence.... The audience must absorb the exception, then the rule, and then usually has to go back to grasp the relationship between the two.[37]

Rather than restating the law precisely as it appears in statutes or regulations, the guidelines instruct agencies to rewrite sentences to "emphasize the positive."[38]

Agencies appear to have heeded this advice. Following enactment of the Plain Writing Act, agency officials have reported that they have rewritten and revised public-facing documents to "improve comprehension" by those who are not attorneys or otherwise experienced in reading legal documents.[39]

Evaluating the Impact on the Public and the Agency
Using plain language to explain what people need to do to follow the law can benefit more than just the members of the public. This is the reason agency officials also consider the potential impact of the language they use on different parties, including

the agency itself. The *Plain Language Guidelines* suggest that, when drafting publications for the public, agency officials should ask, "What's the best outcome for our audience? What do I need to say to get this outcome?"[40] Likewise, the guidelines also instruct agency officials to consider how the text in any public-facing document may impact their specific organization. In other words, agency leaders should also be asking themselves: "What's the best outcome for *my agency*? What do I need to say to get this outcome?"[41]

Condensing Communications for the Internet

Finally, in addition to each of the methods described earlier, agency officials further refine their communications that appear on agency websites and other online platforms. Agency officials do this because, as some have observed, "[o]n the web, people are in a hurry," and they often "skim and scan, looking for quick answers to their questions."[42]

When communicating with members of the public on the internet, PLAIN provides specific advice to agency officials, including:

- "Less is more! Be concise."
- "Use even shorter paragraphs than on paper."
- "Keep the information on each page to no more than two levels."
- "Make liberal use of white space so pages are easy to scan."
- "Eliminate unnecessary words."[43]

This guidance tells us that when agencies explain the law to the public on the internet, their explanations and other statements are even more abbreviated and succinct than those that appear in printed publications.

WHAT IS SIMPLEXITY?

One common characteristic of government agencies' efforts to explain the law to the public can be described as "simplexity." While we are the first scholars to introduce this term in the legal literature, representative descriptions of simplexity from other fields include "[t]he process of simplifying something by obscuring the more complex aspects of the original goal"[44] and "an idea, or concept that appears to be simple to understand, yet is very complex in it's [sic] true description."[45] Later, we distinguish simplexity from simplicity, provide several examples of simplexity in non-legal contexts, and define our usage of the term in this book.

Before defining simplexity, we should first consider simplicity. The dictionary definition of simplicity refers to "the state of being simple, uncomplicated, or uncompounded."[46] In his 2013 book, *Simpler: The Future of Government*, Cass Sunstein notes that the overarching goal of the "large-scale transformation in

American government"[47] that occurred as a result of initiatives such as the Plain Writing Act was to "increase simplicity"[48] through the government's communications with the public.

In the context of fundamental tax reform, government officials have defined simplicity in the negative by stating that it is "not reflected in [taxpayers] ... computing dozens of deductions and credits, and wondering all the while whether other means of saving tax might have been missed through ignorance of the laws."[49] In the same vein, simplicity can occur when legislators eliminate or reject rules that would unduly complicate administration of the law. For instance, some commentators have described changes in the 2017 tax reform legislation, such as the suspension of miscellaneous itemized deductions for individual taxpayers, as temporarily increasing simplicity.[50] Simplicity is, thus, the antithesis of complexity, or, as Sunstein has posited, "simplicity is friendly, and complexity is not."[51]

Simplexity, on the other hand, is distinct from simplicity. Simplexity refers to a concept that appears to be simple but that nonetheless retains underlying complexity. As neurophysiologist Alain Berthoz has written, "[s]implexity is not simplicity. It is fundamentally linked with complexity, with which it shares common roots."[52]

Outside of law, there are a few examples that illustrate the appearance of simplexity. Scientists have used the term to describe the appearance of phenomena whose simplicity obscures underlying complexity, such as a houseplant, whose simple green leaves obscure its underlying "microhydraulics and fine-tuned metabolism and dense schematic of nucleic acids."[53] Similarly, psychology researchers have referred to simplexity as a "cognitive process that compresses information and synthesizes it without losing its complexity."[54]

Commentators have noted that certain literary forms, such as metaphors and fables, are simplex as their accessible narrative conceals deeper, underlying meaning.[55] For instance, Berthoz has argued that simplexity occurs in characters such as the seven dwarves, for "Dopey is not as dopey as he seems" because he is "not a village idiot but a witness and wise presence...."[56] In another artistic setting, simplexity has become a foundational principle of Pixar Animation Studios, producer of acclaimed computer-animated feature films.[57] As one of its lead animators has stated, the studio's artists strive to achieve simplexity by "simplifying an image down to its essence,"[58] which causes complexity of texture, design, and detail to be "masked by how simple the form is."[59]

We now offer our formal definitions of two key terms that we apply throughout the remainder of this book:

Simplicity. We define "simplicity" as occurring when policymakers reform the law by eliminating specific complex provisions or procedures through enactment of statutory changes or issuance of regulations. For instance, we would consider a tax system that repeals specific complex deductions or statutory exceptions or that exempts millions of low-income taxpayers from filing tax returns at all as one that exhibits simplicity.

Simplexity. In contrast, we define "simplexity" as occurring when the government presents clear and simple explanations of law that is, in reality, ambiguous or complex. In other words, when government agencies communicate the law in ways that exhibit simplexity, they present complex or ambiguous law as clear rules, but they do not actually simplify the underlying formal law.

What are some of the sources of simplexity in the government's explanations of the law? One set of sources is statutes and regulations that are ambiguous. When a statute has vague terms, judges and federal agencies must decipher them, which often results in complex, and potentially conflicting, additional rules and standards.

Consider the test for whether a taxpayer has demonstrated that a business expense was "ordinary and necessary."[60] This standard is highly subjective because it depends on taxpayers' individual reasons for incurring expenses. The facts-and-circumstances nature of standards such as this one requires agencies to come up with their own examples and, in some cases, even their own terminology when describing the standards in informal guidance.

Another source of simplexity is the use of statutory standards that focus on the intent or purpose of individual or business actors. These statutes often lead to the issuance of judicial decisions and regulatory examples.[61] Then, in their communications with the public about how the law operates, agencies attempt to summarize the authorities that interpret these statutes, which sometimes results in simplifications that deviate from the underlying formal law.

Last, vague statutory terms may require agencies to offer detailed regulations to define them, but the definition-based content of these regulations may not always carry over precisely to the agencies' informal guidance documents.[62]

Simplexity in IRS Publications

Before examining the application of simplexity in automated legal guidance, it is helpful to examine examples in communications between government agencies and the public more generally. When we started researching this phenomenon in 2017, we first observed the occurrence of simplexity in IRS publications, which are documents that the agency uses to communicate the tax law to individuals, small businesses, and tax professionals. Historically, IRS publications have appeared in printed form and were available at IRS offices, public libraries, and other government buildings. In 2015, however, the IRS announced that, because of budget cuts, the agency would no longer deliver printed copies of IRS publications to public libraries,[63] and instead began posting electronic copies on its website.

The Internal Revenue Service publications provide explanatory information, general guidance, definitions for important terms, and examples intended to show taxpayers how the law applies.[64] Taxpayers who prepare their own individual income tax returns rely extensively on IRS publications and the explanations of the law that they include.[65] For example, the instructions that accompany most IRS forms, such as IRS Form 1040, frequently refer taxpayers to IRS publications that use plain language to explain the content of the forms.[66] While taxpayers tend to rely on the general content on the IRS website as their primary source of guidance from the agency, a large majority of taxpayers (77 percent in 2021) report that IRS publications are "very or somewhat valuable" sources of tax advice and information.[67]

In addition to the guidance received directly from the IRS in its publications, individuals may also encounter this guidance through third-party sources, such as Intuit's TurboTax, which is used by tens of millions of taxpayers every year to complete and file their tax returns with the IRS.[68] In many cases, the advice that TurboTax and its online tax professionals provide is identical to the statements in IRS publications – including IRS statements that deviate from the formal tax law.

Why have companies like Intuit made this choice? By following the IRS's position, as it is stated in the agency's informal guidance documentation, the tax preparation software reduces the likelihood that the IRS will audit its users. Indeed, some companies that sell tax preparation software promise that, in the event of an IRS audit, they will not only refund the purchase price of the program but also provide the customer with no-cost access to trained tax professionals.[69] This type of guarantee further encourages sellers of tax preparation software to avoid conflicting with the IRS position in its informal guidance.

Simplexity permeates IRS publications. Consider the following example as an illustration of how the IRS has used IRS publications to present tax positions that are the subject of judicial ambiguity as if they were unambiguous tax rules.

A classic example of an ambiguous tax law provision that relies heavily on judicial interpretation is the deduction for "ordinary and necessary" trade or business expenses incurred during the taxable year.[70] To claim this deduction, the taxpayer must determine that such expenses are both "ordinary" and "necessary."[71] Explaining what, exactly, these terms mean is a famously difficult task. Indeed, Supreme Court Justice Benjamin Cardozo, in the 1933 case *Welch v. Helvering*, expressed this frustration, writing that "[o]ne struggles in vain for any verbal formula that will supply a ready touchstone."[72]

Despite this inherent legal ambiguity, an IRS publication can serve as a vehicle for providing a ready, extremely clear, touchstone to taxpayers. For example, in 2022, as in many previous years, the IRS presented taxpayers with a straightforward summary of the test for deductibility of business expenses in *IRS Publication 535 (Business Expenses)*.[73] (After the 2022 tax year, the IRS stopped revising this publication.)[74] In *Publication 535*, the IRS stated that "a business expense must be both ordinary and necessary" to be deductible.[75] With respect to the "ordinary" prong, *Publication 535* instructed taxpayers that "[a]n ordinary expense is one that is common and accepted in your industry."[76] This definition imposed an obligation to determine whether other taxpayers operating similar businesses – the taxpayer's "industry" – incur the expense at issue in their business practices (in other words, whether the expense is "common and accepted").[77]

In contrast to the clear rule expressed in *Publication 535*, courts have used various approaches to determine what satisfies the "ordinary" requirement. Several courts have adopted the approach described in *Publication 535*; specifically, they have asked whether other similarly situated taxpayers have incurred the business expense at issue.[78]

Other courts, however, have stated explicitly that taxpayers may treat business expenses as ordinary even if few or no other similarly situated taxpayer in the relevant industry incurs this expense.[79] As one court held, a taxpayer "should not be penalized taxwise for his business ingenuity in [incurring business expenses] which do not conform to the practices of one whom he is naturally trying to surpass in profits."[80] Some courts have viewed such an inquiry as irrelevant to whether an expense is ordinary?[81] In internal memoranda, IRS officials appear to agree, concluding that expenses may satisfy the ordinary prong even if the expenses are not common practice in the industry because "[t]hat which today is a novel method of generating business may be commonplace tomorrow."[82]

In even starker conflict with the IRS's characterization of the "ordinary" prong in *Publication 535*, some courts have held that the "ordinary" requirement is simply meant to clarify that, even though an expense may be necessary, it may not be deductible in the year in question because the expense may relate to the production of income in future tax years.[83] For instance, in one decision, the Supreme Court explained that the "principal function of the term 'ordinary' in Section 162(a) of the Internal Revenue Code is to clarify the distinction, often difficult, between those expenses that are currently deductible and those that are in the nature of capital expenditures...."[84] Citing this language, other courts have refrained from considering whether an expense is "common and accepted" in the taxpayer's industry.[85]

Despite the differing judicial interpretations of the term ordinary under Section 162(a) of the Internal Revenue Code, *Publication 535* presented the taxpayer with an unequivocal definition of an ordinary expense as one that is common and accepted in the taxpayer's industry.[86] Taxpayers who applied the clear rule stated in *Publication 535* may have reasonably concluded that they were not entitled to claim business expense deductions, even if they would have been entitled to do so under one of the alternative judicial interpretations.

For example, assume the owner of a pizza shop was accused of giving customers food poisoning, and the pizza shop owner paid legal fees to retain an attorney to defend against these claims. According to *Publication 535*, if the owner was not able to identify other restaurant owners who paid similar legal fees, the expense did not satisfy the ordinary standard, which means that, consequently, the owner should have foregone a business expense deduction.[87] A more comprehensive understanding of the case law, however, may have supported the deduction. Unfortunately, this taxpayer's area of expertise was pizza, not tax law. As a result, the owner may have forfeited a deduction that was allowable under the tax law.

This example illustrates that there is another side to agency communication through plain language. While its proponents have argued that plain language will lead to greater simplicity and administrability of the law, its use does not make substantive changes to the myriad complexities of the law – technical details, exceptions (and exceptions to exceptions), and ambiguous statutory and judicial language.

Further, and most importantly, the Plain Writing Act only applies to federal government agencies, not to Congress or the courts. Consequently, it places a burden upon agencies to summarize and describe the formal law in easily digestible terms, which can, ironically, cause these agencies to offer descriptions that deviate from the underlying formal law. As the example of the IRS's discussion of the "ordinary and necessary" trade or business standard shows, when agencies attempt to explain the law in plain language, the outcome may not be greater simplicity. Instead, it can result in simplexity that operates to the detriment of members of the public. Whereas simplicity eliminates complexity, simplexity offers only the *appearance* of simplicity.

NOTES

1. See 1 OFF. OF THE SEC'Y, DEP'T OF TREASURY, TAX REFORM FOR FAIRNESS, SIMPLICITY, AND ECONOMIC GROWTH 16 (1984), https://home.treasury.gov/system/files/131/Report-Tax-Reform-v1-1984.pdf [https://perma.cc/7UWC-6S35].
2. See, e.g., Phillippe Compain, *Le pari de la simplexité: Le simple et le complexe en synthèse organique* [*The Challenge of Simplexity: The Simple and the Complex in Organic Synthesis*], 265 L'ACTUALITÉ CHIMIQUE, Apr.–May 2003, at 129, 129.
3. See, e.g., JEFFREY KLUGER, SIMPLEXITY: WHY SIMPLE THINGS BECOME COMPLEX (AND HOW COMPLEX THINGS CAN BE MADE SIMPLE) (2008).
4. Serge Gelalian, *Is Modeling the Primary Activity of the Human Brain?*, 3 PSYCH. RSCH. 175, 184 (2013).
5. See, e.g., ALAIN BERTHOZ, SIMPLEXITY: SIMPLIFYING PRINCIPLES FOR A COMPLEX WORLD 208 (Giselle Weiss trans., 2012).
6. TIM HAUSER, THE ART OF UP 18 (2009) (quoting Pixar animator Ricky Nierva as stating, "[Simplexity] is the art of simplifying an image down to its essence.... 'Simplexity' is about selective detail").
7. See Robert A. Anthony, *Interpretive Rules, Policy Statements, Guidances, Manuals, and the Like – Should Federal Agencies Use Them to Bind the Public?*, 41 DUKE L. J. 1311 (1992); Michael S. Greve & Ashley C. Parrish, *Administrative Law Without Congress*, 22 GEO. MASON L. REV. 501, 532–34 (2015).
8. *Id.*
9. See, e.g., Jessica Mantel, *Procedural Safeguards for Agency Guidance: A Source of Legitimacy for the Administrative State*, 61 ADMIN. L. REV. 343, 354 (2009).
10. Internal Revenue Service Restructuring and Reform Act of 1998, Pub. L. No. 105-206, § 1205, 112 Stat. 685, 722–23 (codified at I.R.C. § 7804); *see also* Leandra Lederman, *Tax Compliance and the Reformed IRS*, 51 KAN. L. REV. 971, 980 (2003) (discussing the Act's ramifications).

11. IRS News Release IR-98-59 (Sept. 24, 1998), https://www.irs.gov/pub/irs-news/ir-98-59.pdf [https://perma.cc/K4UK-MFKW].
12. *Taxpayer Bill of Rights*, IRS, https://www.irs.gov/taxpayer-bill-of-rights (last updated May 1, 2023) [https://perma.cc/TA35-BMTK]; I.R.C. § 7803(a)(3)(A).
13. IRS News Release IR-2014-72 (June 10, 2014), https://www.irs.gov/pub/irs-news/IR-14-072.pdf [https://perma.cc/TDD3-VDUK].
14. Plain Writing Act of 2010, Pub. L. No. 111-274, § 3, 124 Stat. 2861, 2861 (codified at 5 U.S.C. § 301).
15. *Id.* § 3(3), 124 Stat. at 2861.
16. *Id.* § 2, 124 Stat. at 2861; *see also* Exec. Order No. 13,563, 76 Fed. Reg. 3821 (Jan. 18, 2011).
17. *As Others See It: 'Language Bill' Needed*, DAILY GLOBE NEWS (Oct. 12, 2010, 11:00 PM), https://www.dglobe.com/news/as-others-see-it-language-bill-needed [https://perma.cc/5UVB-G6HV].
18. *Id.* § 3(2), 124 Stat. at 2861.
19. Plain Writing Act of 2010 § 4, 124 Stat. at 2861–62.
20. *Id.*
21. *Id.* § 5, 124 Stat. at 2862.
22. *Id.* § 6, 124 Stat. at 2862–63.
23. IRS, PUB. 5206, PLAIN WRITING ACT COMPLIANCE REPORT 2 (2017), https://www.irs.gov/pub/irs-pdf/p5206.pdf [https://perma.cc/GY4G-T6W2] [hereinafter IRS, PUB. 5206].
24. *About*, PLAIN LANGUAGE ACTION & INFO. NETWORK, https://www.plainlanguage.gov/about/ [https://perma.cc/5SJS-U8AH].
25. *Examples*, PLAIN LANGUAGE ACTION & INFO. NETWORK, https://www.plainlanguage.gov/examples/ [https://perma.cc/85QR-Z2WG].
26. IRS, PUB. 5206, *supra* note 23, at 2.
27. *Online Training*, PLAIN LANGUAGE ACTION & INFO. NETWORK, https://www.plainlanguage.gov/training/online-training/ [https://perma.cc/R2ZP-EKAP].
28. *See, e.g.*, U.S. DEP'T OF LAB., 2022 PLAIN WRITING ACT COMPLIANCE REPORT (2022), https://www.dol.gov/general/plainwriting/2022AnnualComplianceReport [https://perma.cc/6NRL-92AM]; U.S. DEP'T OF ENERGY, PLAIN WRITING ACT COMPLIANCE REPORT (2023), https://www.energy.gov/sites/default/files/2023-05/Plain%20Language%20Compliance%20Report%202023.pdf [https://perma.cc/8V3X-D9VC]; U.S. DEP'T OF HEALTH & HUM. SERVS., PLAIN WRITING ACT COMPLIANCE REPORT (2023), https://www.hhs.gov/sites/default/files/2023-plain-writing-complaince-report.pdf [https://perma.cc/3VP5-4DET].
29. Cass Sunstein, *Putting It Plainly*, THE WHITE HOUSE (Apr. 19, 2011, 11:00 AM), https://obamawhitehouse.archives.gov/blog/2011/04/19/putting-it-plainly [https://perma.cc/BTD3-TRMH].
30. *Obama Signs 'Plain Writing' Law*, ABC NEWS (Oct. 17, 2010, 3:16 PM), https://abcnews.go.com/WN/obama-signs-law-understand/story?id=11902841 [https://perma.cc/C8CZ-6KHJ].
31. *See* BLAKE EMERSON & CHERYL BLAKE, ADMIN. CONF. OF THE U.S., PLAIN LANGUAGE IN REGULATORY DRAFTING 41 (2017), https://www.acus.gov/sites/default/files/documents/Plain%20Regulatory%20Drafting_Final%20Report.pdf [https://perma.cc/ZZ45-ZUFP].
32. OFF. OF MGMT. & BUDGET, EXEC. OFF. OF THE PRESIDENT, MEMORANDUM NO. M-11-15, FINAL GUIDANCE ON IMPLEMENTING THE PLAIN WRITING ACT OF 2010 (2011), https://www.whitehouse.gov/wp-content/uploads/legacy_drupal_files/omb/memoranda/2011/m11-15.pdf [https://perma.cc/YR8D-LPCZ]; PLAIN LANGUAGE ACTION & INFO. NETWORK, FEDERAL PLAIN LANGUAGE GUIDELINES (2011), http://

www.plainlanguage.gov/howto/guidelines/FederalPLGuidelines/FederalPLGuidelines .pdf [https://perma.cc/28CL-F39S].
33. *See* IRS, PUB. 5206, *supra* note 23, at 3.
34. *Id.*
35. *See id.* at 3–4.
36. PLAIN LANGUAGE ACTION & INFO. NETWORK, *supra* note 32, at 50.
37. *Id.* at 56.
38. *Id.* at 55.
39. *See* IRS, PUB. 5206, *supra* note 23, at 5.
40. PLAIN LANGUAGE ACTION & INFO. NETWORK, *supra* note 32, at 2.
41. *Id.* (emphasis added).
42. *Checklist for Plain Language on the Web*, PLAIN LANGUAGE ACTION & INFO. NETWORK, https://www.plainlanguage.gov/resources/checklists/web-checklist/ [https://perma.cc/ P6RL-MSCB].
43. *Id.*
44. *Simplexity*, COLLINS DICTIONARY, http://www.collinsdictionary.com/submission/1290/ Simplexity [https://perma.cc/BU6D-TA73 (uploaded archive)].
45. *Simplexity*, URBAN DICTIONARY, http://www.urbandictionary.com/define.php?term=Simplexity [https://perma.cc/BHD9-WTGD].
46. *Simplicity*, MERRIAM-WEBSTER, http://www.merriam-webster.com/dictionary/simplicity [https://perma.cc/BXU6-573T].
47. CASS R. SUNSTEIN, SIMPLER: THE FUTURE OF GOVERNMENT 2 (2013).
48. *Id.*
49. *See* OFF. OF THE SEC'Y, DEP'T OF TREASURY, *supra* note 1, at 15–16.
50. *See, e.g.*, Erica York & Alex Muresianu, *The Tax Cuts and Jobs Act Simplified the Tax Filing Process for Millions of Households*, TAX FOUND. (Aug. 7, 2018), https:// taxfoundation.org/the-tax-cuts-and-jobs-act-simplified-the-tax-filing-process-for-millions-of-americans/ [https://perma.cc/5TEN-VU2K].
51. SUNSTEIN, *supra* note 47, at 1.
52. BERTHOZ, *supra* note 5, at x.
53. KLUGER, *supra* note 3, at 11.
54. Gelalian, *supra* note 4, at 185.
55. *See, e.g.*, BERTHOZ, *supra* note 5, at 208 ("Metaphor ... is a wonderful way of shortcutting language.").
56. *Id.*
57. *See* HAUSER, *supra* note 6, at 18.
58. *Id.* (quoting Pixar animator Ricky Nierva).
59. *Id.*
60. *See* I.R.C. § 162(a); Treas. Reg. § 1.162-1(a).
61. *See* I.R.C. § 183(a); Treas. Reg. § 1.183-2(b).
62. *See, e.g.*, Nina E. Olson, *The Uncertainty of Death and Taxes: Economic Stimulus Payments to Deceased Individuals*, TAX NOTES: PROCEDURALLY TAXING (May 11, 2020), https://procedurallytaxing.com/the-uncertainty-of-death-and-taxes-economic-stimulus-payments-to-deceased-individuals/ [https://perma.cc/5T96-4QX7].
63. *See* Ricardo Torres, *Some Library Patrons Will Have to Pay for IRS Tax Forms This Year*, LAS VEGAS REV.-J. (Feb. 8, 2015, 9:36 AM), https://www.reviewjournal.com/local/local-las-vegas/some-library-patrons-will-have-to-pay-for-irs-tax-forms-this-year/ [https://perma .cc/DYJ2-T6CX].

64. *See Forms, Instructions & Publications*, IRS, http://www.irs.gov/forms-pubs [https://perma.cc/SY3H-XMZD].
65. Treasury Inspector Gen. for Tax Admin., 2011-40-070, The Internal Revenue Service Provides Helpful and Accurate Tax Law Assistance, but Taxpayers Experience Lengthy Wait Times to Speak with Assistors 21 (2011), https://www.taxnotes.com/research/federal/other-documents/treasury-reports/tigta-says-taxpayers-experiencing-long-wait-times-when-contacting-the/vz18?highlight=2011-040-070 [https://perma.cc/TC8Y-NUJY].
66. IRS, Catalog No. 24811V, 1040 (and 1040-SR) Instructions 20 (2023), https://www.irs.gov/pub/irs-pdf/i1040gi.pdf [https://perma.cc/7EXW-DHMZ] ("For details, *see* Pub. 501.").
67. IRS, Pub. 5296, *Comprehensive Taxpayer Attitude Survey (CTAS)* 2021 Executive Report 33 (2022), https://www.irs.gov/pub/irs-pdf/p5296.pdf [https://perma.cc/WT3U-XBF4].
68. *See* Intuit Inc., Annual Report (Form 10-K) (Aug. 31, 2020) (reporting over 50 million customers); Kush Patel, IBISWorld, Rep. No. 54121D, Tax Preparation Services in the US 25 (2019), [https://perma.cc/NCC6-9JNH (private, uploaded archive)].
69. *See, e.g., TurboTax Online Guarantees*, Intuit TurboTax, https://turbotax.intuit.com/corp/guarantees/ [https://perma.cc/9EAN-TS7H].
70. I.R.C. § 162(a); Treas. Reg. § 1.162-1(a).
71. *Deputy v. Du Pont*, 308 U.S. 488, 497 (1940); *Welch v. Helvering*, 290 U.S. 111, 113 (1933).
72. *Welch*, 290 U.S. at 115.
73. IRS, Pub. 535, Business Expenses 3 (2022), https://www.irs.gov/pub/irs-prior/p535--2022.pdf [https://perma.cc/7S55-MZXQ] [hereinafter IRS, Pub. 535].
74. IRS, *Publication 535 is no longer being revised*, Jan. 22, 2024, https://www.irs.gov/forms-pubs/publication-535-is-no-longer-being-revised.
75. *Id.*
76. *Id.*
77. *Id.*
78. *See, e.g., Reffett v. Comm'r*, 39 T.C. 869, 878–89 (1963) (considering whether other coal operators paid the same contingent witness fees as taxpayer).
79. *See, e.g., United Title Ins. Co. v. Comm'r*, 55 T.C.M. (CCH) 34, 45 (1988).
80. *Poletti v. Comm'r*, 330 F.2d 818, 822 (8th Cir. 1964).
81. *Brizell v. Comm'r*, 93 T.C. 151, 158–59 (1989).
82. IRS Field Service Advisory, 1996 WL 33320948 (Sept. 18, 1996).
83. *See, e.g., Comm'r v. Tellier*, 383 U.S. 687, 689–70 (1966).
84. *Id.* at 689.
85. *See, e.g., Raymond Bertolini Trucking Co. v. Comm'r*, 736 F.2d 1120 (6th Cir. 1984).
86. *See* IRS, Pub. 535, *supra* note 73, at 3.
87. *Id.*

4

Simplexity in Automated Legal Guidance

While simplexity exists in many government communications with the public, it is especially pervasive in automated legal guidance. The online tools, virtual assistants, and other technology that we have described in Chapter 2 help the public understand and apply the law by automating the guidance-giving function. While this can increase the efficiency of the government's interactions with the public, these tools sometimes present the law as simpler and clearer than it is. This phenomenon, which we defined in Chapter 3 as *simplexity*, not only leads to the government providing less-precise advice but also, potentially, to users taking inaccurate legal positions.

This chapter describes the results of our research of automated legal guidance tools across the federal government, which we conducted over a five-year period from 2019 through 2023 (which we refer to throughout this chapter as "our research").[1] We first began this study in preparation for a conference on tax law and artificial intelligence in 2019,[2] and were able to expand it significantly, under the auspices of the Administrative Conference of the United States (ACUS), in 2021.[3] ACUS is an independent US government agency charged with recommending improvements to administrative process and procedure. Our goals in this study were to understand how federal agencies use automated legal guidance and to offer recommendations based on our findings. We describe the results of our ACUS study in detail in Chapter 5.

During our research, we examined the automated legal guidance activities of every US federal agency. We found that they used automation extensively to offer guidance to the public, albeit with varying levels of sophistication and legal content. This chapter focuses on two well-developed forms of automated legal guidance currently employed by federal agencies, both of which we examined in detail during our research: the United States Citizenship and Immigration Services' (USCIS) "Emma" and the Internal Revenue Service's (IRS) "Interactive Tax Assistant" (ITA).

As we will describe, Emma is a natural language sorting model, whereas ITA is a decision tree answer model. These are two different models that automated legal guidance can use, although the different capacities of these models could also be combined in the future. Natural language sorting models rely on sophisticated artificial intelligence to understand users' natural language. This feature is why they are very accessible to individual users. By deciphering users' everyday language-based queries, and then providing relevant responses and links to other sources, these tools effectively become substitutes for modern internet search engines such as Google, Yahoo!, and Bing. Decision tree models, on the other hand, provide the same "answer" (a predesigned set of uniform responses) to every user who provides specific inputs or asks specific questions. Although there were differences between the two models, which we identified by providing these tool inquiries based on personal situations of hypothetical users, we found that Emma and ITA both featured a critical similarity: their potential to mislead members of the public about how the law will apply in their individual circumstances.

EMMA (USCIS)

As explained in Chapter 2, the United States Citizenship and Immigration Services (USCIS) has developed Emma, a computer-generated virtual assistant, to answer questions from members of the public about the US immigration system.[4] Emma was launched in December 2015 to provide the public with a new way to receive answers to their questions about the United States immigration process and their own immigration status.[5]

On its website, USCIS informs users that if they need answers to their immigration questions, they should simply click the "Need Help? Ask Emma" link that appears in the upper-right corner of the website. Emma, the agency explains, can provide "immediate responses" to users' inquiries about USCIS services, guide users through the USCIS website, and find information based on users' questions and search terms.[6]

Simplifications of Technical Information

During the time that we used Emma to conduct our research, we found that the tool offered users straightforward explanations in response to their queries. However, Emma often simplified the law, or omitted nuanced discussions or qualifications regarding technical legal information and requirements.

Example: K-visas
For instance, we observed that, when a user asked Emma, "Where is my Visa?" and clicked on "K Visa (Fiancé Visa)," Emma not only opened a webpage called "Green Card for Fiancé(e) of U.S. Citizen" but also provided the following information:

> The K-visa categories for fiancé(e)s of US citizens and their accompanying minor children (K-1 and K-2 visas) were created to speed up the immigration process for such individuals so they could travel more quickly to the United States. By allowing a fiancé(e) and his/her accompanying minor children to be admitted to the United States as nonimmigrants, fiancé(e)s can be spared a long separation from their intended spouse while continuing their processing for an immigrant visa after the marriage takes place.[7]

Emma's statement that K-visas were created "to speed up the immigration process" offered users an explanation of the legislative purpose[8]; however, Emma did not cite any legislative history or provide caveats to accompany this simple, decontextualized statement of legislative purpose. By failing to offer nuanced information on this topic, Emma may have led people to believe that, if they qualified for K-visas, their immigration process would be speedy (or speedier).

As a technical matter, Emma's statement of purpose simplified a complex issue that even the courts have had to use significant care in explaining. For example, when they examined the purpose behind a K-visa in the 2013 case of *Akram v. Holder*, the Seventh Circuit Court of Appeals concluded that "[t]he purpose of a K visa is to allow fiancé(e)s, spouses, and children of citizens to enter the United States temporarily while awaiting permanent visas."[9] Indeed, in explaining this purpose, the *Akram* court emphasized that this temporary allowance is necessary precisely because of the lengthy amount of time – months or years – that it can take for permanent immigrant visas to be processed.[10]

It is likely that, in referring to the speed of the immigration process with K-visas, Emma was only referring to the speed of getting the K-visas themselves. While it is true that these short-term visas can be issued more quickly than permanent visas,[11] this does not mean that the immigration process, as a whole, is sped up for recipients of K-visas. Emma could have offered a more precise explanation of this type of visa – one that emphasized that this visa may simply make it quicker to be able to enter the United States, in part because the permanent immigrant visa process would remain lengthy. Instead, by offering a simpler explanation of the K-visa acquisition process, Emma sacrificed some important nuance that people might end up wishing they would have known.[12]

The simplification at the heart of Emma's explanations may be relatively benign in this case. Users may not have had as full of an understanding of the interaction between K-visas and the length of the entire immigrant visa process. But this lack of comprehensive information was also unlikely to have misled users in a material way, or to have caused users to take positions in conflict with a more nuanced understanding of the law. Moreover, adding additional detail about the K-visa process may have distracted users from the information they likely cared about most – the length of the wait time until they could be reunified with loved ones in the United States.

Answering Questions Too Narrowly

However, in other cases, we found that Emma's simplifications were more problematic. At times, Emma's attempt to communicate in an easily accessible fashion led to answering a question too narrowly, which may have resulted in a failure to warn users that their decisions could possibly result in negative immigration consequences.

Example: Care for Ailing Relative

For instance, we considered a hypothetical permanent resident of the United States who had a sick relative who needed care in another country. The individual wanted to travel abroad to provide the care, which, according to our scenario, could have resulted in an eight-month absence from the United States. Because the individual did not want to jeopardize their immigration status, they visited Emma and typed, "Can permanent residents leave the United States for eight months?"

Emma, in addition to opening the webpage, *International Travel as a Permanent Resident*, offered the following response:

> Permanent residents are free to travel outside the United States, and temporary or brief travel (less than 1 year) usually does not affect your permanent resident status. If it is determined, however, that you did not intend to make the United States your permanent home, you will be found to have abandoned your permanent resident status. Generally, in order to travel outside the United States, you must present a passport from your country of citizenship or your refugee travel document to travel to a foreign country. When re-entering the US, you will be required to present your green card. Please see the page I've opened for you or select from the link(s) provided to learn more about foreign country travel document requirements, requirements for re-entering the United States from abroad, and other general information regarding travel abroad as a permanent resident.[13]

From this straightforward guidance, the individual may have reasonably concluded that they were not risking their immigration status by traveling outside the United States to care for their ailing relative for eight months. However, by offering straightforward guidance regarding the individual's permanent residence question without considering broader potential ramifications, Emma failed to warn the individual about other potential, and significant, negative immigration consequences.

For instance, while the absence would not necessarily jeopardize the individual's permanent residence status, it could undermine their continuous residence in a way that would interfere with their ability to be naturalized as a US citizen. Naturalization, which is often expected to follow in due course from permanent residence status, confers significant benefits, such as the ability to vote, to obtain a US passport, to petition for family members to come to live in the United States, and to receive security against deportation.[14]

To be eligible for naturalization, an individual must have "resided continuously within the United States ... for a period of at least five years after having been lawfully admitted for permanent residence."[15] Critically, absences from the United States between six months and one year "shall disrupt the continuity of such residence ... unless the applicant can establish otherwise to the satisfaction of the Service." The statute goes on to explain that this rule applies regardless of whether the person "document[ed] an abandonment of lawful permanent resident status, and is still considered a lawful permanent resident under immigration laws."[16] As a result, if the individual ends up being absent from the United States for eight months to take care of their ailing relative, they may very well undermine their continuous residence in a way that may disrupt their ability to become a US citizen.

To be sure, in addition to the page entitled *International Travel as a Permanent Resident*, Emma also provided links to more details that could have alerted users to this naturalization issue. Emma provided a link to *Physical Presence Requirements for Naturalization*.[17] In response to a user clicking that link, Emma provided a lengthy discussion of physical presence requirements, as follows:

> During your application for citizenship, you must prove that you were physically present in the United States. If you are applying as a single applicant, you must have been physically present for at least thirty months of the five-year period preceding your application. If you are applying as the spouse of a US citizen, you must have been physically present for at least eighteen months of the three-year period preceding your application. In addition, you must show that you have resided for at least three months immediately before filing your application in the USCIS district or state where you claim to have residency. Also, in addition to the physical presence requirement, there is a separate continuous residence requirement for naturalization. Please see the page that I've opened for more information on this topic.[18]

While the above text would not alert users to any additional concerns about the eight-month absence, there is more concerning information in the additional webpage that Emma opened (which appeared underneath the dialogue box). According to this newly opened page, "[e]xtended absences outside of the U.S. may disrupt an applicant's continuous residence. Absences of more than six months but less than one year may disrupt an applicant's continuous residence unless the applicant can prove otherwise ...."[19]

With good reason, the individual would likely find this statement significantly more concerning than Emma's earlier statement about physical presence. Whereas

Emma indicated that "[p]ermanent residents are free to travel outside the United States, and temporary or brief travel (less than 1 year) usually does not affect your permanent resident status,"[20] the additional webpage then reversed the presumption, indicating that the eight-month absence may disrupt the applicant's continuous residence unless the applicant can prove otherwise.[21]

The problem is that it took several additional steps to find this last bit of information: It involved clicking through a link that was not obviously important, and then going on to read the webpage that ultimately appeared below the dialogue box that offered Emma's answers. Instead of taking these additional steps and clicking every link to check for possible, conflicting information, many users may have reasonably relied on Emma's initial answer. Why? Because that initial answer suggested, in a straightforward way, that the individual's contemplated absence would not have a negative effect on immigration status.

In this case, Emma answered the user's question too narrowly. Our hypothetical individual asked, "Can permanent residents leave the United States for eight months?" This was a question that did not specify what immigration consequences concerned the user. Rather than broadly considering the possible negative immigration consequences that could have flowed from such an outcome (an approach an attorney might take if asked for advice), Emma categorized the question as one dealing with permanent residency only. As a result, Emma provided the individual with an answer about the effect of their absence on permanent residence (which may be minimal) without offering broader, negative consequences that they might face from taking an absence of that length.

In other words, Emma's tendency to categorize questions and then respond to those categories resulted in a failure to warn the user about significant negative immigration consequences of a travel decision.

Lack of Incorporation of Discretionary Guidance

In other cases, the information that Emma provided failed to consider discretionary guidance. During our research, we also asked questions that specifically arose because of the COVID-19 pandemic. The answers we received could, at times, have significantly disadvantaged the person seeking the information.

Example: Quarantine Outside the United States

During the pandemic, many US permanent residents were outside the United States for longer than a year for a variety of reasons: they fled for a safer place to quarantine, they left to take care of an ailing relative, or they were out of the country for some other reason and could not get back in because of pandemic-related travel restrictions.[22]

During our research, we considered a hypothetical immunocompromised permanent resident who left the United States to quarantine at a family cabin in Canada.[23] After being fully vaccinated, the individual wanted to return to the United States but was not sure what impact their relatively lengthy absence had on their immigration status.[24]

The individual posed the following question to Emma: "Can a permanent resident leave the United States for more than a year?" Emma provided the same response given in the previous example, which dictated, in relevant part, that "[p]ermanent residents are free to travel outside the United States, and temporary or brief travel (less than 1 year) usually does not affect your permanent resident status."[25] The negative implication, of course, was that an absence of more than one year was problematic, as it could have affected the individual's permanent residence status.

In this case, if the individual reviewed the webpage that Emma opened underneath the dialogue box, they would have found even more troubling information. The webpage, *International Travel as a Permanent Resident*, provided, among other things:

> If you plan on being absent from the United States for longer than a year, it is advisable to first apply for a reentry permit on Form I-131. Obtaining a reentry permit prior to leaving the United States allows a permanent or conditional permanent resident to apply for admission into the United States during the permit's validity without the need to obtain a returning resident visa from a US Embassy or Consulate abroad. Please note that it does not guarantee entry into the United States upon your return as you must first be determined to be admissible....[26]

Overall, Emma's guidance may have caused the individual to fear that they would not be readmitted to the United States when they attempted to cross the border back from Canada. That anxiety may have been substantial enough to dissuade the individual from trying to return.

However, the guidance that Emma provided would not have accounted for exercises of discretion. When asked about the matter by a reporter, Aaron Bowker, a public affairs liaison with US Customs and Border Protection, responded, "What were you supposed to do if airlines couldn't fly here for six, eight months, right? You couldn't get back here.... These are all things we take into consideration when we're readmitting people into the country."[27] More generally, Bowker explained, "things are handled on a case-by-case basis.... That is really dependent upon the interview with the [U.S. Customs and Border Protection] officer."[28]

By failing to mention the potential exercise of discretion by a US Customs and Border Protection officer when a permanent resident has been out of the country for more than a year, Emma may have discouraged some people from trying to re-enter, even in situations in which immigration officers may have exercised favorable discretion. To be sure, Emma had a difficult task in providing the rule in a situation in which officers may (or may not) exercise discretion. As Bowker elaborated, "It's very hard to paint a blanket brush for everybody saying everything's going to be OK."[29]

However, it is still instructive to compare the advice that a permanent resident receives from accessing Emma with the advice that a permanent resident might obtain from an attorney. If the individual had consulted with an attorney and explained their desire to re-enter the United States, the attorney might have described the general rules about lengths of absences, but also counseled that immigration officers could apply discretion, and advised regarding the nature of the discretion. Instead, Emma provided a responsive answer that may have failed to provide the whole story.

THE INTERACTIVE TAX ASSISTANT (IRS)

As Chapter 2 described, the IRS has turned more and more to the "Interactive Tax Assistant" (ITA) to assist taxpayers with their compliance obligations.[30] As the IRS explains, ITA is "a tax law resource that takes you through a series of questions and provides you with responses to tax law questions."[31] ITA can address inquiries in dozens of categories of tax law, ranging, for example, from a taxpayer's eligibility to deduct medical and dental expenses and claim education tax credits to estimated tax payment obligations.[32]

The Interactive Tax Assistant has often provided taxpayers with accurate answers to simple questions, such as the required forms and deadlines for filing tax returns.[33] However, even though ITA features more tightly controlled user inputs than Emma, both automated legal guidance tools share a critical similarity: As ITA has attempted to respond to questions that are even slightly more complex, it has also presented users with simplified answers that deviate from the formal tax law. Following some of these simplified responses would, at times, have reduced taxpayers' tax liability, whereas at other times following them would have resulted in consequences adverse to the taxpayers' interests.

Below are several illustrations of ITA's responses to taxpayer inquiries, each of which falls into one of three categories: those that are consistent with tax law, those that are favorable to taxpayers, and those that are unfavorable to them.

Consistent with Tax Law

During our research, we found that ITA often delivered accurate responses to taxpayer questions about simple issues that do not involve complex statutes or regulations or conflicting judicial decisions.

Example: Due Dates
For example, we considered a hypothetical single mother who, in early April 2020, was determining whether she could have additional time to file her individual

income tax return, IRS Form 1040. The taxpayer visited ITA and clicked on this topic: "What is the due date of my federal tax return or am I eligible to request an extension?"[34] ITA then asked the taxpayer a series of questions, including "Do you want to know if you are eligible to request an extension, or are you inquiring about the due date of your return (including any extended due dates)?"[35] After the taxpayer answered additional questions regarding residency and refund status, ITA informed the taxpayer that, in 2020, the deadlines for both filing and payment were automatically extended to July 15, 2020, due to the COVID-19 pandemic.[36]

As this example demonstrates, for questions involving basic tax compliance issues, such as deadlines, ITA can aid the taxpayer accurately and efficiently. As soon as the taxpayer responded that she would not be living outside of the United States and Puerto Rico on April 15, 2020, ITA provided the deadline for filing and payment.[37] If, on the other hand, the taxpayer had responded that she would be living outside of the country on that date, ITA would have asked a series of follow-up questions regarding the taxpayer's need for an extension before providing the deadline.[38]

In this example, ITA provided the taxpayer with a personalized answer quickly, and with information that was consistent with the relevant statutory and administrative authorities.

Taxpayer-Favorable Simplifications

We also found that when taxpayers asked ITA questions that involved more complex legal issues, implicated specific aspects of taxpayers' personal situations, or both, the tool also delivered answers that simplify the tax law in ways that are seemingly favorable to taxpayers.

Example: Artificial Teeth Expense

One instance in which ITA may offer taxpayer-favorable deviations is when it uses the existence of certain facts as a proxy for a more complex determination. For instance, we considered a hypothetical aspiring model living in Los Angeles, California, who attempted to alter his physical appearance – specifically, to reduce the spacing between his front teeth. He believed this would help him obtain jobs as a model in print and online advertisements. After having no luck with braces and other orthodontic measures, he visited a maxillofacial surgeon who described a procedure for replacing his four natural front teeth with four artificial teeth, at a cost of approximately $10,000. The aspiring model considered the cost of the surgery and decided that he needed to determine whether he would qualify for any tax credits or other benefits to offset some of the expense.

When he visited ITA to investigate the tax consequences of the surgery, he selected "Can I deduct my medical and dental expenses?"[39] After asking a few questions about the model's adjusted gross income for the year and the amount of the expense, ITA asked a critical, fact-specific question: "What type of expense are you asking about?"[40] From the drop-down menu provided, the taxpayer selected "Artificial Teeth Expenses."[41] After just a few more clicks, ITA informed him that "Your Artificial Teeth Expenses are a qualified deductible expense."[42] Satisfied with this response, the model may have decided to have the surgery and later claim a medical expense deduction on his tax return.

While the taxpayer in this example was able to obtain a definitive answer to his question about the deduction for artificial teeth using ITA, the answer was inconsistent with the formal tax law. Under Section 213(d)(9) of the Internal Revenue Code, taxpayers are not permitted to claim medical expense deductions for cosmetic surgery.[43] In this example, ITA sought simplified inputs by asking about the specific type of expense, artificial teeth, but failed to ask questions about some of the more uncertain features of the statute, such as whether the procedure promoted "the proper function of the body" or treated a condition that resulted from "accident or trauma."[44] At the same time, the taxpayer knew the reasons for the surgery – to improve his chances of securing modeling jobs, not to treat a condition resulting from accident or trauma – but ITA did not have access to this information.

The Interactive Tax Assistant's use of only certain facts (artificial teeth) as a proxy for a more complex inquiry caused it to deliver a taxpayer-favorable answer. Since this answer directly conflicted with relevant statutory authority, it is an answer that could lead the IRS to challenge the taxpayer were it to audit him.

Example: Lead-based Paint Removal Expense
Another feature of ITA that may yield taxpayer-favorable deviations is its failure to describe all the statutory or regulatory requirements that a taxpayer must fulfill to claim a specific tax benefit. We observed this feature during our research, when we considered the hypothetical owner of a small construction company who decided to remove cracking lead-based paint from the walls of her home due to her concern that her children might ingest some of the paint chips.

Before starting the paint-removal process, she researched whether she could qualify for a tax deduction or credit for the expenses involved in the project. She visited ITA and selected the option entitled "Lead-based Paint Removal/Covering Services" under medical and dental expenses.[45] After asking the taxpayer preliminary questions, some of which were about her children, ITA asked, "Was the surface from which the paint was removed in poor repair (peeling or cracking) or within the child's reach?"[46] The taxpayer clicked "Yes," and, in response, ITA informed her that "Your Lead-based Paint Removal/Covering Services are a qualified deductible expense."[47]

The Interactive Tax Assistant provided an answer that appeared to confirm the taxpayer was entitled to a tax deduction; however, this is the type of deduction that the IRS could challenge upon review. An IRS revenue ruling states that taxpayers may deduct the cost of lead-based paint removal as a medical expense; however, the IRS has also required such removal to occur pursuant to a medical doctor's recommendation and as a result of certification by local health authorities.[48] If, during a subsequent audit, the IRS later discovered that the taxpayer did not satisfy these requirements, it could take a contrary position to ITA and deny her claimed deduction.

In this case, ITA simplified the description of the applicable tax law, which was implicit in its questions to the taxpayer, by failing to ask her the necessary questions related to certain factual requirements (such as whether she had received a doctor's recommendation and certification by the health authorities). Worse yet, because ITA asked her a series of detailed and specific questions, it is understandable that the taxpayer would reasonably assume that she could rely on ITA's answer to her inquiry. As a result, ITA may have led this hypothetical taxpayer to take a potentially deniable deduction while, at the same time, causing her to believe she had met all requirements.

Example: Tuxedo Expense

Finally, ITA can deliver taxpayer-favorable deviations by using terms and phrases that do not appear in the statutes or regulations. To examine this phenomenon, we considered a hypothetical individual who served as a maître d' (head waiter) at a French restaurant in Chicago and who was required to purchase and wear a tuxedo to work each evening.

In this scenario, he last purchased three tuxedos, at a cost of $7,500, in 2017. Two years later, in 2019, he heard from a friend at a competing restaurant that the cost of the tuxedos could be tax deductible.[49] The maître d' quickly visited the IRS's website and asked ITA about this issue, clicking on the following category: "Work clothes, protective clothing or uniforms."[50]

After asking a few introductory questions, ITA asked the following question: "Are the clothes suitable for everyday wear?"[51] The maître d' considered this question briefly before clicking "No."[52] He knew that he only wore the tuxedos to work and would not wear them as "everyday wear."[53] ITA promptly informed the maître d', "You can deduct the cost of work clothes and the upkeep of those clothes since you must wear them as a condition of your employment and they are not suitable for everyday wear."[54] He may have followed this advice and filed an amended tax return for 2017, which included the tax deduction for the tuxedos.

While ITA's response that the taxpayer may claim the deduction for his work clothes appears to have been unambiguous, this answer was consistent with neither the relevant case law nor the IRS's official position. As most teachers and students of basic income tax know, individuals who attempted to claim miscellaneous itemized deduction for work clothing expenses (prior to the suspension of the deduction starting in 2018)[55] were required to meet the requirements of a decision issued in 1980 by the Fifth Circuit Court of Appeals, *Pevsner* v. *Commissioner*.[56] In that case, an employee of an Yves Saint Laurent (YSL) boutique in Dallas, Texas, attempted to claim an ordinary and necessary business expense deduction for the cost of YSL clothing that she was required to wear to work.[57] Both the IRS and the court disallowed the deduction under these circumstances because the clothing at issue was "adaptable to general usage as ordinary clothing," even though the taxpayer's employer required her to purchase it.[58] Specifically, applying an objective standard, the court found that clothing was not deductible because it could be worn for "general usage" by an individual, even though the taxpayer in that specific case did not do so.[59]

When ITA asked the taxpayer in the example earlier about the tuxedos, it used a phrase that does not appear in the text of *Pevsner* or statutory or regulatory authority – "everyday wear." This phrase appears to be a simplification of the *Pevsner* test and, presumably, is easier for people who are not tax experts to apply than "general usage."[60] Yet this new language could easily have caused a taxpayer like the maître d' to consider whether he wore, or could wear, the tuxedos *every day* rather than whether he could wear them to an event where this type of clothing was the norm, such as weddings or other formal events. If the IRS were to audit the maître d', it could have rejected the business expense deduction by applying the *Pevsner* test. In this case, the subtle changes to the relevant judicial test that appear in ITA's questions caused ITA to deliver dubious legal guidance to the taxpayer.

Taxpayer-Unfavorable Simplifications

In addition to providing taxpayers with answers that simplify the law in taxpayer-favorable ways, we also found that ITA presented guidance that simplified the tax law in ways that, if followed by taxpayers, would have resulted in less favorable tax consequences.

Example: College Athletic Scholarship

One of ITA's most frequent types of taxpayer-unfavorable simplifications occurs when it answers a taxpayer inquiry without incorporating potential statutory or administrative exceptions.

For instance, we considered a hypothetical high school competitive swimmer who received a swimming scholarship to a university with an NCAA Division I swim team. The student received a scholarship offer letter from the university that stated that the student would receive the scholarship if she was eligible to participate in swim meets, which would require her to meet certain physical fitness and health requirements. The letter also stated that the students could be required to participate in fundraising and promotional events throughout the academic year.

The student's parents visited ITA to learn whether they were required to report their daughter's swimming scholarship as taxable income and selected the topic related to academic scholarships, fellowships, and grants.[61] At that point, ITA asked whether they considered the scholarship to be a "payment for services" that the student was "required to perform as a condition of receiving the scholarship."[62]

After considering the university's requirement that their daughter participate in swim meets and fundraising events, the parents selected "All" in response to this question.[63] The parents went on to answer additional questions posed by ITA, and after this process was finished, ITA stated that "[t]he [scholarship] payment must be included in income" because it "was received for services you were required to perform...."[64]

Like the other examples described in this chapter, ITA's response, while clear and simple, may also have been inconsistent with the applicable tax law. In the past, the IRS has considered whether athletic scholarships that require participation in competitions are "qualified scholarships," which are excluded from gross income.[65] In Revenue Ruling 77-263, the IRS clarified that an athletic scholarship is not taxable if it is not cancelled "in the event the student cannot participate," including due to events such as injury or ill health.[66]

Despite this guidance and the judicial decisions it references, ITA did not ask any questions of the parents regarding the substantive terms of their daughter's scholarship. Instead, ITA only inquired whether the taxpayer was receiving the scholarship "for services."[67] Consequently, if the parents followed the guidance offered by ITA because of their responses, ITA could have influenced their decision to report the scholarship as taxable income, even though they could have had legal grounds for excluding it.

Example: Teeth Whitening Expenses
When ITA uses certain facts as a proxy for a more complex determination, it also may incorrectly indicate that a tax deduction or credit is disallowed. During our research, we considered a hypothetical taxpayer who was a cancer survivor and who experienced several side effects from months of chemotherapy, including developing discolored patches on her teeth.[68] After receiving approval from her oncologist, the taxpayer spent over $1,000 on professional teeth-whitening services from her dentist to address the discoloration.

The taxpayer researched whether she could claim a medical expense deduction for the teeth-whitening services, which were not covered by dental insurance. She contacted her friend, an accountant, to inquire about the deduction. Her accountant visited the ITA website and, from the categories of questions, selected medical and dental expenses.[69] The accountant then clicked on an option called "Teeth Whitening Expenses," under which ITA stated that "Teeth Whitening Expenses are not a deductible expense."[70] After the accountant explained the IRS position, based on ITA's response, the taxpayer may have followed this response and not have attempted to claim the medical expense deduction for the teeth whitening.

Despite the unambiguous nature of ITA's response, the IRS has implied, in more formal guidance, that teeth-whitening expenses could be deductible in certain circumstances. In Revenue Ruling 2003-57, the IRS stated that the cost of teeth whitening is not deductible medical care when the procedure is not used to treat discoloration that is "caused by a disfiguring disease or treatment."[71] In other words, if the reason for the procedure was merely to improve the taxpayer's appearance and was not due to a disease or treatment for the disease, then the expense was "cosmetic surgery," which does not fit within the definition of medical care.[72]

Here, however, the taxpayer experienced tooth discoloration because of the chemotherapy that had treated her cancer. Yet ITA never asked questions regarding the facts surrounding the teeth-whitening expense and instead assumed that teeth whitening is a purely cosmetic expenditure. As a result, ITA presented a simplified output – teeth whitening expenses are not deductible – that may have incorrectly caused the taxpayer to forgo the medical expense deduction.

Example: Charitable Contributions

As we have seen, when ITA asks questions without defining terms or providing additional context, it may deviate from the formal tax law in a way that is not favorable to the taxpayer. During our study, we considered a hypothetical taxpayer whose father received treatment at a local hospital for a serious medical injury resulting from an automobile accident. After the medical treatment of the taxpayer's father, the taxpayer decided to make a charitable contribution to the tax-exempt foundation that receives donations on the hospital's behalf. When making a $2,000 charitable gift to the hospital foundation, the taxpayer noted that the gift was in honor of his father (and included his father's name with the gift).

In considering whether he could deduct this gift, the taxpayer visited ITA.[73] During the exchange, ITA posed the following question: "Was your contribution to the qualified organization intended for a specific person, other than for a person in foster care or a student living in your home?"[74] After considering this question, the taxpayer clicked "Yes" because he did intend for his gift to honor a "specific person," his father. In response, ITA quickly informed the taxpayer that "[y]ou are not eligible to claim a deduction ... for [this] charitable contribution" because it was "intended for a specific person."[75] After receiving this response, together with ITA's explanation, the taxpayer may have decided not to claim the charitable contribution deduction.

In this example, ITA may have caused a taxpayer to refrain from claiming a deduction to which he was legally entitled because of its vague and confusing questioning. Specifically, ITA asked if the gift was "intended for a specific person," but did not include any explanation of this term or provide any examples of what this term meant.[76] By contrast, the written IRS publication on this topic, *IRS Publication 526 (Charitable Contributions)*, describes the meaning of this term, specifically stating that "[p]ayments to a hospital that are for a specific patient's care or for services for a specific patient" are not deductible as charitable contributions.[77]

If the taxpayer had received this additional explanation, he might have concluded that his gift was not "intended for a specific person" because it was not payment for services for his father. Without explanation of all terms in its questions, ITA can cause taxpayers to enter responses that lead to deviations from the tax law that are, in the end, contrary to the taxpayer's interests.

WHY AUTOMATED LEGAL GUIDANCE EXACERBATES SIMPLEXITY

As the earlier examples illustrate, while automated legal guidance can enable administrative agencies to offer clear and simple answers to the public, it can also cause people to follow responses that diverge in critical ways from the underlying law. This can also be true of simplexity in traditional written legal guidance to the public.[78] But automated legal guidance tools, such as ITA and Emma, can create more powerful and pervasive forms of simplexity than traditional written legal guidance for several reasons: automated legal guidance presents personalized communication; it often offers even less qualified explanations of the law than exists in written legal guidance; and it delivers information to requesting individuals almost immediately.

As a useful analogy, imagine a student who is having trouble with their computer and needs assistance figuring out what to do. The student has three options for getting help: a computer manual, a phone conversation with a representative from the computer company, or an online discussion with the computer company's chatbot. The first form of assistance is akin to the type of written, informal guidance that agencies have provided the public for decades. The second form is like the oral, informal guidance agencies provide the public through human representatives. And the third form is closest to automated legal guidance.

The student may encounter simplexity in all three forms of assistance – it is very hard to explain the mechanics of a computer problem to someone who is not an expert. But the process of searching the computer manual and discussing the problem with the human service representative is also likely to force the student to explore multiple options. Contrast this with the student's experience with a chatbot that asks de-contextualized questions and then, in response, provides a one-screen "answer" to what is wrong with the computer. This latter form of assistance may offer the student an even more constrained set of information. If this is all the information the student gets, the student may be even more likely to be affected by simplexity.

Of course, in the context of a problem with a computer, if the student uses the answer the chatbot provides to try a certain fix, and it doesn't work, the student can try again. In contrast, the individual who takes a tax return or immigration position or relies on a chatbot in making other important decisions about government obligations and benefits may not have that luxury. This makes the impact of simplexity in the context of automated legal guidance particularly important.

Personalization

Automated legal guidance, unlike the guidance in static printed publications, delivers personalized, rather than generic, information to people in response to their direct inquiries. For instance, when individuals seek guidance from ITA, they answer a series of questions, such as whether they are looking to deduct medical expenses that had been reimbursed by health insurance. In nearly all cases, the questions use second-person pronouns (*i.e.*, "you" or "yours"). After receiving and processing these responses, ITA presents the taxpayer with an output that most reasonable people would believe is tailored to their circumstances, especially because these answers use language that makes it seem like the system is responding to the taxpayers directly (*e.g.*, "*Your* artificial teeth expenses are a qualified deductible expense.")[79]

Behavioral research shows that personalized communication can have a greater impact on individuals' beliefs and actions than generic statements. Online advertisers, political campaign consultants, and telemarketers often use second-person pronouns because they "enhance consumer involvement and brand attitude as a result of increasing the extent that consumers engage in self-referencing."[80] Similarly, marketing researchers have found that when a solicitation contains the individual's name in the subject line, individuals are significantly more likely to open an email and ultimately respond positively to the solicitation.[81]

How do these findings relate to what government agencies are programming their automated tools to do? Part of the motivation behind personalization of guidance, whether by government or private-sector actors, is to induce reliance and satisfaction from users. By requiring users to input personal information, such as their own adjusted gross income and other personal details, and presenting outputs with personalized language, these agencies are attempting not only to provide relevant information but also to convince users that this information has directly addressed their inquiries.

Because of the nature of the medium and the interactions, automated legal guidance achieves the desired level of personalization much more effectively than static written publications. Even though static publications can use second-person pronouns, people know that these publications are written in a generalized way so that they are applicable to all potential readers. The text on the page may use the words "you" or "your," but it clearly does not vary depending upon the specific reader.[82]

As communication research has shown, personalized messages, including those that use second-person pronouns, are not always more effective than generalized messages.[83] Indeed, it is the reader's perception that matters. The key feature that allows advertisers to affect consumers' behavior is that the recipient of the information perceives that it is personalized. Automated legal guidance offers this possibility in a way that static, written publications do not. ITA, for example, asks a series of questions that solicit specific information, including personal details such as the user's income, marital status, and children, before it provides guidance to the taxpayer.[84] Questions that seek personal information and that are directly addressed to the taxpayer may allow ITA to achieve perceived, even if not actual, personalization.[85] In line with behavioral research, this perceived personalization may increase the impact of automated legal guidance and its inherent simplicity.

Nonqualified Statements

Another reason why simplicity in automated legal guidance may be particularly impactful is that this type of guidance can offer nonqualified answers. For example, when our hypothetical aspiring model sought information regarding expenses for his artificial teeth, he wanted to learn whether he could qualify for a tax deduction or credit. The problem was that, once he selected "artificial teeth" from the list of possibilities under medical and dental expenses, ITA responded with a nonqualified statement that the expense was deductible.

Despite the possibility that the IRS could characterize the expense as cosmetic surgery, ITA did not provide a qualified answer, which would have read something like this: The expense is deductible as long as the procedure was "necessary to ameliorate a deformity arising from, or directly related to, a congenital abnormality, a personal injury resulting from an accident or trauma, or disfiguring disease."[86] This formulation would have alerted the taxpayer that he would have to satisfy additional statutory or regulatory requirements to claim a medical expense deduction. Instead, whenever taxpayers complete the questions that ITA poses, the tool adopts a binary approach (e.g., deductible or nondeductible) in analyzing the inquiry and presents its response as the "answer."[87]

The Internal Revenue Service publications, in contrast, often include general discussion of the requirements and exceptions that apply to specific tax treatment. For example, IRS Publication 502 uses plain language to describe the tax treatment of medical expenses.[88] It explains that artificial teeth expenses are deductible, but, in text that is nearby, describes rules regarding cosmetic surgery.[89] The publication informs readers that "[g]enerally, you can't include in medical expenses the amount you pay for cosmetic surgery."[90] It then provides a number of examples, involving procedures such as breast cancer surgery, that describe when an expense is, and is not, cosmetic surgery. IRS publications at least offer the possibility that a taxpayer would read text addressing both artificial teeth and cosmetic surgery and conclude that additional research is necessary.

Some automated legal guidance tools issue even less qualified responses than static agency publications provide. For example, ITA provides taxpayers with simple and direct "answers" that taxpayers can follow. These responses, however, are far removed from a broader legal context. This makes it easier for members of the public to receive answers that they can apply easily and upon which they feel they can rely. But it also can make it even less likely that users of automated legal guidance will be responsive to nuances and complexities in the underlying law.

Immediate Responses

Finally, automated legal guidance can deliver information more immediately than static written publications. For example, when taxpayers start the process of submitting information to ITA, the initial screen provides an "[e]stimated completion time" for each question.[91] When we conducted our research, the estimates for questions about basic topics, such as filing dates and the amount of the applicable standard deduction, were generally less than ten minutes.[92] Even for more complex topics, such as the deductibility of medical and dental expenses, we received estimates of fifteen minutes.[93] Further, if taxpayers respond to questions quickly, the total time it would take to receive an answer to the initial inquiry can be significantly less than these estimates.

The Internal Revenue Service publications, in contrast, can number in the hundreds of pages and require readers to consider numerous exceptions, requirements, and examples.[94] Even the online versions of IRS publications contain hyperlinks to other IRS publications, which require additional reading and review.[95] Assessing the information from these written publications takes not only a lot of time but also a lot of skill.

Individuals may rely more on automated legal guidance than other types of advice because of its ability to deliver information promptly and without charge. Marketing research shows that consumers value automated systems when they deliver requested information in as little time as possible.[96] This is a significant reason why government agencies have attempted to emulate the private sector in developing automated systems.

One effect of the immediate nature of automated legal guidance tools' responses is that they may counteract individuals' interest in conducting additional research or contacting third-party advisors for advice. In contrast, if someone reads apparently conflicting statements in a static publication (such as a statement that artificial teeth are deductible but cosmetic surgery is not), that person might be encouraged to ask an expert for guidance (assuming the taxpayer could afford this service).

For this and all the other reasons discussed earlier, automated legal guidance can provide the government with greater power to shape individuals' understanding of, and compliance with, the law than static publications.

* * *

As this chapter illustrates, federal government agencies are increasingly using automated tools to communicate the law to the public. These tools, which are already being extensively used by some agencies, and are in development or in more nascent stages in others, have the potential to significantly increase the reach of these organizations' digital guidance efforts.

Automated legal guidance tools can answer questions from the public about the law in a straightforward fashion. Ideally, their ability to do so provides useful guidance to the public while also freeing up constrained agency resources, allowing agency officials to focus on more difficult inquiries. However, as we have illustrated through numerous examples in this chapter, these tools can also systematically create divergences from a more comprehensive understanding of the law. Depending on the case, these answers can either benefit or disadvantage their recipients.

We should emphasize that the examples that we identified in this chapter are merely that – examples. Because so many more examples may be identified, a broader phenomenon comes into focus: in attempting to provide straightforward answers to the public's questions, automated legal guidance tools often only offer part of a more complex story. Sometimes, the answers that these tools provide will fit the question exactly and provide all the information relevant to the inquiry, or may, at least, be close enough, in that they do not mislead users in a material way. However, on other occasions, automated tools will fail to provide comprehensive answers to people's questions in ways that are much more problematic. They may only offer an abbreviated description of legal requirements, or provide overly simplistic summaries. They may categorize the question and respond with answers that fit in that category, while failing to identify a deeper or broader legal issue. They may also engage in other simplifications that make the advice understandable, but misleading.

These deviations are critical because they are inherent to automated legal guidance. The very goal of providing straightforward responses to legal inquiries necessitates deviations from the law when the law itself is not straightforward. Moreover, the more effective the automated legal guidance tools are in encouraging users to follow their guidance, the more these tools may exacerbate the impact of these deviations from the law.

NOTES

1. *See* Joshua D. Blank & Leigh Osofsky, *Legal Calculators and the Tax System*, 16 OHIO ST. TECH. L. J. 73 (2020) [hereinafter Blank & Osofsky, *Legal Calculators*]; Joshua D. Blank & Leigh Osofsky, *Automated Legal Guidance*, 106 CORNELL L. REV. 179 (2020) [hereinafter Blank & Osofsky, *Automated Legal Guidance*]; JOSHUA D. BLANK & LEIGH OSOFSKY, AUTOMATED LEGAL GUIDANCE AT FEDERAL AGENCIES (2022) (report to the Admin. Conf. of the US) [hereinafter BLANK & OSOFSKY, GUIDANCE AT FEDERAL AGENCIES], https://www.acus.gov/projects/automated-legal-guidance-federal-agencies [https://perma.cc/265T-Q28Y]; *see also* Joshua D. Blank & Leigh Osofsky, *Automated Agencies*, 107 MINN. L. REV. 2115 (2023) [hereinafter Blank & Osofsky, *Automated Agencies*].

2. *See* Blank & Osofsky, *Legal Calculators*, *supra* note 1; Blank & Osofsky, *Automated Legal Guidance*, *supra* note 1.
3. *See* BLANK & OSOFSKY, GUIDANCE AT FEDERAL AGENCIES, *supra* note 1; *see also* Blank & Osofsky, *Automated Agencies*, *supra* note 1.
4. *Meet Emma, Our Virtual Assistant*, U.S. CITIZENSHIP & IMMIGR. SERVS., https://www.uscis.gov/tools/meet-emma-our-virtual-assistant [https://perma.cc/UB4R-TKMD] (last updated Apr. 13, 2018).
5. Aaron Boyd, *USCIS Virtual Assistant to Offer More "Human" Digital Experience*, FED. TIMES (Nov. 16, 2015), https://www.federaltimes.com/it-networks/2015/11/16/uscis-virtual-assistant-to-offer-more-human-digital-experience [https://perma.cc/M8UM-ZAEP].
6. *See Meet Emma, Our Virtual Assistant*, *supra* note 4.
7. *See Meet Emma, Our Virtual Assistant*, U.S. CITIZENSHIP & IMMIGR. SERVS., https://www.uscis.gov/tools/meet-emma-our-virtual-assistant [click "Ask Emma"; then type: "Where is my Visa?"; then click send; then click "K Visa (Fiance Visa)"] [https://perma.cc/2P4W-QENP (uploaded archive)] [hereinafter *Emma*, Where is my Visa?]; *Green Card for Fiancé(e) of U.S. Citizen*, U.S. CITIZENSHIP & IMMIGR. SERVS., https://www.uscis.gov/green-card/green-card-eligibility/green-card-for-fiancee-of-us-citizen [https://perma.cc/56G7-YRMF] (last updated Feb. 8, 2018).
8. *Emma*, Where is my Visa?, *supra* note 7.
9. *Akram v. Holder*, 721 F.3d 853, 859 (7th Cir. 2013).
10. *Id.* at 855.
11. *Id.*
12. Interestingly, the webpage to which Emma refers users does not discuss the impact of K-visas on the speed of the immigration process at all. *Green Card for Fiancé(e) of U.S. Citizen*, *supra* note 7.
13. *Meet Emma, Our Virtual Assistant*, U.S. CITIZENSHIP & IMMIGR. SERVS., https://www.uscis.gov/tools/meet-emma-our-virtual-assistant (click "Ask Emma"; then type: "Can permanent residents leave the United States for eight months?"; then click send) [https://perma.cc/BP6U-UP3T (uploaded archive)] [hereinafter *Emma*, Eight Months]; *International Travel as a Permanent Resident*, U.S. CITIZENSHIP & IMMIGR. SERVS., https://www.uscis.gov/green-card/after-we-grant-your-green-card/international-travel-as-a-permanent-resident [https://perma.cc/W4L8-SG9Q] (last updated Jan. 11, 2018).
14. Elizabeth Carlson, *Handling the Complex Naturalization Process*, 15–06 IMMIGR. BRIEFINGS 1, 1 (2015).
15. 8 C.F.R. § 316.2(a)(3) (2022).
16. 8 C.F.R. § 316.5(c)(1)(i) (2022).
17. *Emma*, Eight Months, *supra* note 13.
18. *Id.* (click "Physical Presence Requirements for Naturalization") [https://perma.cc/5YT5-MLUC (uploaded archive)].
19. *Continuous Residence and Physical Presence Requirements for Naturalization*, U.S. CITIZENSHIP & IMMIGR. SERVS (May 25, 2021) https://www.uscis.gov/citizenship/continuous-residence-and-physical-presence-requirements-for-naturalization [https://perma.cc/2CPB-EDAP]. A user may also get to this information by reading the text that appears on the webpage *International Travel as a Permanent Resident*, which appears underneath the dialogue box of Emma's first answer. *International Travel as a Permanent Resident*, *supra* note 13. However, the text is hidden inside a tab that is labeled "What if my trip abroad will last longer than 1 year?" *Id.* As a result, a user is relatively unlikely to find the text in this way.
20. *Emma*, Eight Months, *supra* note 13.

21. *Continuous Residence and Physical Presence Requirements for Naturalization, supra* note 19.
22. Joel Rose, *Permanent Residents Who Left the U.S. During the Pandemic Worry They Can't Come Home,* NPR (July 24, 2021, 7:01 AM), https://www.npr.org/2021/07/24/1019423852/permanent-residents-left-u-s-pandemic-return [https://perma.cc/FX6M-LN3C].
23. This hypothetical is based on one of the stories detailed in the NPR article. *See id.*
24. *Id.*
25. *Meet Emma, Our Virtual Assistant,* U.S. CITIZENSHIP & IMMIGR. SERVS., https://www.uscis.gov/tools/meet-emma-our-virtual-assistant (click "Ask Emma"; then type: "Can a permanent resident leave the United States for more than a year?"; then click send) [https://perma.cc/5YE6-E3HQ (uploaded archive)].
26. *International Travel as a Permanent Resident, supra* note 13. This text would also appear underneath the dialogue box in response to an inquiry to Emma about being absent for eight months. *Emma,* Eight Months, *supra* note 13.
27. Rose, *supra* note 22.
28. *Id.*
29. *Id.*
30. *See Interactive Tax Assistant (ITA),* IRS, https://www.irs.gov/help/ita [https://perma.cc/SB4C-FAQ3] (last updated Jan. 16, 2024); *see also* TREASURY INSPECTOR GEN. FOR TAX ADMIN., 2011-40-070, THE INTERNAL REVENUE SERVICE PROVIDES HELPFUL AND ACCURATE TAX LAW ASSISTANCE, BUT TAXPAYERS EXPERIENCE LENGTHY WAIT TIMES TO SPEAK WITH ASSISTORS 15–16 (2011), https://www.taxnotes.com/research/federal/other-documents/treasury-reports/tigta-says-taxpayers-experiencing-long-wait-times-when-contacting-the/vz18?highlight=2011-040-070 [https://perma.cc/27HG-PUM2 (uploaded archive)].
31. *Id.* at 15.
32. *See id.*
33. *See Interactive Tax Assistant (ITA), supra* note 30.
34. *See* Blank & Osofsky, *Automated Agencies, supra* note 1 at n. 152–56.
35. *See Id.*
36. *Id.*
37. *Id.*
38. *Id.*
39. *Interactive Tax Assistant (ITA), supra* note 30; *Can I Deduct My Medical and Dental Expenses?,* IRS, https://www.irs.gov/help/ita/can-i-deduct-my-medical-and-dental-expenses [https://perma.cc/5X3N-WS8D] (last updated Jan. 16, 2024).
40. *Can I Deduct My Medical and Dental Expenses?, supra* note 39 (click "Begin"; then click "Continue"; then input the tax year; then select "Yes"; then select "No"; then select "Yes"; then select "No"; then select marital status and filing status) [https://perma.cc/EJ3T-4P3N (uploaded archive)].
41. *Id.* (from "What type of expense are you asking about?" select "A"; then select "Artificial Teeth Expenses") [https://perma.cc/P97Z-8UYM (uploaded archive)].
42. *Id.* (from "Artificial Teeth Expenses," select "Continue"; then select "All"; then select "None"; then select "None"; then select "Self") [https://perma.cc/FE99-5JMS (uploaded archive)].
43. *See* I.R.C. § 213(d)(9).
44. *See id.*
45. *Interactive Tax Assistant (ITA), supra* note 30; *Can I Deduct My Medical and Dental Expenses?, supra* note 39 (click "Begin"; then click "Continue"; then input the tax year; then select "Yes"; then select "No"; then select "Yes"; then select "No"; then select

marital status and filing status; then select "L"; then select "Lead-Based Paint Removal/Covering Services") [https://perma.cc/6QEV-UZBZ (uploaded archive)] [hereinafter Lead-Based Paint].
46. Lead-Based Paint, *supra* note 45 (from "Lead-Based Paint Removal/Covering Services" select "Continue"; then select "Yes"; then select "Yes") [https://perma.cc/XEV7-EJBR (uploaded archive)].
47. *Id.* (from "Was the surface from which the paint was removed in poor repair (peeling or cracking) or within the child's reach?" select "Yes"; then select "All"; then select "None"; then select "None"; then select "Dependent"; then select "Yes"; then select "No") [https://perma.cc/2LH7-A3KK (uploaded archive)].
48. *See* Rev. Rul. 79–66, 1979-1 C.B. 114.
49. *See* I.R.C. § 162(a) (2018); IRS, Pub. 529: Miscellaneous Deductions 12 (2019), https://www.irs.gov/pub/irs-prior/p529–2019.pdf [https://perma.cc/5W73-RLWG].
50. *See* Blank & Osofsky, *Automated Legal Guidance*, *supra* note 1 at n. 173–78.
51. *See id.*
52. *See id.*
53. *See id.*
54. *See id.*
55. I.R.C § 67(g).
56. 628 F.2d 467 (5th Cir. 1980).
57. *Id.* at 468–69.
58. *Id.* at 469.
59. *Id.* at 470–71.
60. *Pevsner*, 628 F.2d at 469.
61. *Interactive Tax Assistant (ITA)*, *supra* note 30; *Do I Include My Scholarship, Fellowship, or Education Grant as Income on My Tax Return?*, IRS, https://www.irs.gov/help/ita/do-i-include-my-scholarship-fellowship-or-education-grant-as-income-on-my-tax-return [https://perma.cc/5N43-HQUL] (last updated Jan. 16, 2024).
62. *Do I Include My Scholarship, Fellowship, or Education Grant as Income on My Tax Return?*, *supra* note 61 (click "Begin"; then click "Continue"; then input the tax year; then select "Yes" and "No"; then select "Yes"; then select "None"; then select "Qualified expense") [https://perma.cc/3NZ7-XYCT (uploaded archive)] [hereinafter Payment for Services].
63. *Id.*
64. *Id.* (from "What portion of the scholarship, fellowship or grant was a payment for services you were required to perform as a condition of receiving the scholarship, fellowship or grant?" select "All"; then select "No") [https://perma.cc/DG3C-FRR7 (uploaded archive)]
65. *See* Rev. Rul. 77-263, 1977-2 C.B. 47. For further discussion, see Richard Schmalbeck & Lawrence Zelenak, *The NCAA and the IRS: Life at the Intersection of College Sports and the Federal Income Tax*, 92 S. Cal. L. Rev. 1087, 1125 (2019).
66. Rev. Rul. 77-263, 1977-2 C.B. 47.
67. Payment for Services, *supra* note 62.
68. For discussion, *see Oral Complications of Chemotherapy and Head/Neck Radiation (PDQ®)–Patient Version*, Nat'l Cancer Inst., https://www.cancer.gov/about-cancer/treatment/side-effects/mouth-throat/oral-complications-pdq [https://perma.cc/HK8M-Y7NL] (last updated Dec. 6, 2023).
69. *Interactive Tax Assistant (ITA)*, *supra* note 30; *Can I Deduct My Medical and Dental Expenses?*, *supra* note 39.

70. *Can I Deduct My Medical and Dental Expenses?, supra* note 39 (click "Begin"; then click "Continue"; then input the tax year; then select "Yes"; then select "No"; then select "Yes"; then select "No"; then input marital status and filing status; then select "T"; then select "Teeth Whitening Expenses") [https://perma.cc/469L-WZ7L (uploaded archive)].
71. Rev. Rul. 2003–57, 2003-1 C.B. 959.
72. *Id.*; *See* I.R.C. § 213(d)(9).
73. *Interactive Tax Assistant (ITA), supra* note 30; *Can I Deduct My Charitable Contributions?*, IRS, https://www.irs.gov/help/ita/can-i-deduct-my-charitable-contributions [https://perma.cc/5ZCM-4X2X] (last updated Jan. 16, 2024).
74. *Can I Deduct My Charitable Contributions?, supra* note 73 (click "Begin"; then click "Continue"; then input the tax year; then select "Yes"; then select "Yes"; then select "Yes") [https://perma.cc/Y2WN-AELG (uploaded archive)].
75. *Id.* (from "Was your contribution to the qualified organization intended for a specific person, other than for a person in foster care or a student living in your home?" select "Yes") [https://perma.cc/U59S-XX42 (uploaded archive)].
76. *See supra* note 74 and accompanying text.
77. IRS, Pub. 526: Charitable Contributions 6 (2019), https://www.irs.gov/pub/irs-prior/p526--2019.pdf [https://perma.cc/2XZD-Y9NV].
78. *See, e.g.*, IRS, Pub. 502: Medical and Dental Expenses 5 (2020), https://www.irs.gov/pub/irs-prior/p502--2020.pdf [https://perma.cc/YH4K-LC65] (stating that "[y]ou can include in medical expenses the amount you pay for artificial teeth"). Interesting new research tests the impact of simplexity in the tax context. Professor Emily Cauble surveyed over 2,000 US adults to determine the impact that informal IRS guidance had on them. The study showed that, as a result of simplexity, a substantial share of people interpret informal IRS guidance in a way that does not align with the actual tax law. Moreover, they did so with a high degree of (false) confidence and wrongly believed that tax law would afford them legal relief when they relied to their detriment on informal guidance. The study tested simplexity in ITA, as well as in excerpts from written IRS publications, and in hypothetical dialogues between taxpayers and an IRS helpline representative. Emily Cauble, *The Impact of Informal Guidance* (draft on file with authors).
79. *See supra* note 42 and accompanying text (emphasis added).
80. Ryan E. Cruz, James M. Leonhardt, & Todd Pezzuti, *Second Person Pronouns Enhance Consumer Involvement and Brand Attitude*, 39 J. Interactive Mktg. 104, 104 (2017).
81. *See, e.g.*, Navdeep S. Sahni, S. Christian Wheeler, & Pradeep Chintagunta, *Personalization in Email Marketing: The Role of Noninformative Advertising Content*, 37 Mktg. Sci. 236, 237 (2018) (finding that including the name in the subject line "increased the probability of the recipient opening the email by 20%").
82. *See, e.g.*, IRS, Pub. 535: Business Expenses 6 (2022), https://www.irs.gov/pub/irs-prior/p535--2022.pdf [https://perma.cc/UQ6S-RCWN] ("Generally, *you* can deduct the full amount of a business expense if it meets the criteria of ordinary and necessary and it is not a capital expense" (emphasis added)).
83. *See* Cong Li, *When Does Web-Based Personalization Really Work? The Distinction Between Actual Personalization and Perceived Personalization*, 54 Computs. Hum. Behav. 25, 25 (2016).
84. *See, e.g., supra* note 40 and accompanying text (the fourth question from ITA asks: "Do you know the amount of adjusted gross income reported on this return?") [https://perma.cc/B8HH-AVG6 (uploaded archive)].
85. *See* Li, *supra* note 83, at 28–32.
86. I.R.C. § 213(d)(9)(A).

87. *See supra* note 70 and accompanying text.
88. *See* IRS, Pub. 502, *supra* note 78, at 15.
89. *Id.* at 5, 15.
90. *Id.* at 15.
91. *See, e.g., supra* note 39 (providing an estimated completion time of fifteen minutes for the question whether "I [can] Deduct My Medical and Dental Expenses").
92. *See, e.g.*, How Much Is My Standard Deduction?, IRS, https://www.irs.gov/help/ita/how-much-is-my-standard-deduction [https://perma.cc/8N8G-8HRV] (last updated Jan. 16, 2024) (providing an estimated completion time of five minutes).
93. *See supra* note 91.
94. *See, e.g.*, IRS, Pub. 17: Your Federal Income Tax (2020), https://www.irs.gov/pub/irs-prior/p17–2020.pdf [https://perma.cc/NJG7-EZ7Q] (277 pages).
95. *See Publications Online*, IRS, https://www.irs.gov/publications [https://perma.cc/W9KX-YKDD] (last updated Feb. 21, 2024).
96. *See, e.g.*, Jesper Falkheimer & Mats Heide, Strategic Communication: An Introduction (2018).

5

View from the Inside

Interviews with Federal Agency Officials

As we have shown, the federal government, motivated by the rise of automated customer service, has turned to automation to engage with the public. Automation makes it less expensive for the government to offer a multitude of important public services, including, critically, providing information about how the law applies. Additionally, in today's online world, automation helps the government meet consumer expectations. After the mother we introduced at the beginning of the book is finished doing her banking business on her phone, she can keep on tapping to access information about her disability benefits, her student loan obligations, her federal tax return, and more. She may even "speak" with a virtual government representative, such as FSA's Aidan, or get answers to her specific tax questions from the IRA's virtual assistant, ITA.

Our research has identified how this automation, while both convenient and important, has also exacerbated the "simplexity" that underlies federal government agencies' explanations of complex law to the public. Specifically, the automated legal guidance tools that these agencies have introduced often, for various reasons, flatten out the nuances in the law. Consequently, people may end up making decisions without having all the necessary information; for example, when it comes to taxes, they may forgo deductions, credits, and other benefits to which they are entitled by the underlying Internal Revenue Code provisions, regulations, case law, and other authorities.

Later in this book, we will turn to a wholesale evaluation of automated legal guidance and will explore not only what the benefits and costs of these tools are, but also how we can ameliorate the costs while preserving some of the benefits. External evaluation of these tools, however, is not enough. Instead, we must also consider how agency officials who are designing these tools and supervising their use understand them. What benefits do these officials think these tools offer the public, what concerns do they have about them, and what do these views tell us more broadly?

To obtain these insights, in Fall 2021, we conducted interviews with federal agency officials. The Administrative Conference of the United States (ACUS) facilitated these conversations, and we are very grateful for ACUS's support. Our gratitude also extends to the agency officials who spoke with us and generously shared their knowledge and perspectives.

Based on what we learned during these interviews, we can better appreciate how automated legal guidance tools are designed with user-friendliness as a fundamental goal. This is a goal that makes a lot of sense. If the private sector's use of automation is among the government's chief motivators for the transformation of government guidance, the metaphorical bar will be high for automated legal guidance to allow users to get information as easily and quickly as it takes to order a caramel Frappuccino from a virtual Starbucks barista, as just one example of today's automation.

We caution, however, that there are important differences in scope and complexity between the federal government explaining the law to the public and a coffee franchise offering the customer an online opportunity to order a beverage. Our interviews also revealed, at times, a failure to appreciate some of what is unique about the federal government's efforts to automate its guidance-giving function and some of the inevitable risks and pitfalls that arise as a result. The interviews we describe in this chapter, while helping us better appreciate the role of automated legal guidance, also highlight the need to think more carefully about its design and deployment.

INTERVIEWS BACKGROUND AND METHODOLOGY

We conducted these interviews as part of a study that ACUS selected us to complete regarding automated legal guidance. Here, we provide some of the background for these interviews, including the role of ACUS, and discuss our interview approach.

Administrative Conference of the United States

The Administrative Conference of the United States is itself an independent federal agency. It is headed by a chairperson, whom the President appoints by and with the advice and consent of the Senate. ACUS's other members include the chairperson (or designee) of each independent board or regulatory commission, the head (or designee) of each executive department designated by the President, and other appointees who provide broad representation, including certain individuals appointed based on their expertise in administrative law and procedure.[1]

The Administrative Conference of the United States has a number of charges, including, most notably, studying "the efficiency, adequacy, and fairness of the administrative procedure used by administrative agencies" and making "recommendations to administrative agencies ... and to the President, Congress, or the Judicial Conference of the United States, in connection therewith, as it considers appropriate."[2] ACUS may also "collect information and statistics from administrative agencies and publish such reports as it considers useful for evaluating and improving administrative procedure."[3]

The "Assembly of the Conference" is the designation for the ACUS meeting in plenary session,[4] and it has the power to, among other things, "adopt such recommendations as it considers appropriate for improving administrative procedure" of federal administrative agencies.[5]

Our Charge from ACUS

Pursuant to its authority, in the summer of 2021, ACUS selected us to conduct a study of federal government agencies' use of automated legal guidance. We were asked to draft a report on this topic and present our findings and recommendations at ACUS's plenary session (as well as at preceding committee meetings).[6] ACUS's full assembly would then consider our recommendations, together with any potential administrative procedure reforms stemming from them.

In terms of our research focus, ACUS specifically asked us to:

- Identify best practices for agencies to use when implementing automated tools to deliver legal guidance to members of the public;
- Explore the types of automated legal guidance agencies issue and the circumstances in which different types of automated legal guidance are most effective;
- Explore how agencies oversee the programs providing such guidance to ensure that the information they provide is accurate and useful; and
- Explore how agencies can make certain that recipients of such guidance understand its limitations, and do not rely on it to their detriment.

Interviews Methodology

In Fall 2021, as part of our research for ACUS, we interviewed officials who have direct or supervisory responsibility for well-developed automated legal guidance tools in use by federal agencies (namely, Aidan, Emma, and ITA). We also spoke with several individuals from the GSA who supported agencies in developing these tools. These interviews, and in particular those with GSA officials, confirmed for us that, at present, USCIS, IRS, and FSA have the most well-developed automated legal guidance tools. However, we learned that many other federal agencies are currently contemplating adopting these tools as well, and that experts expect the use of this technology to grow increasingly common among federal agencies over time.

After identifying people who were capable of speaking to us in depth about current, well-developed uses of automated legal guidance by the federal government, we engaged in ten interviews with agency officials on the topic. Because, as we discovered, the number of individuals in charge of each project at each agency tends to be small (usually a few people), the total number of interviewees available and willing to speak with us reflected this number. If a group of multiple people played similar roles in the development or supervision of an automated legal guidance tool, the agency tended to be hesitant for us to speak with all of them, and instead made a particular representative available to us on behalf of the group. We expect that the number of individuals involved with these tools, as well as the quantity of various differing perspectives, will grow as the technology expands across the federal government.

We believe that the interviews provided a reasonably comprehensive picture of the views of people who were significantly involved in the development and supervision of the federal government's automated legal guidance tools at the time. At the same time, the relatively small number of interviewees intricately involved in developing automated legal guidance tools, and thus able to speak to us about them, is an important finding in its own right. As we detailed in Chapter 2, millions of people are using the federal government's automated legal guidance tools every year to understand their legal rights and obligations. Yet, our study found that decisions about these tools are being made by a relatively small number of officials within agencies, often without a lot of supervision by higher-level agency officials. This suggests that some of the choices being made about automated legal guidance, which is influencing millions of people a year in their understanding of the federal law, are relatively insular at present. We hope that our study will unearth some of these decisions and encourage greater contemplation of how they are made.

The interviews lasted approximately an hour each and covered a range of questions that generally fell into a few categories:

- How and why the agency developed a tool
- How the agency solicited feedback and conducted evaluations regarding the tool's performance and efficacy
- How the agency makes decisions about presenting complicated legal information in an accessible fashion
- How the guidance these automated tools offer relates to agency guidance generally

We used a semi-structured interview approach, meaning that we had a general list of questions that we planned to ask each interviewee. Prior to each interview, we tailored the questions somewhat based on the person's role in providing automated legal guidance for the agency. For instance, we would plan to use examples from a particular automated legal guidance tool when interviewing an agency official who developed that tool. We also asked different questions depending on the interviewee's direct involvement in either developing the tool, supervising the tool's activities or performance, or supervising the provision of agency guidance more generally.

Beyond the preplanned tailoring of the questions, we also allowed the interview itself to dictate some of the direction of our conversation. If, for example, an interviewee brought up their own example of how the tool operated or was designed to explain how the team thought about an issue, we would continue the conversation by talking about that example, rather than forcing the interview back to our preplanned questions. In this way, we started with a tailored, but somewhat standard, set of expectations for the interviews, but remained open to varying the conversation based on the responses we were receiving.

AGENCY INTERVIEWS

High-Level Summary

From our interviews, we learned that agency officials working with automated legal guidance are not adequately apprised of some of the issues that we had identified in our own research. For instance, agencies generally favored focusing on the product's usability, which often came at the cost of potentially obscuring some of the ways that the guidance may deviate from formal law. Agencies focused on usability, rather than accuracy, because of a belief that users had little ability, inclination, or both, to read complex material, particularly in the context of the subject matter of the content and the format in which it was delivered. As a result, agency officials believed that automated guidance needed to offer answers that were as simple as possible. In this way, we found little appreciation for the concept of "simplexity" that we discussed in Chapter 3.

As we have explored in this book already, there is good reason to think agency officials are onto something with their concerns about users' capacity to read and absorb complex legal material. As Chapter 2 described, there is a mismatch between extremely complex law and increasing expectations that most transactions, especially those that take place online, should involve minimal cognitive load. From our interviews, we learned how agency officials tried to make things seem even easier and more straightforward as the technology got more sophisticated, especially with the introduction of chatbots and virtual assistants. In this way, the trends from the private sector that we explored in Chapter 1 appeared to have influenced agency officials' ways of approaching automated legal guidance.

Across the board, we found that agencies conducted limited evaluations of these tools and solicited feedback that was focused on customer usability rather than fundamental questions about how the guidance dovetails with the underlying law. We also heard agencies express little concern regarding the ways that their guidance may be a poor fit in a given circumstance or for how users may be relying on the guidance in ways that may ultimately leave users vulnerable. Further, we learned that no agency currently publishes an archive of changes that their employees have made to their automated tools' questions and answers, nor do any appear to have plans to do so in the future. We heard minimal concern about how the public may view statements by the government as an authoritative and binding form of law, even if agency officials do not think that the statements fill this role. In this regard, agencies do not appear to appreciate the government's distinct and unique responsibilities in this area, particularly in contrast to other types of automated systems.

The various agencies, we learned, have different models for developing and overseeing automated legal guidance. Some agencies employ less sophisticated technology, using a decision tree "answer" model, while others have opted for more sophisticated technology, and use a natural language "sorting" model. This creates varying potential paths for automated legal guidance. For example, the natural language "sorting" model is more similar to private sector innovation; however, while it offers greater possibilities, it also presents unique risks.

That said, all automated legal guidance presently in use by the federal government stops well short of the most advanced technology possible, as we mentioned in Chapter 2. In this way, the federal government seems to be cognizant of some of the potential harms of turning over its guidance-giving responsibility to technology entirely and is, at least for now, retaining some human control in the process. However, there should be no expectation that things will stay the way they are indefinitely, and the variation in models that we observed offers food for thought in contemplating how automated legal guidance may evolve in the future.

We also learned what agency officials consider to be the successes and problems with their automated legal guidance tools. Agencies view high user numbers and percentages of questions that users report as having been responsive as indicative of success. However, at least in some cases, agencies see the lack of reduced question traffic elsewhere within the agency as a problem.

Focusing on variables such as visitor traffic and user experience again shows the influence of private sector-like standards. Much as a private company such as Amazon worries a great deal about user experience, so too, according to our interviewees, was this quality an important metric of success for agencies' development of automated legal guidance. Those we interviewed expressed less of an appreciation of the fact that, due to the complexity of the law that makes automated legal guidance systems important and impactful, users of these systems may not always be good judges of what, under the circumstances, is actually a useful response to a question.

Findings on Particular Topics

The high-level summary earlier provides an instructive overview of the views of agency officials who have developed automated legal guidance. Using these tools to provide accessible guidance is a task that agency officials clearly take seriously. Later, we describe in more detail our findings on particular topics. These findings elaborate on how agencies develop automated legal guidance, as well as what benefits and costs officials consider, and what costs they do not.

Models for Development and Coordination within Agencies

The basic technological platform for an automated legal guidance tool is available through several outside vendors or contractors. At the time of our interviews, federal agencies were generally acquiring their platforms from these providers, rather than developing them themselves. Typically, following this acquisition, the agency works with the outside vendor to input the appropriate content (*i.e.*, questions and answers) and to refine the technology for the desired user experience. All agency officials with whom we spoke stressed that strict government protocols regarding privacy and accessibility are followed when working with an outside vendor.

While this technology acquisition model seemed commonplace, agencies differed in how they coordinated and allocated work on the product itself within the organization. In some cases, the team of agency officials who work on it may be relatively small, relying heavily on a separate, centralized agency process for the development of the guidance content itself. In this model, the technology may be under the direction of a "product owner," or a key person who is accountable for the technology.

This tool development framework requires the product owner to work with other teams within the agency (such as the content or policy team) to populate the tool initially with information, and to keep it updated. While this information population and updating process seemed to vary by agency, the content itself generally had to be cleared centrally, or by agency counsel. Some agencies use a type of central information bank, from which content is disseminated and used in a variety of channels, such as on the federal agency's website, by the agency's chatbot, and, potentially, even by the agency's call center.

It was not always clear to us who was responsible for monitoring the law for any changes that might implicate the content that was used by an automated legal guidance tool. We often heard about many different people and groups who might be involved in updates and changes to agency guidance: the product owner, the policy team, the content team, a chief operating officer, content specialists, counsel, working groups, a design team, a communication team, or someone else. There was, however, some general understanding across agencies that content or area specialists were responsible for monitoring any updates that needed to be made, and that these changes would be pushed out to all the appropriate channels, including chatbots and websites. As one agency official summarized, "there's different methods of intake, but at a very high level we make sure that the appropriate teams are consulted before we publish any content out in the public space."

It was clear, however, that certain unique difficulties arise when it comes to updating content that had already been published. As another agency official conceded, "I think it's easier when there's an active change. I think what's harder for us is when we put out guidance that maybe gets outdated, but there hasn't been really proactive statutory change." This interviewee also stressed that change to guidance could come about in different ways, including from a program office (or an office responsible for administering a particular program), but that changes were passed through many different groups, including counsel.

Even under this centralized guidance development model, the product owner or team responsible for the automated legal guidance tool might suggest that specific modifications be made to the centrally created agency guidance. These changes would then have to be approved across various chains of authority. Such modifications might be made to render the content more appropriate for users' expectations regarding readability on an automated legal guidance tool. However, in the end, the overall expectation remained that the team responsible for the automated legal guidance tool was not creating content from scratch. Rather, the team was using content that had been centrally created, which was also being used and applied in other ways throughout the agency as well.

An alternative model that we observed featured a greater degree of autonomous guidance content development. In this model, a larger team may be dedicated to the automated legal guidance tool, and this team's responsibilities may include developing material that is unique for use with this technology. As a result, the content provided by the agency's automated guidance tool may differ from content available elsewhere, including elsewhere on the website and through the call center. In any event, the agency's legal counsel would still be heavily involved in vetting any content developed by this team.

Indeed, the development of unique content for an automated legal guidance tool involves a laborious and lengthy process, in part because the content must be created from scratch. Under this model, rather than updates being pushed through to the technology from some sort of centralized agency content bank, the team responsible for the technology must monitor the law and propose any changes to the content. Only after those changes are approved by legal counsel would they be integrated into the tool itself, and available to be provided to the tool's users.

Usability of the Guidance

Agency officials across the board emphasized that an important purpose of offering information through an automated legal guidance tool is to make complex information easier for the public to understand and use. This is not surprising, in light of not only the background for the development of automated legal guidance discussed in Chapter 2 but also the origins of this technology in private sector automation.

One official noted that their agency learned, by testing the technology, that "people don't read and they don't want a lot of content." Accordingly, the agency focused on providing a "super concise" answer that is really "high level" in response to a user question, together with a link to more detailed information if the visitor wanted to access it. The conciseness of answers is particularly important because, if the agency were to put all the applicable legal requirements in a chat bubble, "most people likely are not going to read it." This observation reflects some of the ways that private sector automation has seemed to both reflect and threaten our capacity for complex decision-making, as discussed in Chapter 1.

Another agency official summed up the situation even more plainly: "We have the data to present to show that we can not only say [that] we think that they don't read, [but that] we know that." This data included usability tests, in which the agency would provide an answer to a question and then the user would follow up and ask the question that was already answered in the information that had already been provided. The data also included feedback from users, who complained that the agency, by providing too much content, had a negative impact on users, and that the agency should focus instead on "trying to solve their problems."

This desire to have their problems "solved" echoed some of the ways that consumers in the private sector can expect things like complex investment advice with the click of a button, with little input or involvement required by the consumer. This sort of feedback from users required the agency to "cut down on the number of words so that users don't feel overwhelmed by that kind of content."

At least one agency official attributed users' expectations in this regard to their experience with other online platforms that provide "short, quick information." Another agency official explained that this struggle mirrored the difficulties the agency has with issuing guidance generally, in that:

> [O]n the one hand, you want that information disclosed ... and on the other hand, the more disclosures we have, the more people don't read them and they get overwhelmed by the amount of paperwork so there's kind of a pendulum on that, where one administration will add a lot of these disclosures and then next question will take them away and come back again.

In the context of automated legal guidance tools, agencies seemed to place a premium on particularly concise answers, especially in light of what users have shown to be their expectations for this sort of platform.

Control of Answers by the Agency

Machine learning and other forms of artificial intelligence may enable technological tools over time to develop, at least somewhat autonomously, more accurate or sophisticated responses to user inquiries. However, all agency officials with whom we spoke indicated that generative artificial intelligence capabilities are not currently used to offer guidance to the public through an automated legal guidance tool. Indeed, many officials stressed that, in developing these tools to offer guidance to the public, the agencies needed to be sure that all of the information the technology supplied was authoritative and correct.

As a result, at present, these automated guidance tools have not been equipped with the capability to develop their own responses to questions. Rather, all questions and responses are vetted within appropriate agency channels. One individual with whom we spoke indicated that this approach was consistent with the pressure on federal agencies to get the answers right, and agencies' accompanying reluctance to employ technologies that might impose risk.

However, while generative artificial intelligence has not been employed (yet) in automated legal guidance systems used by federal government agencies, this does not mean that agency tools are not sophisticated in important ways. Perhaps the most important example of this is that agency tools can interpret natural language questions from visitors to select relevant answers from their response banks. These tools can also learn what a helpful response was to a question by receiving feedback on whether or not a user was satisfied with a response. Of course, by eventually combining this information with more sophisticated artificial intelligence technology, they may be better able to provide direct answers to the questions asked over time.

Differences in Inputs and Outputs Offered
Consistent with our own observations, we also heard about different models for the inputs and outputs for automated legal guidance tools.

USCIS's Emma represents one type of model, in which the goal of the automated tool is to assess what topic area a user is asking about by analyzing the user's natural language query, and then to direct the user to the relevant information about that topic area. While the particular information offered by the automated legal guidance tool should be responsive to the user's inquiry, the automated legal guidance tool does not attempt to provide a personalized answer.

The IRS's ITA represents another automated tool model. Here, the platform exercises greater control over the information that users enter. Specifically, it offers a series of prompts with set response options and then provides an "answer." In this way, tools such as ITA are really a digitized, accessible, version of a decision tree model.

In agencies that adopted the first model, agency officials emphasized that their tools did not tell users what to do. For instance, as one agency official explained, "[I]f you look across social media and how we engage with customers, we don't typically tell users how to act. We provide tools that can help them make decisions, but there is never a case where you will see [the tool] tell users they are eligible." The official stressed that their agency's information is "somewhat neutral" in this regard, in that it "provide[s] the information/the criteria for eligibility, but ... never ... a personalized response[.]"

Agency officials who employed the first model also emphasized that the information that their tool provided was just that – mere information – and not law. As one agency official emphasized, "At no time does our [tool] provide any legal advice." Instead, according to agency officials who developed this type of tool, it merely provided "information about the ... process."

The Information Is Correct
Regardless of differences in the types of answers offered by different agencies, agency officials were generally in agreement as to their high confidence in the

correctness of the responses. This confidence was a result of the intensive vetting process that is used for all questions and answers.

Regarding the accuracy issue, one agency official emphasized that "none of the content itself could ever be inaccurate. It's just a matter of ... they didn't give the answer that the user would want.... But again, we never produce content that isn't approved so it just might not be the right topic area ... when it's marked inaccurate."

People Do Not/Cannot Rely On It/No Archiving

Perhaps most interestingly, some agency officials with whom we spoke suggested that users did not actually rely upon the information their tools provide. The explanation was that the tool only offered general information. If a user wanted to take a legal position, these agency officials argued, they would have to take additional steps, such as filling out a form. According to this reasoning, a user would be required to undergo that additional process to claim that they had relied on agency guidance.

As one agency official explained:

> [The tool] provides accurate information based on our policy and our guidance.... It is not saying, hey, this is something that we tell you that is specifically for you and it is a binding agreement.... The work that we do, it is mostly providing validated information to the user around any questions ... we are just providing information that you already have available on the website.

However, when asked, the same agency official indicated that there are no general disclaimers that tell users that the information they get is neither binding, nor something that users can or should rely upon. Instead, the agency "stand [s] by our internal process, first and foremost, to push out and publicize the content that we put on our site.... [The tool] is not providing new information that is not already accessible or available on the website."

Other agency officials did not reject as strongly the idea that users, in fact, rely upon the information given by automated legal guidance tools. However, they all agreed that, as a matter of law, users could not, in fact, rely upon such tools. This was true even for forms of the technology that provided more personalized "answers" to users. Guidance from such tools, as agency officials pointed out, is not considered to be the type of "published" guidance that would support a legal reliance argument.

Relatedly, agency officials with whom we spoke indicated that their tools do not provide publicly accessible archives of old answers that would allow a user to refer to an answer that the tool provided on a prior date. While some agencies maintained archives of old authority, no agency officials believed that a bank of questions and answers supplied on a prior date was available to the public, at least not through the automated legal guidance tool itself.

Evaluation Methods

We heard about a variety of methods for evaluating an agency's automated legal guidance tool. One agency stressed that it used internal metrics to evaluate whether the answer given was the answer the user would have wanted. This same agency stressed that the tool was not capable of giving a "wrong" answer, because all the answers had been internally vetted. Rather, the agency designed the internal metrics to determine whether the answer given by the tool accurately matched the answer the user would have wanted, based on the question that the user was asking. The agencies also frequently surveyed the users about their experience. The feedback sought focused not only on usability but also on whether the tool provided the answer that the user had been seeking. One important metric was the rate at which a tool responded "I don't know" to user inquiries, especially if a primary goal of the tool was to direct users to the relevant information in response to their questions. In evaluating this data, agencies paid particular attention to how frequently the tool responded, "I don't know," and how it could happen less often by having the tool offer additional information. To these agency officials, reducing their system's "I don't know" rate over time was an important measure of success.

In general, our interviewees explained that the feedback users provided was often "technical," such as suggestions about being able to use the interface more easily. In general, agencies reported positive feedback from users, who appreciated the additional assistance.

Successes and Challenges

We also made a point of asking interviewees about successes and challenges that they had experienced with their automated tools. In response, we heard that one of the most significant accomplishments of these tools was that they had expanded the agencies' abilities to serve the public by offering 24/7 answers in an agile way. Agency officials pointed to considerable increases in user statistics over time, together with favorable user ratings, as indicators of the success of these systems. Agency officials were also forthcoming about challenges they had identified, which included ensuring that the tools had sufficient content to provide users all the answers they wanted, and maintaining the tools adequately over time.

All of the agencies acknowledged the limits to the types of information automated legal guidance tools could provide, particularly in comparison to an agency's other available options. Human agency officers can answer more complicated questions. Automated legal guidance tools cannot currently offer that same level of response to user inquiries. This is due not only to constraints in developmental resources but also because only certain types of information can be offered in an automated, non-authenticated environment. Thus, these tools currently can only address a relatively narrow set of questions and provide a limited number of responses. Nonetheless, our interviewees uniformly believed that the tools were a positive addition to the ways that the agencies can interact with, and respond to, public queries.

AGENCY INTERVIEWS IN CONTEXT

The interviews we conducted provide a richer understanding of what agency officials are thinking in developing automated legal guidance. Consumer expectations for automation highly motivate agency officials who design these tools. Concerns about the public's ability to understand complex legal material also influence these agency officials.

As a result, automated legal guidance tools attempt to ease public interaction with and understanding of complex federal laws and regulations. In this way, they serve as a partial realization of some of the many government customer service initiatives discussed in Chapter 2.

How do these tools, and the agencies that offer and maintain them, accomplish this objective?

- As the 21st Century Integrated Digital Experience Act recognized, "the public expects their digital interactions with the government to be on par with their favorite consumer websites and mobile apps,"[7] and the work that agencies have been doing in this area is helping the federal government meet that expectation.
- They keep in mind President Biden's order that agencies should be driven by "human-centered design methodologies" for digital services and OMB's subsequent circular that "all services and tasks [should be] made available through digital channels [including websites, mobile apps, email, text messaging, and social media."[8]
- By paying particular attention to user feedback regarding whether they feel they got their questions answered, agencies are aligned with the OMB's focus on "user testing" as a means of assessing digital tools.[9]

Across the board, the attention that agency officials pay to the private sector analog, together with their commitment to user satisfaction, reflects President Clinton's longstanding executive order to provide "the highest quality of service delivered to customers by private organizations providing a comparable or analogous service."[10]

However, because agencies are committed to making their tools similarly easy to use as those deployed by private sector businesses, agency officials have been less focused on ways that explaining complex law cannot be made easy, or ways that making it seem easy may sell short some of its underlying complexity. To put it most starkly, navigating difficult legal questions, such as figuring out whether you can take a tax deduction, or whether you can leave the country without jeopardizing your immigration status, is necessarily a lot more complicated than choosing a new coffee drink. Further, the potential consequences of trying to make these legal decisions can be exponentially greater than a decision about your daily caffeine choice. Of course, we do not think that agency officials equate the two – they do not. However, the government's heavy emphasis on the private sector model has trickled down into the development of automated legal guidance, such that the emphasis is on making things easier, and more usable, without as much focus regarding the risks in increasing ease of use.

So, what is lost in this process? Chapters 6–8 will elaborate. The views we heard during our interviews with agency officials about automated legal guidance not offering "law" and not being relied upon, even though millions of people are using this guidance, should give us pause. We should also consider some of the unclear lines of supervision over automated legal guidance tools, in addition to the fact that evaluation of these tools focuses on whether users "liked," or found helpful, a response, rather than focusing on additional evaluation by agency lawyers regarding how apt the responses were for the questions posed.

It is true that users probably approach automated legal guidance with some amount of understanding that it might not be providing the full story. A lawyer would never confuse this type of guidance for the underlying statutes, regulations, case law, and other sources that comprise the formal, underlying law. Members of the public, who are more likely to make up the actual user base for these tools, may also be unlikely to misconstrue these tools in this way. If an individual seeking to understand their immigration status had a choice between thoroughly researching the underlying law and getting some basic information available from Emma, that person would likely choose the former. But the reason people turn to automated legal guidance is often because they do not have access to this underlying law and cannot afford to hire an attorney.

The bottom line is that the government is providing an assortment of "answers" and detailed information in response to questions that people pose online. To do this, the government is using systems that sometimes even have digital faces and names to make them appear more human. This creates an underlying difficulty, in that the distinction between what *is* the law and what is information *about* the law is likely to become blurry. In this regard, the fact that the government is speaking matters in people's understanding of what they are being told. As we will discuss, the failure to include meaningful disclaimers, or to make clear to people that they may not be receiving the full legal story from the automated legal guidance, only makes this problem worse.

NOTES

1. 5 U.S.C. § 593(b).
2. *Id.* § 594(1).
3. *Id.* § 594(3).
4. *Id.* § 595(a).
5. *Id.* § 595(a)(1).
6. Joshua D. Blank & Leigh Osofsky, Automated Legal Guidance at Federal Agencies (2022) (report to the Admin. Conf. of the US) [hereinafter Blank & Osofsky, Guidance at Federal Agencies], https://www.acus.gov/projects/automated-legal-guidance-federal-agencies [https://perma.cc/265T-Q28Y].

7. *21st Century Integrated Digital Experience Act*, DIGITAL.GOV, https://digital.gov/resources/21st-century-integrated-digital-experience-act/ [https://perma.cc/8V4R-DGQM] (last updated Feb. 5, 2024, 1:48 PM).
8. Exec. Order No. 14,058, 86 Fed. Reg. 71357, 71357–58 (Dec. 13, 2021); OFF. OF MGMT. & BUDGET, EXEC. OFF. OF THE PRESIDENT, OMB CIRCULAR NO. A-11, PREPARATION, SUBMISSION, AND EXECUTION OF THE BUDGET 280–83 (2023), https://www.whitehouse.gov/wp-content/uploads/2018/06/a11.pdf [https://perma.cc/SW3K-SCVK].
9. Exec. Order No. 14,058, 86 Fed. Reg. 71357, 71358 (Dec. 13, 2021).
10. Exec. Order No. 12,862, 58 Fed. Reg. 48257, 48257 (Sept. 11, 1993).

6

How Automated Legal Guidance
Helps Agencies and the Public

Now that we have seen how federal agencies use automated legal guidance to communicate with the public, we should consider *why* these agencies have embraced this form of communication. What are some of the advantages of offering automated legal guidance compared to other possibilities, such as providing increased human customer service? Alternatively, why have government agencies decided to use technology to deliver guidance to members of the public, rather than seeking to completely automate various acts of legal compliance?

Automated legal guidance provides significant administrative benefits to federal government agencies. As our interviewees confirmed, federal agencies save a lot of money by delivering customer service through online tools, such as chatbots, especially compared to the expense involved in employing human agents to answer phone and in-person inquiries. Using the technology of automated legal guidance can also allow agencies to reach broader swaths of the population much more quickly than they would by relying on other forms of customer service. Additionally, compared to individual human customer service representatives, who might deliver guidance that differs depending upon an individual's question and the relevant context, automated legal guidance can provide uniform answers to specific inquiries consistently.

Likewise, when members of the public turn to automated legal guidance to understand the law, they enjoy important compliance-related benefits. Automated legal guidance helps people more easily comprehend complex, lengthy, and ambiguous statutory and regulatory provisions. It can also promote transparency by allowing individuals to understand how agency officials interpret the law, especially when that law is ambiguous. Finally, people can refer to automated legal guidance to get information about the law quickly and cheaply, without having to spend time and money to consult with lawyers, accountants, and other professional advisors.

The rise of simplicity in automated legal guidance can itself also provide civic participation benefits. In addition to the administration and compliance benefits described earlier, by using simplicity to explain the law, the government offers members of the public an opportunity to engage with the law. This is especially evident relative to alternative systems the government could use, such as automating compliance altogether. As we will discuss, under an automated compliance system, the government would not even try to explain the law to the public, but rather would simply apply complex law in an automated fashion. While automated compliance itself may have some benefits (in terms of reduced administration costs), it would reduce public knowledge of and engagement with the law. Automated legal guidance offers an alternative.

This chapter explores how automated legal guidance helps both federal agencies and members of the public. It outlines several specific benefits, including administrative efficiency, communication of complex law in plain language, transparency regarding agency interpretations of the law, internal and external consistency regarding agency communications, and public engagement with the law.

ADMINISTRATIVE EFFICIENCY

Federal agencies face tremendous pressure to assist members of the public who are attempting to comply with the law. As described in Chapter 3, agencies must provide people with "plain language" explanations and instructions regarding complex law, and they must accomplish this even as some agencies have diminished funding and labor resources. In light of this communication mandate, automated legal guidance provides agencies with several administrative efficiency benefits.

A significant administrative benefit of automated legal guidance is that it can allow federal agencies to deliver information to members of the public more quickly than when they use printed publications and human customer service representatives to provide guidance. For instance, the IRS's ITA can answer questions about tax deductions and credits from taxpayers in as little as fifteen minutes. In this regard, federal agencies' automated tools often emulate the speed and efficiency with which private sector chatbots deliver information to customers.

Printed IRS publications, by contrast, may require that taxpayers devote many more minutes, or even hours, to read and apply the law to their own situation. These publications can number hundreds of pages in length and require readers to consider myriad exceptions, requirements, and examples.[1] Further, trying to speak with an IRS customer service representative on the phone is not necessarily a preferable solution, albeit for different reasons. In 2022, IRS customer service representatives answered only about 10 percent of the calls they received.[2] Wait times for the calls that were answered averaged twenty minutes, although many callers just gave up on waiting.[3] Indeed, the difficulty in reaching a human being at the IRS has become so formidable that some taxpayers have resorted to hiring companies to repeatedly call the agency until they can actually get through, which, of course, further exacerbates access difficulties for other callers.[4]

The speed and availability of automated legal guidance is especially helpful during times when human customer service representatives are not available. For example, the IRS officials we interviewed confirmed that during the COVID-19 pandemic, people turned to ITA for guidance in significantly higher numbers because IRS offices were closed for long periods of time. The round-the-clock availability of automated legal guidance may only prove to be more valuable in the event of future public health emergencies or other situations where federal agency offices are closed, such as shutdowns of the federal government. Much like private sector businesses,[5] federal agency officials have explicitly endorsed the significant expansion of automated guidance as a way to respond to the availability barriers that occur with human customer service representatives.[6]

Another administrative benefit of automated legal guidance is that, as explained in Chapter 4, agencies are able to use this technology to deliver information in a way that appears to be personalized to individual users. When consulting federal agencies' automated tools, such as Emma and ITA, users input information in response to questions and receive seemingly personalized answers.[7] These statements emulate the type of service that a human customer service agent might provide to someone during an interaction in-person or over the phone. The personalized nature of automated legal guidance may reduce the potential for users to continue to call hotlines or visit service centers to seek clarification from human agents.

Another administrative benefit of automated legal guidance is that it is significantly less expensive than human customer service representatives. Many of the government officials we interviewed cited the cost savings of automated legal guidance. Instead of spending money on hiring and training a large staff to answer people's inquiries, federal agency officials can instead allocate budgetary funds to developing automated legal guidance tools. Whether they develop automated legal guidance tools in-house or hire third-party vendors to develop them, federal agencies incur upfront costs, but also gain the benefit of having products that can provide service to the public over many years. This feature of automated legal guidance is especially attractive as annual funding from Congress may be lacking, or at least unstable.[8]

Finally, automated legal guidance tools can streamline the processes for third parties who may be assisting people with their legal compliance obligations. For example, consider the annual requirement to file an IRS Form 1040 (US Individual Income Tax Return), together with its related schedules and forms. Even when taxpayers turn to tax accountants and other return preparers to complete these tax returns, those professionals turn to the IRS's automated legal guidance tools themselves.

Why is this? While legal education for tax lawyers focuses on statutes, regulations, and case law, many educational programs for accountants and other tax-return preparers instead teach them to follow IRS statements regarding the tax law in the agency's informal publications.[9] In addition, as discussed in Chapter 3, when individuals purchase third-party software, such as Intuit's TurboTax, to complete and file their tax returns,[10] the program often follows the IRS's positions from sources such as ITA.[11] By assisting third-party advisors, automated legal guidance tools further reduce the burden on federal agencies to provide human customer service assistance to the public.

COMPLEX LAW IN PLAIN LANGUAGE

When automated legal guidance tools provide individuals with accurate information about legal rules and obligations, they can help them understand complex rules and procedures in the underlying formal law. This allows people to interpret and apply complex formal law to achieve practical ends, such as filing an amended tax return, applying for a green card, or requesting a discharge of federal student loan debt. These tools can also streamline the inquiry process for third parties, such as accountants, lawyers, and other advisors, who are assisting users with their legal compliance obligations.

Assistance from Automated Legal Guidance

Automated legal guidance can help individuals, especially those who lack access to counsel, understand their entitlements, obligations, and restrictions under the formal law, including statutes and regulations.

When individuals visit the IRS's ITA automated guidance tool, they can quickly find answers to questions about their tax compliance obligations, such as whether they must file a tax return, when they must file it, and whether they are entitled to an extension. In 2020, this proved to be enormously helpful, to both the agency itself and to individual taxpayers, when the country was enmeshed in the COVID-19 global health emergency.

For instance, as we described in an example in Chapter 4, after answering only a few questions about residency and refund status, ITA could inform a taxpayer that, because of the pandemic, both the filing and payment deadlines were automatically extended to July 15, 2020.[12] ITA's ability to consider residency was especially key. A taxpayer who stated that they would not be living outside of the US and Puerto Rico on April 15, 2020, was given the deadline for filing and payment by ITA.[13] If, on the other hand, the taxpayer stated that they would be living outside of the country on that date, ITA was programmed to ask a series of follow-up questions regarding the taxpayer's need for an extension before providing the deadline.[14] ITA made it a lot easier to understand the confusing statutes, together with temporary changes in the underlying, formal law, that governed those filing and extension dates.[15]

In addition, automated legal guidance also provides individuals who do not have access to professional advisors explanations of the formal law in plain language. It costs a lot of money to retain the services of an accountant or a lawyer. For example, whereas paid preparers tend to charge in the hundreds of dollars to prepare a tax return and tax software costs a fraction of that price,[16] tax lawyers cost hundreds of dollars an hour, and those who work in large firms or in major cities can charge substantially more than that.[17] One would have to have a very large amount of tax liability at stake to justify paying a tax lawyer's fees. Further, the larger the amount at stake, the more valuable that service may be. Automated legal guidance tools like ITA can help fill a substantial gap by explaining complex underlying formal law, whether it involves issues like filing deadlines or eligibility for the earned income tax credit, to members of the public free of charge.

TRANSPARENT INTERPRETATIONS OF THE LAW

Another benefit of automated legal guidance tools is that they can promote and further transparency when it comes to how agencies interpret the law. With this information, members of the public and their advisors can observe how agency officials view unsettled legal issues when deciding whether to pursue different actions and legal positions.

Transparency occurs where the government makes information that it holds, including how it interprets the law, "available for examination and scrutiny."[18] Information transparency allows the public to perform two actions that are critical to democratic governance. First, it empowers individuals, often through their representatives, to engage in informed debate and deliberation about the government's plans and actions.[19] Second, transparency ensures that the public can monitor the government and hold it accountable for its actions.[20] This second point is especially important regarding agencies: when they are transparent regarding their own interpretations of the law, people can consider and question whether these government actors are fulfilling their enforcement and administration responsibilities appropriately.

Agency explanations of the law embedded in many automated legal guidance tools offer a preview of how the government would apply the law during investigations, audits, and litigation. This advance view is most illuminating where the law is ambiguous. For example, ITA's definition of "ordinary" business expenses under Section 162(a) of the Internal Revenue Code, discussed earlier, provides taxpayers with insights about the IRS's probable reactions before taxpayers file their tax returns. Taxpayers can consider these IRS simplifications, and then respond either by foregoing the tax position at issue and the potentially resulting tax controversy or, conversely, by claiming the tax position and preparing to contest the IRS's interpretation.

Explanations provided by automated legal guidance tools can also further agencies' obligations to disclose information about their interpretations of the law in other contexts. For instance, under Section 6110 of the Internal Revenue Code, the IRS is required to publicly disclose all "written determination[s]," including private letter rulings, tax-exempt determination letters, and technical advice memoranda.[21] Congress enacted this provision to prevent the IRS from creating "secret law" in internal communications and in private letter rulings, which would only be accessible to "a few major tax practitioners" who frequently interacted with IRS officials.[22]

By sharing agencies' interpretations of the law with the public, automated legal guidance tools effectively prevent agencies from shielding their interpretations of ambiguous or complex formal law from public view. While an agency's internal agency documents often describe the agency's view of the law in technical terms that are understandable only to lawyers and other experts,[23] automated legal guidance tools provide this information to the public in a much more accessible and simplified way.

CONSISTENCY

A key purpose of automated legal guidance is to make agency communication more uniform and consistent. For example, as described in Chapter 3, IRS officials adopted a web-based internal guide, the Interactive Tax Law Assistant (ITLA), in 2008, and human IRS assistants were required to use it to respond to taxpayers' telephone inquiries. Prior to this, IRS assistants would often attempt to find the answers to taxpayers' inquiries by reviewing IRS publications and other documents. Once IRS officials and oversight organizations determined that these assistants were providing different, sometimes inaccurate, information to taxpayers about interpretation of the tax law and taxpayers' compliance obligations, they developed ITLA. After introducing ITLA, there was a significant increase in the consistency and accuracy of information that IRS assistants delivered. Following the success of this internal guidance tool, the IRS introduced its public-facing automated legal guidance tool, the Interactive Tax Assistant (ITA), in 2010.

As this example demonstrates, automated legal guidance tools allow agencies to provide more consistent information about the law to the public. Information delivered in person and over the phone by human agents, on the other hand, can be varying and conflicting. By employing automated legal guidance tools, agencies can ensure that all users receive the same responses to common inquiries.

When agencies provide inconsistent messaging regarding the law, they can face public frustration and criticism. Most people do not want to receive different answers to their inquiries about government programs such as, for example, green cards, tax credits, and federal student loans; they certainly do not want to receive the wrong information if it will prevent them from enjoying benefits to which they are entitled. By delivering consistent messages regarding their policies and legal interpretations, the perceived legitimacy of agencies may increase.[24] Automated tools allow these agencies to lessen, if not prevent, the possibility that individual human customer service representatives will provide people with conflicting information and guidance.

These tools may encourage agency officials to enforce the law more consistently as well. Some scholars have argued that agencies function more effectively "when central officials can advise responsible bureaucrats how they should apply agency law."[25] These tools can provide consistent messaging about an agency's legal interpretations not only to the public but also to the organization's own employees, as the tools' use by the IRS demonstrates.

There is an important caveat to consider regarding consistency: the agencies must retain control over the information that their automated legal guidance tools provide to the public. Right now, these tools operate on a spectrum, on which the government retains varying degrees of control over the information they provide.

The IRS operates at one end of this spectrum in that it retains significant control over information by using ITA, which incorporates a decision-tree model. The agency has preprogrammed every statement of ITA so that it always provides the same response to every inquiry that involves the same facts. This level of consistency makes this tool highly trustworthy.

Other types of automated tools, however, may behave differently. For example, Open AI's ChatGPT (Chat Generative Pretrained Transformer), which first launched in November 2022, functions by communicating with users in a conversational tone and searching the web to respond to users' inquiries. By its very nature, this type of chatbot technology may deliver highly variant responses, because it relies on the specific words and requests that the users enter into its interface. If consistency in information delivery is a high-priority goal, this user interface model may not be ideal. Consequently, when introducing automated legal guidance tools, agency officials should carefully consider how the model they choose may impact the consistency of its responses to users.

PUBLIC ENGAGEMENT WITH THE FORMAL LAW

A final benefit of automated legal guidance is that it allows people to engage with formal law. This benefit becomes apparent if we compare automated legal guidance with an alternative system: automation of individuals' legal compliance activities.

Agencies' current uses of automated legal guidance, such as ITA and Emma, tend to rely on simplexity, together with a relatively primitive use of technology, to make the law more comprehensible to individuals who will apply it.[26] ITA, for instance, does not fill out taxpayers' tax returns, or even learn from the experience of providing information to users. Rather, it uses preprogrammed technology to answer questions, thereby enabling taxpayers (or their advisors) to file their own tax returns. Likewise, Emma, the virtual assistant for the USCIS, does not actually file a green card application for people who visit the website. Rather, Emma simply answers questions about the various eligibility, procedural, and other requirements for doing so.

The rapidly changing technology landscape, however, may begin a new regulatory era, in which government agencies introduce systems that automate individuals' compliance obligations *without* explaining the underlying law. Indeed, as artificial intelligence continues to evolve, it may be possible for an agency to create targeted rules for every situation, which would essentially collapse guidance and enforcement.[27]

How would this work? Agencies could do this by issuing "microdirectives," which would automatically tailor and communicate the law in a way that would be responsive to all relevant factors.[28] Consider, for example, individually tailored speed limits. A government agency could use artificial intelligence to factor in a driver's experience and accident history, the weather, the speed of other cars, along with all other relevant variables, to communicate (through some sort of interface in the car) what speed the driver is legally required to go at every moment in time.[29] Of course, at this point, human drivers might be considered to be superfluous; instead, driverless cars could be programmed to go the legal speed dictated by the artificial intelligence, given all of the attendant circumstances.[30]

Consider the potential impact of such technical evolutions on the legal system. In this scenario, the use of simplicity in these tools may be a waystation to something much more transformative: a world in which artificial intelligence can make decisions about how federal law applies, without any required human analysis.[31]

How and why would such an alternative system work, and how could simplicity help us get there? In the law, rules and standards are typically used to calibrate the law appropriately to given situations. At some point, however, the combination of uncertainty from standards and complexity from rules exceeds human capacity to understand what the law is. One solution to the problem is to use artificial intelligence to remove the legal explanation process. By gathering the applicable facts and then mapping them onto algorithms about how the law applies in given situations, artificial intelligence could dictate what the legal requirements or outcomes are in a given situation, without any need to explain the law.[32] This could generate the benefits of careful tailoring that can come from complex law (for instance, a unique speed requirement that depends on all relevant conditions at the time), without requiring human beings to engage in the difficult process of understanding very complex law.

Would the shift to automated compliance be desirable? Understanding the role of simplicity in today's government-provided automated legal guidance is critical to evaluating what would be gained and what would be lost. Simplexity helps communicate law in a way that is easy to understand for those who would not otherwise understand it. As we have seen, however, it has costs as well, primarily with regards to ironing out nuances in the law that serve important values. Simplifying these nuances may, without proper targeting, confer disproportionate advantages on different groups.

In contrast, automated compliance need not have the same ironing-out effect. If artificial intelligence is going to monitor our actions to determine our legal responsibilities without any understanding required on our part, then the law need not be presented or applied to us in an oversimplified way. The rules could be as complex as artificial intelligence can process, which may be extraordinarily complex – certainly far more so than the current legal system, which assumes some amount of application by human beings. In this way, pure automation could, given some underlying motivating framework, reach more accurate individualized results than any existing legal system.[33]

One of the principal costs of pure automation, however, would be the precise benefit that automated legal guidance, powered by simplicity, offers: the ability for people to access the formal law. Simplicity may offer an overly simplified version of the law, but it does attempt to communicate the law to people. More advanced artificial intelligence that eschews the need for such communication may ultimately erode human beings' understanding of the law that governs them.[34] Indeed, we may already be seeing this when it comes to taxes. There has been an ongoing lament regarding how the advent of tax return preparation software has eroded not only taxpayers' understanding of the tax law but also the sense of civic virtue that accompanies filing a tax return.[35] This lament is sometimes accompanied with a suggestion that the technology perversely encourages Congress to make exceedingly complicated law, pacified by the notion that software, rather than people, will have to apply it.[36] At a more general level, automation that no longer attempts to communicate the law may bypass some of the costs of simplicity, but there are several potential costs: members of the general public will have an even lower sense of what the law is, how its effects are being allocated, and how to challenge it.

All of this does not suggest that we should respond to the arrival of automation by burying our heads in the sand. It does suggest that automated legal guidance, powered by simplicity, may be an important alternative to (1) an imprecise legal system and (2) an automated legal system that eliminates the need for human beings to understand the law that is being applied. In situations where the law is complex and explanations of it are important, automated legal guidance has a critical role to play.

NOTES

1. *See, e.g.*, IRS, PUB. 17, YOUR FEDERAL INCOME TAX: FOR INDIVIDUALS (2021), https://www.irs.gov/pub/irs-prior/p17-2021.pdf [https://perma.cc/G54M-UJT8].
2. *See* Michelle Singletary, *This Tax Season, IRS Answered Just 10 Percent of Taxpayer Calls*, WASH. POST (June 24, 2022, 7:42 AM), https://www.washingtonpost.com/business/2022/06/24/irs-taxpayer-calls/ [https://perma.cc/KZ4V-M548].
3. Michelle Singletary, *If You Call the IRS There's Only a 1-in-50 Chance You'll Reach a Human Being*, WASH. POST (Apr. 23, 2021, 7:00 AM), https://www.washingtonpost.com/business/2021/04/23/irs-1040-hotline [https://perma.cc/C677-7RCL].
4. TAXPAYER ADVOC. SERV., NATIONAL TAXPAYER ADVOCATE ANNUAL REPORT TO CONGRESS 69 (2021), https://www.taxpayeradvocate.irs.gov/wp-content/uploads/2022/01/ARC21_Full-Report.pdf [https://perma.cc/23B3-4ZMR (uploaded archive)].

5. *See, e.g.,* Aakrit Vaish, *Five Reasons Why Chatbots Are the Future of Customer Service,* ENTREPRENEUR (Jan. 5, 2019), https://www.entrepreneur.com/article/325830 [https://perma.cc/AL6P-H84V]; *AI for Customer Service,* IBM, https://www.ibm.com/watson/ai-customer-service [https://perma.cc/D4AX-QQQ5].
6. *See, e.g.,* IRS, PUB. 5426, TAXPAYER FIRST ACT: REPORT TO CONGRESS 47 (2021), https://www.irs.gov/pub/irs-pdf/p5426.pdf [https://perma.cc/29JF-QEQF].
7. *See* Chapter 4, "Why Automated Legal Guidance Exacerbates Simplexity."
8. *See* Jim Tankersley & Alan Rappeport, *New Details in Debt Limit Deal: Where $136 Billion in Cuts Will Come From,* N.Y. TIMES, https://www.nytimes.com/2023/05/29/us/politics/debt-ceiling-agreement.html [https://perma.cc/AG5P-VKL5 (private, uploaded archive)] (last updated June 2, 2023).
9. *See, e.g.,* LOC. GOV'T SERVS. DIV., GA. DEP'T OF REVENUE, BASIC ACCOUNTING WORKSHOP 83 (2017), https://dor.georgia.gov/document/training-program/basic-accounting-workshop/ [https://perma.cc/XSN2-TZDT].
10. *See* Intuit Inc., Annual Report (Form 10-K) (Aug. 31, 2020) (reporting over 50 million customers); KUSH PATEL, IBISWORLD, REP. NO. 54121D, TAX PREPARATION SERVICES IN THE US 25–26 (2019), [https://perma.cc/8MXK-L7UH (private, uploaded archive)].
11. *TurboTax Online Guarantees,* INTUIT TURBOTAX, https://turbotax.intuit.com/corp/guarantees [https://perma.cc/C7LF-PAMW].
12. *See* Joshua D. Blank & Leigh Osofsky, *Automated Agencies,* 107 MINN. L. REV. 2115 (2023) at n. 152–56.
13. *Id.*
14. *Id.*
15. *See, e.g.,* I.R.C. § 6072(a); Treas. Reg. § 1.6072(a) (Time for filing returns of individuals, estates, and trusts).
16. For instance, Intuit TurboTax's most popular paid option was priced at eighty-nine dollars in 2023–2024. *See* INTUIT TURBOTAX, https://turbotax.intuit.com/personal-taxes/online/ [https://perma.cc/UB6A-KXRD].
17. *See, e.g., How Much Does a Tax Attorney Cost,* CROSS L. GRP.: BLOG (Jan. 16, 2017), https://www.crosslawgroup.com/blog/hiring-tax-attorney-worth-cost/ [https://perma.cc/953D-GMLZ]; Tom Grupa, *Average Cost of Tax Attorney Fees,* THERVO (Oct. 28, 2022), https://thervo.com/costs/average-cost-of-tax-attorney-fees [https://perma.cc/NG2X-KUJK]; *What Is the Average Cost of Hiring a Tax Attorney?,* SUPERMONEY, https://www.supermoney.com/what-average-cost-hiring-tax-attorney/ [https://perma.cc/3478-98MD] (last updated Oct. 31, 2022).
18. Frederick Schauer, *Transparency in Three Dimensions,* 2011 U. ILL. L. REV. 1339, 1343, 1348–50.
19. *See, e.g.,* Mark Fenster, *The Opacity of Transparency,* 91 IOWA L. REV. 885 (2006); Schauer, *supra* note 18, at 1347; Jeremy Waldron, *Accountability: Fundamental to Democracy* 11 (N.Y.U. Sch. of L. Pub. L. & Legal Theory Rsrch. Paper Series, Working Paper No. 14-13, 2014), http://papers.ssrn.com/sol3/papers.cfm?abstract_id=2410812 [https://perma.cc/E8BZ-W6ZN (uploaded archive)]; Lawrence B. Solum, *Legal Theory Lexicon 015: Transparency,* LEGAL THEORY LEXICON, https://lsolum.typepad.com/legal_theory_lexicon/2003/12/legal_theory_le_1.html [https://perma.cc/HPM8-U8SD (uploaded archive)] (last updated Apr. 9, 2023).
20. *See* Fenster, *supra* note 19, at 898; *see also* Rachel E. Barkow, *Overseeing Agency Enforcement,* 84 GEO. WASH. L. REV. 1129, 1176–79.
21. I.R.C. § 6110.

22. 1 OFF. OF TAX POL'Y, DEP'T OF THE TREASURY, REPORT TO THE CONGRESS ON SCOPE AND USE OF TAXPAYER CONFIDENTIALITY AND DISCLOSURE PROVISIONS 27 (2000), https://home.treasury.gov/system/files/131/Report-Taxpayer-Confidentiality-2010.pdf [https://perma.cc/C478-4RDB].
23. See About IRS Written Determinations, IRS, https://www.irs.gov/uac/About-IRS-Written-Determinations [https://perma.cc/R77D-A2XM] (last updated Oct. 13, 2023).
24. See, e.g., Nadine van Engen et al., *Do Consistent Government Policies Lead to Greater Meaningfulness and Legitimacy on the Front Line?* 2019 PUBL. ADM. 97, 110.
25. Peter L. Strauss, *Publication Rules in the Rulemaking Spectrum: Assuring Proper Respect for an Essential Element*, 53 ADMIN. L. REV. 803, 808 (2001).
26. *Cf., e.g.,* DAVID FREEMAN ENGSTROM, DANIEL E. HO, CATHERINE M. SHARKEY & MARIANO-FLORENTINO CUÉLLAR, ADMIN. CONF. OF THE U.S., GOVERNMENT BY ALGORITHM: ARTIFICIAL INTELLIGENCE IN FEDERAL ADMINISTRATIVE AGENCIES 7 (2020), https://law.stanford.edu/wp-content/uploads/2020/02/ACUS-AI-Report.pdf [https://perma.cc/KR8A-HKNL].
27. *See, e.g.,* Anthony J. Casey & Anthony Niblett, *The Death of Rules and Standards*, 92 IND. L. J. 1401, 1410–12 (2017).
28. *See id.* Relatedly, other scholars have begun to contemplate the prospect of using big data and advances in artificial intelligence to create "personalized law," which crafts appropriate legal rules (such as disclosure requirements and mandatory contract provisions) to best suit particular individuals. *See generally, e.g.,* Christoph Busch, *Implementing Personalized Law: Personalized Disclosures in Consumer Law and Data Privacy Law*, 86 U. CHI. L. REV. 309 (2019); Omri Ben-Shahar & Ariel Porat, *Personalizing Mandatory Rules in Contract Law*, 86 U. CHI. L. REV. 255 (2019); Omri Ben-Shahar & Ariel Porat, *Personalizing Negligence Law*, 91 N. Y. U. L. REV. 627, 674–85 (2016); Ariel Porat & Lior Jacob Strahilevitz, *Personalizing Default Rules and Disclosure with Big Data*, 112 MICH. L. REV. 1417 (2014).
29. *See* Casey & Niblett, *supra* note 27, at 1404.
30. *See, e.g., Driverless Cars Are Taking Longer Than We Expected. Here's Why.*, N.Y. TIMES (July 14, 2019), https://www.nytimes.com/2019/07/14/us/driverless-cars.html [https://perma.cc/MNY8-69BX (private archive)].
31. *But see, e.g.,* Niva Elkin-Koren & Michal S. Gal, *The Chilling Effect of Governance-by-Data on Data Markets*, 86 U. CHI. L. REV. 403, 404–5 (2019).
32. *See* Busch, *supra* note 28, at 314. For discussion of the impact of algorithmic mediation and public understanding of the law, *see* Dan L. Burk, *Algorithmic Fair Use*, 30 U. CHI. L. REV. 238 (2019).
33. *See, e.g.,* Louis Kaplow, *A Model of the Optimal Complexity of Legal Rules*, 11 J. L. ECON. & ORG. 150 (1995) (suggesting that increased legal complexity can increase accuracy).
34. *But see* Cary Coglianese & David Lehr, *Regulating by Robot: Administrative Decision Making in the Machine-Learning Era*, 105 GEO. L. J. 1147 (2017).
35. *See, e.g.,* Lawrence Zelenak, *Justice Holmes, Ralph Kramden, and the Civic Virtues of a Tax Return Filing Requirement*, 61 TAX L. REV. 53, 56–65, 70 (2007).
36. *See, e.g.,* LAWRENCE ZELENAK, LEARNING TO LOVE FORM 1040: TWO CHEERS FOR THE RETURN-BASED MASS INCOME TAX 113–14 (2013).

7

The Hidden Costs of Automated Legal Guidance

Automated legal guidance tools offer many administrative benefits to both the public and government agencies. However, these tools can also have drawbacks. In Chapter 4, we discussed some of our prior research on automated legal guidance. This research revealed that automated legal guidance tools can provide quick, accurate answers to simple legal questions but can also present simplified descriptions that deviate from the formal law. Our research also found that agency officials were insufficiently attuned to the often subtle ways in which automated legal guidance can create these simplifications.

When agencies' chatbots and other automated tools dispense legal information that may not be exactly accurate, the public usually does not receive any notice of these potential deviations. During our research, we found, among other omissions, that agencies have failed to inform users of the following:

- that the law is uncertain or unsettled because of conflicting judicial treatment;
- that agencies cannot be legally bound to follow the statements provided by their automated tools; and
- that there are legal limitations on using statements provided by automated legal guidance tools as defenses against noncompliance penalties that could occur after audits or other investigations.

The federal government's embrace of automated tools has had an ironic effect. While, at first blush, they appear to make legal compliance obligations easier, they also exacerbate a two-tiered legal system in the United States. For individuals who cannot afford lawyers, accountants, and other professional advisors, these tools are rapidly becoming primary sources of information about the law – even if this information diverges from what the underlying law actually is. This information is especially influential on those who are using it because the information appears to come directly from government agencies in a highly personalized form.

Conversely, individuals who have access to sophisticated counsel may pay little attention to chatbots and other interactive tools on agency websites. They do not need to rely on automated legal guidance tools to learn about their legal obligations because they can afford to pay advisors to ensure that they are doing everything correctly. Thus, the need to rely upon automated legal guidance when making legal compliance decisions is not uniform among the population. As a result, automated legal guidance imposes certain costs that are borne by a segment of the population that already has fewer resources.

This chapter illuminates some of the hidden costs of the federal agencies' use of automated legal guidance to explain the law to the public. It highlights the following features of these tools:

- they make statements that deviate from the formal law;
- they fail to provide notice to users about the accuracy and legal value of their statements; and
- they induce reliance in ways that impose inequitable burdens among different user populations.

We also consider how policymakers should weigh these costs against the benefits of automated legal guidance when contemplating whether to adopt, or increase, agencies' use of these tools.

WHY THE GOVERNMENT'S VOICE MATTERS

Before exploring the hidden costs of automated legal guidance, we should pause to consider the significance of the government's voice in these communications. Why does it matter that the government, rather than a third-party advisor or for-profit business, uses automated tools to provide guidance to members of the public?

When it comes to free or low-cost informal legal advice, there are, after all, plenty of nongovernment sources available online. For instance, DoNotPay.com is an online service that describes itself as an "AI Consumer Champion," which "uses artificial intelligence to help you fight big corporations, protect your privacy, find hidden money, and beat bureaucracy."[1] In some ways, these types of private services may create some of the same issues as the government's automated legal guidance tools, such as providing advice that differs from the underlying law. There are, however, many significant differences between advice offered by government agencies and that offered by these private parties.

Many people may feel more compelled to follow the agencies' automated guidance, rather than that offered by a private actor, because they fear the consequences of conflicting with the government's view of the law. For example, individuals consistently report that a "fear of audit" exerts at least some influence over their decisions to report and pay their taxes honestly,[2] even though the overall audit rate for individual taxpayers, as of 2022, was 1 percent or less.[3] The IRS has reported that fear of audit is an even greater influence among Gen Z and Millennial taxpayers compared to more senior generations.[4] Therefore, when automated tools such as ITA describe the IRS's interpretation of the tax law, or issue a directive, many individual taxpayers are likely to follow that guidance rather than risk a potential audit. However, people who receive legal advice from free or low-cost online services may have a different reaction. They might be more likely to question that guidance, especially if it includes caveats, warnings, and disclaimers. It might also be unclear to them whether following this third-party advice will prevent them from contradicting a position the government would take.

People may also believe that legal guidance provided by the government is more trustworthy and reliable than that from third-party sources. In our research, we found that individuals often ask the government's automated tools questions related to important and sensitive personal issues, including immigration status, tax liability, student debt, and medical care.[5] According to the agency officials we interviewed, users provided positive feedback after using the tools to obtain answers to their legal questions.

One reason that individuals trust advice from these tools especially may be that they know that the source is the government itself rather than a third party. Private parties, on the other hand, can be profit-motivated, inconsistent, or short-lived, all of which could impact how much people trust the advice they provide. At its foundation, government guidance is supposed to help the public. When individuals turn to agencies' automated tools, they receive what they believe are accurate and helpful encapsulations of the government's views, rather than mere predictions of agencies' interpretations of the law.

Another important distinction between government- and third-party advice is the possibility of redress if the advice turns out to be wrong. When people use third-party services to obtain advice, whether they are online legal services, software such as Intuit's TurboTax, or even lawyers and accountants, compensation may be available if these services provide them with erroneous or incomplete guidance. Users can demand a refund of fees, or even sue their lawyers for malpractice. Far fewer possibilities for redress exist, however, when it comes to statements by the federal agencies' automated legal guidance tools. Individuals who are misled by these tools regarding their tax obligations or immigration-related requirements, for instance, may face significant legal consequences. As we will discuss further in this chapter, members of the public may not even be able to use the guidance offered by these tools to defend against certain sanctions for noncompliance.

DEVIATIONS FROM THE FORMAL LAW

The government's voice is especially powerful when it leads people to develop beliefs and pursue actions, even if the message conveyed conflicts with the underlying formal law. As documented in Chapter 4, federal agencies' automated legal guidance tools can deliver answers to users that are consistent with the law, but they can also provide guidance that deviates from the law, in ways both subtle and significant. These tools have, at times, presented unsettled formal law as unambiguous, added administrative gloss to the formal law, and omitted discussion of statutory and regulatory exceptions and requirements.[6] In these cases, automated tools have provided descriptions of the law that deviate from the statutes that Congress enacted, regulations that agencies have adopted, or doctrine that judges have articulated.

Paradoxically, this simplification can have the effect of *diminishing* people's knowledge of the formal law. In theory, someone could view statements provided by agencies' chatbots, virtual assistants, and other automated tools merely as one step of their research into legal questions. However, one of the primary purposes of automated legal guidance is to ensure that people need not spend time reviewing the text of statutes, regulations, and judicial decisions. Another important goal is to provide information about the law for those who do not have the means to seek legal advice from lawyers and other expert advisors. Because unsettled legal areas are often neither acknowledged nor explained in this type of guidance, most people would not know when these agency explanations differ from the formal law.

The result of this dynamic is that the government may be harming some people who rely on this form of guidance. For instance, these individuals may forfeit valuable benefits, such as tax deductions, to act in accordance with advice provided by automated legal guidance tools. Users' responses can also go the other way. For example, someone could have followed advice provided by USCIS's Emma regarding travel outside the United States, even though it may have been inconsistent with the relevant formal law. When people do this, they may face unwelcome surprises if the government later challenges their actions.

Deviations from the formal law also limit the public's ability to debate the law and to hold the government accountable for its actions.[7] First, when government agencies use automated legal guidance tools to simplify complex statutory law or unsettled case law to help members of the public comply with the law, public debate regarding the law may emerge from an artificial foundation of certainty and clarity. For example, in the tax context, Congress appears to have deliberately included ambiguous requirements regarding medical expense deductions to allow courts to consider individual cases.[8] Yet, ITA has often provided unambiguous answers in response to certain inquiries regarding medical expense deductions.[9] To the extent that automated legal guidance encourages the public, or even a large segment of the public, to follow the government's simplified approach, automated legal guidance forecloses more refined and comprehensive development of law. Second, automated legal guidance tools may contribute to the public's unwillingness to challenge the government for enacting overly complex or vague rules. By presenting the law as clear and simple, automated legal guidance tools create an end-run around public review and challenge of the actions of Congress and federal agencies.

As Chapter 8 will describe, there are limited opportunities for the public to hold agencies accountable for providing guidance to the public that conflicts with the formal law. However, US federal administrative law does provide some ways for the public to hold government agencies accountable. Chief among these are notice-and-comment procedures, which require agencies to publish notices of their intent to create legislative rules and offer people the opportunity to comment on these rules before they finalize them.[10] These procedures are structured to ensure accountability, in addition to transparency and nonarbitrariness, of federal government agencies when these agencies promulgate legislative rules.

Why is this important? Legislative rules include agency statements of law that can bind both the agency and the public.[11] It is often challenging to distinguish legislative rules, which formally bind both the agency and the public, from an agency's interpretative statements about the law, which are not subject to notice-and-comment requirements.[12] In any event, the automated legal guidance tools we studied did not go through notice-and-comment requirements. Yet, many users are likely to follow statements made by automated legal guidance. In our research, we found that agencies were insufficiently attentive to this reliance, believing that because users *shouldn't* be bound by automated legal guidance, they were not, in fact, relying on it. In other words, there was a significant, unrecognized tension between agencies' promotion of automated legal guidance as a way for users to apply the law and the belief that users could not rely, and were not relying, on the information it provided.

LACK OF NOTICE TO USERS

During our research, we observed that, when it comes to automated legal guidance, federal agencies often have omitted certain important information. These omissions include, but are not limited to, the following:

- the ways underlying formal law may differ from the information provided by the automated legal guidance tools;
- instances in which agency officials have revised the questions and responses offered by these tools; and
- the limited legal authority of the statements that these tools have offered.

This section describes each of these types of omissions and their potential impacts on users.

Formal Law

By providing clear and simple answers, automated legal guidance often has portrayed the law as unambiguous. A particularly notable example of this, which was discussed in Chapter 4, involves USCIS's Emma, which may have led some noncitizen users to believe that they could leave the United States for personal reasons and return without risking their US residency status.[13]

A significant issue is that, when automated legal guidance tools have answered users' questions in a straightforward fashion, they have not provided users with notice of the formal law upon which these answers are based. Further, they have not signaled to users that the formal law related to the inquiry may be the subject of conflicting judicial decisions. Some tools we reviewed contained introductory disclaimers regarding the formal law;[14] however, they rarely provided citations to the supporting statutes and regulations, or otherwise indicated that the law may be unsettled. Further, during our research, we did not find agency explanations as to *why* their automated guidance varied from the underlying formal law. This silence is surprising, especially if the agencies intended to deviate from the underlying formal law.

This type of omission is not the standard operating procedure for the government. Consider, by contrast, the legislative process. After Congress passes tax legislation, for instance, the Joint Committee on Taxation issues a report that describes present law, the newly enacted provision, and, importantly, the reasons for change to existing tax law.[15] Moreover, this type of notification procedure is not limited to Congress. Agencies also occasionally provide public announcements regarding changes to their legal interpretations. This happened, for example, in 2013, when the IRS adopted a new interpretation of the terms "married" and "marriage." The agency issued a public revenue ruling to this effect, explaining that its motivation for this change was to apply "the most natural reading" of the terms in light of the Supreme Court's decision in *United States* v. *Windsor*,[16] in which the Supreme Court held that the Defense of Marriage Act (DOMA) was unconstitutional.[17] We did not find, however, that agencies issued similar explanations during our review of their automated legal guidance tools.

Agency Revisions

Second, when federal agencies have revised the questions and answers provided by their automated legal guidance tools, they have not notified users of these changes or their effective dates. Compared to static, printed publications, it is very difficult to determine when an agency has made changes to any aspects of its automated legal guidance tools.[18] For instance, when users visit ITA, most of the topics require a user to respond to over a dozen questions before receiving an answer to their initial inquiry.[19] However, when the IRS edits ITA's questions and answers, neither ITA itself, nor the IRS website, offers any notice of the agency having done so.

The lack of notification of revisions to statements provided by automated legal guidance tools differs starkly from government transparency in other areas. In both houses of Congress, for example, bills that amend a law that is currently in force must provide a "comparative print" that shows textual deletions and additions.[20] As one legislative official explained it, the "comparative print can be of great aid in ascertaining the intended effect of amendatory legislation."[21]

Here, too, this documentary transparency is not limited to Congress. For example, when issuing final regulations, the Treasury Department explicitly describes changes made to "previously issued guidance," including prior proposed regulations.[22] Although agencies use this notification procedure elsewhere, they do not do so in their automated legal guidance, which means that users are highly unlikely to be aware that agency officials have made revisions. Consequently, different users may receive different answers in response to the same questions, depending upon when they accessed agencies' automated tools, which may cause some to pursue compliance actions that conflict with the automated tools' latest statements. The result? Some users will be consulting the wrong information when attempting to comply with the law, or when responding to subsequent audits or challenges by agency officials.

Disclaimers

Finally, federal agencies' automated legal guidance tools have lacked adequate disclaimers and warnings to users related to reliance on the information they provide. This is a critical omission, given that the guidance offered by these tools cannot bind the government, nor can people use the guidance to defend against noncompliance penalties.

This is not to say that there are no disclaimers whatsoever. Some automated legal guidance tools, such as ITA, tell users that their answers are not "written advice."[23] However, we found no ITA warning stating that users cannot rely on ITA-provided statements to bind the IRS or to assert certain tax penalty defenses, such as the "reasonable basis" defense.[24] Other tools, such as FSA's Aidan, offer no disclaimers at all related to the advice that the tool offers through its chat function.[25] The absence of warnings may provide users with a false sense of confidence that they can rely upon the answers that these tools provide, in addition to failing to apprise them of the risk they undertake by following the guidance.

UNEQUAL ACCESS TO JUSTICE

A surprising hidden cost of the government's shift to automated legal guidance is that this form of customer service can aggravate inequities in access to the law based on wealth, income, education level, language fluency, and other factors. Because formal law, such as statutes, regulations, and case law, is nearly impossible for nonlawyers and other experts to understand, most people lack meaningful access to it.[26] To fulfill their compliance obligations, most people rely on informal law, including automated legal guidance offered by federal agencies. Yet high-income, wealthy, and well-connected individuals can gain access to the formal law by hiring lawyers,[27] which creates, in effect, a two-tiered legal system.

This section discusses how a two-tiered legal system develops and persists, and how automated legal guidance can exacerbate the expanding access to justice gap by creating this type of system.

Two-Tiered Legal Systems in General

Many people have come to believe that, in the United States, there is a "two-tiered" legal system, in which the government's disparate enforcement of the law perpetuates systems of supremacy and subordination.[28] Well-known inequities exist in myriad areas of the law, including criminal law,[29] property law,[30] policing,[31] immigration,[32] and judging.[33] Inequitable substantive and enforcement aspects of the law, in turn, undermine social justice.

Another important, though underappreciated, inequity in the legal system relates to the various, inequitable forms of law to which people have access. Formal law, such as statutes, regulations, and case law, is binding on the government, but is nearly impossible for most people to understand without the assistance of a lawyer, accountant, or other professional. By contrast, informal law, such as automated legal guidance, instructions regarding required forms, FAQs on government websites, and other administrative guidance, is easier for most people to understand, yet it does not bind the government. This two-tiered system of law both dovetails with and exacerbates the inequities in substance and enforcement of law that others have identified.

The United States also has, in effect, a two-tiered system of legal drafting. Inordinately complex statutes, regulations, and case law offer the law in great detail for the relative few who can understand them. At the same time, federal agencies offer significantly simplified, plain-language explanations of the law for everyone else. This results in a "private" system of law for the few and a "public" system of law for the rest. The small number of people and businesses who have the expertise and resources to hire attorneys to decipher the formal law can access interpretations offered by a private, exclusive market. Those who lack the resources to access this private market instead get the public option: explanations of the formal law in plain language offered by government agencies.

The Expanding Access to Justice Gap

The gap between these private and public options, which is already significant, is likely to continue to expand over time. As the world becomes more complex, so too must the statutes and regulations that attempt to respond to it.[34] This remains true despite periodic efforts at regulatory reductions – indeed, recent presidential administrations have attempted to diminish the volume of unnecessary or overly burdensome regulations.[35] By any measure, however, regulation has continued apace,[36] resulting in a steady accretion over time.[37]

Simultaneously, the federal government's legislative process is plagued by a growing level of chaos. Congress has become increasingly polarized, making legislation much more difficult to pass. This has resulted in a rise in the use of "unorthodox legislation" to accomplish legislative objectives.[38] This includes extreme legislative bundling, deterioration of expert and committee control, and increased use of rapid-fire changes and post-committee amendments.[39] Taken together, these phenomena result not only in less quality control but also more inadvertent, unanswered questions, as well as statutory mistakes.[40]

While some forces push regulatory and statutory complexity in an upward direction, others pressure agencies to offer seemingly clearer, easy-to-use guidance to the public. Specifically, the rise of automation in the private sector and increasing technological capacity, as described in Chapter 2, are shaping expectations with respect to the law as well. Individuals and businesses that rely on agencies' explanations are thus expecting greater ease of use, at the same time that the law itself grows more complex. The government is responding with more, and more innovative, attempts to simplify interactions with the law, thus yielding a greater gap between different ways of accessing the law.

Who Uses Informal Law?

Acknowledging the expanding gap between ways that people access the law is an important development in and of itself. What makes this recognition even more pressing is the possibility that different access options may not be distributed evenly across the population. Rather, they are likely distributed based on factors such as income level, and may even correlate with other demographic characteristics, such as rurality, gender, disability, and race.

The access to justice literature offers ways to begin thinking about this possibility. While much more empirical work remains to be done in this area,[41] it is clear that low-income Americans, who generally do not have the same access to higher education as those in higher income categories,[42] also suffer from inadequate access to lawyers. Further, people who live in poverty are more likely to have legal problems than middle- or high-income individuals,[43] and often lack the assistance of adequate legal counsel to help them resolve these problems. A 2017 study by the Legal Services Corporation, a US government agency that supports civil legal aid initiatives, found that low-income individuals received no or inadequate legal assistance 86 percent of the time.[44] This is due to a complex set of factors beyond a lack of financial resources, including a dearth of available legal counsel, unawareness that legal assistance could help, and a desire to address the situation independently. Additionally, many low-income people in the United States do not trust or have faith in the legal system, due to prior experiences with the police, the courts, and government agencies.[45]

How does this relate to the law access gap created by two-tiered legal drafting? Accessing the complex, underlying law is only available through attorneys, to whom low-income people often lack access for various reasons. Instead, people living in poverty are much more likely to go it alone, relying on the simplified, no-cost explanations offered by the government to learn how to claim benefits and follow requirements.

In connection with her access to justice research, Professor Sara Sternberg Greene conducted interviews to learn more about how these dynamics play out when it comes to filing for federal disability benefits. One of the people she interviewed offered the following testimonial:

> I hated going and filling out all that paperwork for disability. I really needed it, I could hardly get up, my back was that shot. I got it, but they made me feel dumb. I resoluted there and then I'd get back on me feet. And I did. I do things for myself.[46]

A low-income individual who proceeds in this way, without the assistance of a lawyer, is highly unlikely to be able to access the complicated statutory and regulatory regime of the disability benefits system. They are much more likely to trudge through forms, relying on simplified explanations provided in them by the government, in addition to experiences and tips shared by family and friends.[47]

Besides income, lack of access to formal law may correlate with other demographic characteristics. For instance, the access to justice literature has examined the extent to which a person's rurality, disability, and status as a veteran can affect the likelihood of receiving legal assistance.[48] This literature also suggests that a person's race may impact their likelihood of having access to a lawyer.[49] In the end, all of this shows that the two-tiered system of law may discriminate between members of the public in problematic ways.

How Automated Legal Guidance Widens the Access to Justice Gap

At first glance, the federal government's introduction of automated tools appears to be a pure benefit to those individuals most in need of legal assistance. These tools offer fast, often personalized, responses to users' inquiries about the law free of charge. However, if we look more closely at the differences between this type of guidance and the formal law, another picture emerges. Although automated legal guidance uses plain language and deemphasizes technical terminology, it diverges from formal law in significant ways. These differences can cause automated legal guidance to widen the access to justice gap.

Adverse Guidance

In some cases where the law is unsettled, complex, or ambiguous, federal agencies have adopted interpretations that are adverse to users' interests.[50] Chapter 4 provided multiple examples of this, offering hypothetical examples of individuals who received answers to their questions about immigration requirements and the availability of tax deductions from Emma and ITA, respectively.

As a practical matter, people who lack access to legal counsel will follow the guidance that the government's automated legal guidance tools provide, even if doing so is contrary to their own personal interests.[51] By contrast, where the formal law is ambiguous, individuals and businesses who have access to advice from lawyers and accountants are far less likely to follow, or even receive, guidance that is adverse to their interests.

Consider again an example we described in Chapter 4, where a hypothetical couple attempted to determine whether their daughter's college swimming scholarship was excludable from taxable income.[52] In that example, the daughter received a competitive swimming scholarship offer from an NCAA Division I university, which would have required her to participate in swim meets and fundraising events for the university.

When the parents consulted ITA for advice, in response to a question that asked about the extent to which the scholarship was "payment for services" required as "a condition for receiving the scholarship," the couple clicked "all." Based on that response, ITA indicated that the scholarship was fully taxable. Faced with such a clear "answer" from ITA, the couple most likely would have included the scholarship in taxable income, even though the IRS has provided more nuanced, as well as contrary, interpretations in other published guidance. As we described, the IRS has stated in other guidance that college athletic scholarships are not taxable if they will not be cancelled in the event of student injury and other events. Without consulting third-party experts familiar with the underlying law, such as tax lawyers or accountants, the parents may have been misled by the IRS's automated legal guidance tool.

By contrast, wealthy individuals and businesses who have access to the formal law through sophisticated advisors are much less likely to be practically bound by statements provided by automated legal guidance tools that are disadvantageous to their interests. For example, in the tax context, under the "reportable transaction" disclosure rules, the IRS may designate potentially abusive tax strategies as "listed transactions" or "transactions of interest." Taxpayers and their advisors are required to disclose information regarding their participation in these strategies.

In 2021, the US Supreme Court heard a case, *CIC Services, LLC v. IRS*,[53] about these types of designations. The case involved a tax advisor in Tennessee who specialized in advising clients regarding microcaptive insurance strategies. In serving the clients, the advisor attempted to prevent the IRS from designating this type of tax strategy as a "transaction of interest,"[54] using formal law to fight against the IRS's position. The advisor's primary argument was that the IRS had not completed the notice-and-comment process, as required by the Administrative Procedure Act, in designating the tax strategy as a transaction of interest.[55] The Court agreed with the tax advisor and ruled against the IRS in a unanimous decision.[56]

In this example, taxpayers who had access to sophisticated legal counsel were able to benefit from the formal law: their advisor was able to fight the IRS's legal position, using principles rooted in administrative law and their interaction with the tax law.

Not Legally Binding

In contrast to the statutes, regulations, and other types of formal law, federal agencies are not bound (required) to take positions during audits, challenges, and litigation that are consistent with statements expressed by automated legal guidance tools.[57] Only formal law, access to which is frequently available only to those who can afford to hire legal counsel, is binding on federal agencies.[58]

Consider, for instance, the hypothetical taxpayer described in the introduction to this book who attempted to determine whether the taxpayer could deduct expenses for tuition for an MBA.[59] According to the scenario presented, this person hoped to pursue managerial opportunities and pay increases within their own company and wanted to know whether the MBA would be deductible. To answer this question, the taxpayer visited the IRS website and ITA, which asked the taxpayer several questions.

One of those questions was, "Was the education necessary in order to meet the minimum educational requirements of your trade or business or your employer's trade or business?"[60] The hypothetical taxpayer answered "no" because they did not believe that an MBA was a minimum educational requirement for the type of management role that they hoped to pursue in their current company. After answering a few more questions, the taxpayer received an affirmative answer from ITA: "Your work-related education expenses are deductible."[61]

The Interactive Tax Assistant appeared to deliver the answer that the taxpayer was hoping to receive. However, if the IRS ended up auditing the taxpayer, it could have challenged the deduction for MBA tuition and related expenses. There have been dozens of cases, some of which the IRS won and others that it lost, where the agency rejected taxpayers' attempts to deduct this type of education expense.[62] Yet, in this example, ITA asked the taxpayer a series of binary questions. It did not ask any follow-up questions that could have explored the taxpayer's rationale for pursuing the MBA, the type of trade or business the taxpayer had been conducting, and how the taxpayer would use the knowledge gained during MBA studies in the future. Despite this, ITA provided the taxpayer with what could reasonably be viewed as a clear, definitive statement on a screen featuring a heading that contained the word "Answer": the education expenses were deductible.[63]

In the event of an audit, the taxpayer would not be able to argue that the IRS should be bound by statements provided by ITA. The courts have consistently held that administrative guidance cannot alter the meaning of the formal tax law, statutes, and regulations.[64] In these holdings, the Tax Court's opinion in the case *Miller* v. *Commissioner*[65] is frequently cited and quoted. In *Miller*, the court clearly established the following rule: "[t]he authoritative sources of Federal tax law are the statutes, regulations, and judicial decisions; they do not include informal IRS publications."[66]

Further, the IRS takes the position that the Internal Revenue Bulletin (IRB), a weekly government publication, is the IRS's authoritative instrument for announcing official IRS rulings and procedures and for publishing Treasury Decisions and other items.[67] The IRS has informed its employees internally that they must follow everything that is published in the IRB, and taxpayers may rely on it.[68] However, the IRS does not publish statements provided by ITA, or any forms of automated legal guidance, as official statements in the IRB.[69]

If the taxpayer in this example had been able to consult with a tax lawyer to access formal law, they may have received advice that could have allowed them to defeat a challenge by the IRS. As a result of the frequent litigation between the IRS and taxpayers over the deductibility of MBA expenses, tax lawyers advertise that, in exchange for a fee, they advise clients on how to structure their affairs before claiming this deduction.[70]

Sources that a tax attorney would likely consult before advising a client in this matter, for example, include the Treasury Regulations. These contain ten specific, illustrative examples of situations where taxpayers deducted work-related education expenses, each of which is accompanied by analysis from Treasury officials.[71] If the taxpayer had been able to afford to speak with a tax lawyer, the lawyer might have reviewed these regulations and advised the taxpayer, for example, to engage in managerial activities and to document these efforts *before* applying to any online MBA programs.[72] The tax lawyer would also be familiar with the relevant case law that specifically discusses education expense deductions and would use that knowledge to help the taxpayer plan for the degree program and prepare documentation in the event of an IRS audit as well.

On a much larger scale, wealthy individuals and business taxpayers can access formal tax law to assist with tax planning in situations in which the stakes are far higher than the MBA student's deduction for tuition. In June 2021, for example, the *New York Times* published an exposé of the private equity industry's efforts to use "fee waivers" to convert the two percent management fee that they earned from ordinary income, which, at the time, was taxed at a top ordinary income tax rate of 37 percent, to a different type of income that was taxed at a net capital gain rate of 20 percent.[73] This was not the first time the private equity industry attempted to lower its tax burden; it had already successfully used the "carried interest" tax planning gambit to ensure that the bulk of private equity fund managers' fees were taxed at the lower capital gain rate.[74] Despite already having this tax victory, the private equity industry wanted to get more of fund managers' fees eligible for this lower rate of taxation.[75]

To accomplish this, sophisticated advisors working for the private equity firms relied on a deeply ambiguous and complicated set of tax rules regarding the receipt and taxation of partnership profits interest.[76] The advisors had to rely on a number of different provisions related to the taxation of partnership earnings, including

Internal Revenue Code sections, legislative history underlying such sections, case law, and more.[77] The combined complexity and ambiguity of these provisions made the aggressive planning possible.[78]

Penalties for Noncompliance

Finally, in some cases, automated legal guidance tools, like other types of informal law, do not enable users to claim defenses against penalties for noncompliance.

Returning to the MBA education expense deduction example, if the IRS asserted civil tax penalties against the taxpayer for claiming it, it would have been difficult for the taxpayer to show reliance on IRS statements in informal tax guidance to defend against these penalties. If the IRS asserted an accuracy-related tax penalty, such as negligence due to "disregard of rules and regulations,"[79] the taxpayer might have attempted to defend against this penalty by claiming, for example, that they had a "reasonable basis" for the tax position.[80] However, to assert this defense, the taxpayer must demonstrate that they reasonably relied upon written statements contained in one of a limited number of authorities, including the Internal Revenue Code, Treasury Regulations, IRS Revenue Rulings, judicial decisions, and items published by the IRS in the IRB.[81] Because statements made by ITA are not published in the IRB, they cannot be used for a reasonable-basis defense.[82] Nor would it have been likely for the taxpayer to successfully raise a "reasonable cause and good faith" defense, which is provided by statute,[83] because they would have had difficulty obtaining a complete written record of communication with ITA to show that the misunderstanding of the law was reasonable.

Even if the taxpayer had used third-party tax return preparation software, rather than ITA, to determine whether they could claim a deduction for the MBA tuition expenses, it is unlikely that they could have shown reliance on answers delivered by that software as a defense against accuracy-related tax penalties. These products, such as Intuit's TurboTax, often republish statements from informal IRS guidance and mimic the questions and answers that ITA provides.[84] As the Tax Court has commented when considering a taxpayer's attempt to rely on tax preparation software, this technology is "only as good as the information one inputs into it."[85] Consequently, many courts have held that taxpayers who have relied on TurboTax when completing their returns cannot use it as a tax penalty defense.[86]

On the other hand, people who accessed formal law with the assistance of counsel may be able to use statements in these sources to establish penalty defenses.[87] These individuals may also have the resources necessary to pay for written opinions from legal counsel to avoid the imposition of certain civil penalties for noncompliance.[88] For instance, regarding the private equity fee waivers mentioned earlier, because of the ambiguity of the legal issues involved, combined with the fact that the planning occurred based on the advice of counsel, the private equity firms were able to take advantage of the "reasonable cause and good faith" defense against civil tax penalties.

EVALUATING AUTOMATED LEGAL GUIDANCE

Taking all of this into account, those who try to rely on federal agencies' automated legal guidance tools are at a disadvantage relative to those who can access the formal law. When, for example, automated legal guidance discourages people from claiming benefits or positions to which they are entitled, there is typically no government challenge to apprise them of their lost benefits. The taxpayer who does not claim a tax deduction to which they were arguably entitled, or the immigrant who does not try to re-enter the United States despite the fact that agency discretion may have worked in their favor, has lost an important government benefit.

In contrast, when informal law encourages someone to claim benefits or positions that are arguably too advantageous, relative to the formal law, the government may very well challenge that individual (such as in a tax audit or a review of immigration status). Automated legal guidance will offer little protection when fighting that challenge, especially when compared to the protection that might have been available had that reliance been based on formal law.

Further, while the "super concise"[89] guidance offered by automated legal guidance may be able to reach more people, it also significantly increases the need for simplicity, which means it has the tendency to create even larger deviations from the formal law. Likewise, other features of automated legal guidance that make it more likely to be used also render these deviations even more significant. That its personalized design makes it more likely to influence users, combined with the fact that the advice is instantaneous and relatively decontextualized, makes recipients less likely to turn to other sources for guidance. Finally, when compared to talking to an agency official on the telephone, automated legal guidance in its present form has less capacity to elevate users to a higher tier of authority if it would be appropriate to do so under the circumstances. Automated legal guidance, consequently, may encourage users to follow guidance that may be unduly disadvantageous or expose them to legal risk.

In this regard, automated legal guidance tools reflect the federal agencies' trade-off between (1) representing the law accurately and (2) presenting it in accessible and understandable terms. Many of the benefits of automated legal guidance are double-edged. Its extreme conciseness, apparent personalization, lack of broader context, and instantaneous responses make automated legal guidance a particularly usable, and likely to be used, form of guidance. But these same features also increase the possibility that users will miss legal nuances.

Critically, our research has revealed that agencies seem insufficiently attuned to this tradeoff; specifically, agency officials do not adequately appreciate the ways that automated legal guidance (1) affects users and, in the process, (2) can obscure what the law is. Regarding this first point, we were struck by the views in agency management that users were not relying on the guidance or, alternatively, that users should not rely on such guidance, despite heavy user traffic to the guidance tool. Indeed, some agency officials believed that users did not actually rely upon the information provided by their tools because the automated legal guidance is "just providing information that you already have available on the website."[90]

As to the second point, we were surprised by agency officials' beliefs that it was not possible for the automated legal guidance to be "wrong." As we explained in our findings in Chapter 5, one agency official stressed that the agency's automated legal guidance tool was not capable of giving a "wrong" answer, because all the answers had been internally vetted.[91] Likewise, there was general agreement regarding the correctness of the responses provided by these tools. One agency official even went as far as to explain, "none of the content itself could ever be inaccurate. It's just a matter of did, they didn't give the answer that the user would want basically to answer the question ...."[92]

This combination of believing that automated legal guidance would have little influence (despite responding to millions of user inquiries), and that it was not possible for it to mislead users about the law or how it applies to users' particular circumstances, explains some of the other issues we identified with it. For instance, these beliefs help explain the following:

- the lack of adequate disclosure to users informing them that they should not rely on the guidance;
- the lack of evaluation methods designed to identify ways that descriptions of the law might be misleading users with unique circumstances;
- the failure to archive guidance as it changes; and
- the failure to provide users with a record of the information that they received from these tools.

In response to federal agencies' growing use of informal administrative guidance, government officials and policymakers have attempted to institute reform measures. For example, in 2019, President Trump signed an executive order prohibiting federal agencies from creating binding rules through the issuance of guidance documents.[93] (President Biden subsequently revoked this executive order on his first day in office.[94]) At the agency level, in 2020, the US Department of Justice added a rule to its internal manual that states that lawyers cannot rely on guidance documents in any civil or criminal cases.[95] Other agencies, such as the Food and Drug Administration, have implemented "[g]ood [g]uidance [p]ractices," in which the agency commits to seek public input before issuing guidance, in addition to seeking suggestions for guidance projects from stakeholders.[96]

While each of these reform measures is designed to increase the efficiency, fairness, and transparency of agencies' issuance of administrative guidance, they do not address the access-to-justice gap between those who can rely on access to formal law through sophisticated advisors and those who have no other option than to consult informal law, such as automated legal guidance. Policy reforms that are designed to limit the use of informal administrative guidance, such as President Trump's 2019 executive order,[97] would exacerbate the access-to-justice gap, given how unlikely it is that middle- and low-income individuals and small businesses would be able to understand the formal law in the absence of this guidance. Further, policies that focus on the government's use of informal administrative guidance to support enforcement and litigation, such as the US Department of Justice's guidance policy,[98] do not relieve concerns by those individuals who rely on this guidance that the government could take contrary enforcement actions in the future. Finally, these policy responses do not offer new legal defenses to penalties and other sanctions for those individuals and businesses that have taken actions in reasonable reliance on statements provided by automated legal guidance tools. Thus, these reforms leave in place the need for automated legal guidance and do little to ameliorate its contribution to a two-tiered legal system.

APPRECIATING TRADEOFFS, RELATIVE TO ALTERNATIVES

In relation to alternative systems of communicating the law, automated legal guidance is not uniquely problematic. It does, however, present distinct costs and benefits. Automated legal guidance serves as one solution to a difficult problem: the need for the law to address complex problems, combined with the public's lack of ability or inclination to understand a complex legal system.

There are other potential solutions to this problem, each of which presents their own tradeoffs. Indeed, these potential solutions exist along a spectrum. At one end is a very simple legal system. Not only would this system be easier for the public to understand, but it would also avoid certain democracy- and equity-related problems that arise when presenting the law as simpler than it really is. However, a simpler legal system would also be less capable of ensuring that benefits and costs are assigned to the correct individuals, which itself may undermine equity and other goals the legal system would like to accomplish.[99]

At the other end of the spectrum is a complex legal system that the government does not try to explain to the public at all. In this type of system, sophisticated artificial intelligence could simply impose the law on people. While this system would be more capable of targeting the right benefits and costs to specific individuals, implementing a legal system the government cannot explain and the people cannot understand raises significant concerns related to democracy and the rule of law.[100]

Having a complex legal system that the government attempts to explain in simple terms, including through automated legal guidance, represents a point more in the middle of the spectrum. Given all of the variables, this may be the best option, but only as long as its implementation is thoughtfully conceived and executed. However, there will be tradeoffs. Relative to alternatives, the central tradeoff for automated legal guidance is that it cannot adequately describe how complex law applies to everyone's circumstances. Instead, it obscures the complexity, and even intensifies the effects of simplicity through its use, as compared to other forms of legal guidance that are less easy to transmit to the public.

Why does this matter? Because, at worst, automated legal guidance threatens to systematically discourage the most vulnerable members of the public from realizing benefits to which they are entitled. While many members of the public may have the resources or wherewithal to access other forms of legal advice, the costs of automated legal guidance will tend to be borne to the greatest extent by those members of the public who use it as their first and last stop in understanding the legal system – indeed, because of wide-ranging societal inequities, by the people who can least afford to be disadvantaged in this way.

At present, agency officials are not adequately apprised of this tradeoff. Significant design choices are being made, such as the choice to present users with "answers" in a decision tree answer model, or to picture the automated legal guidance as a person or other being (in the cases of Emma and Aidan), without considering how these choices are influencing public views regarding the law. As automated legal guidance grows and evolves, the federal government has a responsibility to more seriously consider how its choices to explain the law may affect public behavior, especially when its communication methods necessarily involve deviations from the underlying legal rules.

In one example of this, not realizing that automated legal guidance can mislead members of the public about how the law applies in their circumstances may cause agencies to fail not only to apprise the public of its limits but also to robustly evaluate such guidance outside of just relying on user experience surveys. Additionally, not appreciating the tradeoffs of automated legal guidance reduces the government's ability to consider when its use is appropriate relative to alternative approaches. In this regard, understanding automated legal guidance and its attendant tradeoffs is not only relevant when agencies choose to use this method of communication. Rather, understanding the costs and benefits of this approach, relative to others, is central to the more general task of designing and communicating a legal system.

NOTES

1. DoNotPay, https://donotpay.com [https://perma.cc/UH8C-6XUD].
2. *See* IRS, Pub. 5296, Comprehensive Taxpayer Attitude Survey (CTAS) 2021: Executive Report 28 (2021), https://www.irs.gov/pub/irs-pdf/p5296.pdf [https://perma.cc/9ZNQ-KE9Q].
3. *See* IRS, Pub. 55–B, Internal Revenue Service Data Book, 2022, at 33 (2023) https://www.irs.gov/pub/irs-pdf/p55b.pdf [https://perma.cc/69WL-XSLG].
4. *See* IRS, Pub. 5296, *supra* note 2, at 7, 29.
5. *See* Chapter 4, "Emma (USCIS)" and "Interactive Tax Assistant (ITA)."
6. *See id.*

7. *See, e.g.*, Letter from Thomas Jefferson to Charles Yancey (Jan. 6, 1816), https://founders.archives.gov/documents/Jefferson/03-09-02-0209 [https://perma.cc/WP4X-6H6W] ("[I]f a nation expects to be ignorant & free, in a state of civilisation, it expects what never was & never will be."); *see also* JOHN RAWLS, A THEORY OF JUSTICE 14–15 (rev. ed. 1999) (theorizing that justice is the product of a social contract between individuals and government); Frederick Schauer, *Transparency in Three Dimensions*, 2011 U. ILL. L. REV. 1339, 1343 (emphasizing, in the abstract, the importance of government transparency).
8. *See* I.R.C. § 213(a).
9. *See* Chapter 4, "Interactive Tax Assistant (ITA)."
10. *See, e.g.*, Shu-Yi Oei & Leigh Osofsky, *Legislation and Comment: The Making of the § 199A Regulations*, 69 EMORY L. J. 209, 220–21 (2019).
11. *See, e.g., Chrysler Corp. v. Brown*, 441 U.S. 281, 295 (1979); Michael Asimow, *Nonlegislative Rulemaking and Regulatory Reform*, 1985 DUKE L. J. 381, 383.
12. 5 U.S.C. § 553 (requiring notice-and-comment rulemaking for legislative rules but exempting interpretative rules); *see also Cmty. Nutrition Inst. v. Young*, 818 F.2d 943, 946 (D.C. Cir. 1987).
13. *See* Chapter 4, "Emma (USCIS)."
14. *See id.*
15. *See, e.g.*, STAFF OF THE JOINT COMM. ON TAXATION, 112TH CONG., JCS-2-13, GENERAL EXPLANATION OF TAX LEGISLATION ENACTED IN THE 112TH CONGRESS (Comm. Print 2013), https://www.jct.gov/publications/2013/jcs-2-13/ [https://perma.cc/H34Y-MGGP (uploaded archive)].
16. 570 U.S. 744 (2013).
17. Rev. Rul. 2013-17, 2013-2 C.B. 201.
18. *See* TAXPAYER ADVOC. SERV., NATIONAL TAXPAYER ADVOCATE OBJECTIVES REPORT TO CONGRESS: FISCAL YEAR 2021, at 48 n.3 (2021), https://www.taxpayeradvocate.irs.gov/wp-content/uploads/2020/08/JRC21_FullReport.pdf [https://perma.cc/7SYY-F75D (uploaded archive)].
19. *See* Chapter 4, "Interactive Tax Assistant (ITA)."
20. *See* RICHARD S. BETH, CONG. RSCH. SERV., RS20617, HOW BILLS AMEND STATUTES 2 (2003), https://fas.org/sgp/crs/misc/RS20617.pdf [https://perma.cc/4KPV-PSJR] (describing House Rule XIII, cl. 3(e)(1) (the "Ramseyer Rule") and Senate Rule XXVI, ¶ 12 (the "Cordon Rule")).
21. *Id.*
22. *See, e.g.*, T.D. 9655, 2014-1 C.B. 541, 541–42 (2014).
23. *See* Chapter 4, "Interactive Tax Assistant (ITA)."
24. *See* Treas. Reg. § 1.6662-4(d)(3)(iii).
25. *See* Chapter 2, "Automated Legal Guidance."
26. *See* LEGAL SERVS. CORP., THE JUSTICE GAP: MEASURING THE UNMET CIVIL LEGAL NEEDS OF LOW-INCOME AMERICANS 13 (2017), https://www.lsc.gov/sites/default/files/images/TheJusticeGap-FullReport.pdf [https://perma.cc/A6N9-X9MP]; REBECCA L. SANDEFUR, AM. BAR FOUND., ACCESSING JUSTICE IN THE CONTEMPORARY USA: FINDINGS FROM THE COMMUNITY NEEDS AND SERVICES STUDY 3 (2014), https://www.americanbarfoundation.org/uploads/cms/documents/sandefur_accessing_justice_in_the_contemporary_usa._aug._2014.pdf [https://perma.cc/W3D3-HVU8] [hereinafter SANDEFUR, ACCESSING JUSTICE]; Sara Sternberg Greene, *Race, Class, and Access to Civil Justice*, 101 IOWA L. REV. 1263, 1298 (2016).
27. *See, e.g.*, Jesse Drucker & Danny Hakim, *Private Inequity: How a Powerful Industry Conquered the Tax System*, N.Y. TIMES, https://www.nytimes.com/2021/06/12/business/

private-equity-taxes.html [https://perma.cc/ELR2-24VW (private, uploaded archive)] (last updated Sept. 8, 2021).
28. *See, e.g.,* Jeffrey Deskovic, *Looking Back: Our Two-Tiered Justice System*, DAVIS VANGUARD (Dec. 27, 2020), https://www.davisvanguard.org/2020/12/looking-back-our-two-tiered-justice-system/ [https://perma.cc/XRV3-8ACA].
29. *See, e.g.,* SENT'G PROJECT, REPORT TO THE UNITED NATIONS ON RACIAL DISPARITIES IN THE U.S. CRIMINAL JUSTICE SYSTEM (2018), https://www.sentencingproject.org/publications/un-report-on-racial-disparities/ [https://perma.cc/SR24-UD2A].
30. *See, e.g.,* K-Sue Park, *Conquest and Slavery in the Property Law Course: Notes for Teachers* (July 24, 2020) (unpublished manuscript), https://papers.ssrn.com/sol3/papers.cfm?abstract_id=3659947 [https://perma.cc/X56L-PJNV (uploaded archive)] (describing the history of slavery and subordination at the heart of property law).
31. *See, e.g., Mahoney v. Owens,* 818 F. App'x 894, 899 (11th Cir. 2020) ("Racism in policing is a particularly brutal facet of our country's mistreatment of Black people.").
32. *See, e.g.,* Jayashri Srikantiah & Shirin Sinnar, Essay, *White Nationalism as Immigration Policy*, 71 STAN. L. REV. ONLINE 197, 198–203 (2019).
33. *See, e.g.,* Justin D. Levinson, Mark W. Bennett & Koichi Hioki, *Judging Implicit Bias: A National Empirical Study of Judicial Stereotypes*, 69 FLA. L. REV. 63, 110–11 (2017) (finding negative, implicit bias by judges against certain groups, with impacts on judicial outcomes).
34. *See, e.g.,* Nicholas Bagley, *The Procedure Fetish*, 118 MICH. L. REV. 345, 401 (2019).
35. *See, e.g.,* Exec. Order No. 12,866, 58 Fed. Reg. 51735, 51739–40 (Sept. 30, 1993); Exec. Order No. 13,563, 76 Fed. Reg. 3821 (Jan. 18, 2011); Exec. Order No. 13,771, 82 Fed. Reg. 9339 (Jan. 30, 2017); Exec. Order No. 13,777, 82 Fed. Reg. 12285, 12286 (Feb. 24, 2017).
36. *Reg Stats*, GW REGUL. STUD. CTR., https://regulatorystudies.columbian.gwu.edu/reg-stats [https://perma.cc/K5V9-TV4S]; Jason Webb Yackee & Susan Webb Yackee, *Testing the Ossification Thesis: An Empirical Examination of Federal Regulatory Volume and Speed, 1950–1990*, 80 GEO. WASH. L. REV. 1414, 1422 (2012).
37. *See* J. B. Ruhl & James Salzman, *Mozart and the Red Queen: The Problem of Regulatory Accretion in the Administrative State*, 91 GEO. L. J. 757, 761 (2003) (discussing such complexity).
38. BARBARA SINCLAIR, PARTY WARS: POLARIZATION AND THE POLITICS OF NATIONAL POLICY MAKING (2006).
39. Leigh Osofsky, *Agency Legislative Fixes*, 105 IOWA L. REV. 2107, 2115–17 (2020); *see also* BARBARA SINCLAIR, UNORTHODOX LAWMAKING: NEW LEGISLATIVE PROCESSES IN THE U.S. CONGRESS (5th ed. 2016) (providing background).
40. Osofsky, *supra* note 39, at 2117–18.
41. *See* Rebecca L. Sandefur, *What We Know and Need to Know about the Legal Needs of the Public*, 67 S. C. L. REV. 443, 453 (2016) (describing courts' development of "plain language forms" for tasks like pleadings).
42. *See* LEGAL SERVS. CORP., *supra* note 26, at 18.
43. SANDEFUR, ACCESSING JUSTICE, *supra* note 26, at 3.
44. LEGAL SERVS. CORP., *supra* note 26, at 6.
45. *Id.* at 7; SANDEFUR, ACCESSING JUSTICE, *supra* note 26, at 12–13.
46. Greene, *supra* note 26, at 1298; *see also* Gillian K. Hadfield, *Higher Demand, Lower Supply? A Comparative Assessment of the Legal Resource Landscape for Ordinary Americans*, 37 FORDHAM URB. L. J. 129 (2010).
47. SANDEFUR, ACCESSING JUSTICE, *supra* note 26, at 11 (finding that people handled civil justice situations through the help of family or friends twenty-three percent of the time).

48. *See, e.g.*, LEGAL SERVS. CORP., *supra* note 26, at 8 (identifying rate of civil legal problems in these groups, among others); *see also, e.g.*, Lisa R. Pruitt et al., *Legal Deserts: A Multi-State Perspective on Rural Access to Justice*, 13 HARV. L. & POL'Y REV. 15 (2018).
49. *See, e.g.*, Brian Libgober, *Getting a Lawyer While Black: A Field Experiment*, 24 LEWIS & CLARK L. REV. 53, 54 (2020); Amy Myrick, Robert L. Nelson, & Laura Beth Neilsen, *Race and Representation: Racial Disparities in Legal Representation for Employment Civil Rights Plaintiffs*, 15 N. Y. U. J. LEGIS. & PUB. POL'Y 705 (2012).
50. *See* Chapter 4, "Emma (USCIS)" and "Interactive Tax Assistant (ITA)."
51. *See id.*
52. *See id.*
53. 141 S. Ct. 1582 (2021).
54. *Id.* at 1588; IRS Notice 2016-66, 2016-47 I.R.B. 745 (designating strategy as transaction of interest).
55. *CIC Servs.*, 141 S. Ct. at 1588; IRS Notice 2016-66, 2016-47 I.R.B. 745.
56. *CIC Servs.*, 141 S. Ct. at 1594. For further discussion, *see* Kristen A. Parillo, *Supreme Court's CIC Services Opinion Clarifies Scope of AIA*, TAX NOTES (May 18, 2021), https://www.taxnotes.com/tax-notes-today-federal/litigation-and-appeals/supreme-courts-cic-services-opinion-clarifies-scope-aia/2021/05/18/6o1cw [https://perma.cc/YE2Z-HDYL (private, uploaded archive)]; and Daniel Hemel, *Treasury Needs to Act Fast to Save the Tax-Shelter Disclosure Regime*, SUBSTANCE OVER FORM (May 18, 2021), https://substanceoverform.substack.com/p/treasury-needs-to-act-fast-to-save [https://perma.cc/8UC8-JTJ9]. The Court's holding in *CIC Services* is consistent with the arguments presented by Professor Kristin Hickman in her amicus brief in this case. *See* Brief of Amicus Curiae Professor Kristin E. Hickman in Support of Petitioners at 2–19, *CIC Servs., LLC v. IRS*, 141 S. Ct. 1582 (2021) (No. 19-930).
57. *See, e.g., Miller v. Comm'r*, 114 T.C. 184, 194–95 (2000).
58. *See, e.g., id.* at 194–95; *United States v. Josephberg*, 562 F.3d 478, 498 (2d Cir. 2009) (stating that the only authoritative sources for the IRS are statutes, regulations, and judicial decisions); *Carpenter v. United States*, 495 F.2d 175, 184 (5th Cir. 1974); *Adler v. Comm'r*, 330 F.2d 91, 93 (9th Cir. 1964); *Zimmerman v. Comm'r*, 71 T.C. 367, 371 (1978), *aff'd Zimmerman v. Comm'r*, 614 F.2d 1294 (2d Cir. 1979); *Johnson v. Comm'r*, 620 F.2d 153, 155 (7th Cir. 1980).
59. *See* Introduction.
60. *Are My Work-Related Education Expenses Deductible?*, IRS, https://www.irs.gov/help/ita/are-my-work-related-education-expenses-deductible [https://perma.cc/83R5-ZFNP] (last updated Jan. 16, 2024); *Id.* (click "Begin"; then click "Continue"; then select a tax year; then select "Yes") [https://perma.cc/33NV-V9G3 (uploaded archive)].
61. *Id.* (from "Was the education necessary in order to meet the minimum educational requirements of your trade or business or your employer's trade or business?" select "No"; then select "No"; then select "No"; then select "Yes"; then select "No") [https://perma.cc/Y2EC-9P8C (uploaded archive)].
62. *See, e.g., Link v. Comm'r*, 90 T.C. 460, 463–64 (1988), *aff'd*, 869 F.2d 1491 (6th Cir. 1989) (denying graduate education expense deduction); *Schneider v. Comm'r*, 47 T.C.M. (CCH) 675 (1983) (denying MBA work-related education expense deduction); *Sherman v. Comm'r*, 36 T.C.M. (CCH) 1191 (1977) (same); *see also Allemeier v. Comm'r*, 90 T.C.M. (CCH) 197 (2005), *supplemented by* 91 T.C.M. (CCH) 758 (2006) (allowing MBA work-related education expense deductions).
63. *See supra* note 61.
64. *See supra* note 58.

65. 114 T.C. 184 (2000).
66. *Id.* at 195. For cases citing *Miller* for the proposition that administrative guidance by the IRS is not binding on the government, see, for example, *Dorsey v. Comm'r*, 91 T.C.M. (CCH) 907 (2006); *Dunnigan v. Comm'r*, 110 T.C.M. (CCH) 320 (2015); and *Blodgett v. Comm'r*, 104 T.C.M. (CCH) 500 (2012).
67. IRS Interim Guidance Mem. SBSE-04-0517-0030, IRM 4.10.7.2.4 (Jan. 10, 2018).
68. *Id.* (adding "Caution" statement to subsection of *Internal Review Manual*).
69. *See* Kristin E. Hickman, *IRB Guidance: The No Man's Land of Tax Code Interpretation*, 2009 MICH. ST. L. REV. 239, 240 (2009); Leslie Book, *Giving Taxpayer Rights a Seat at the Table*, 91 TEMP. L. REV. 759, 768 (2019).
70. *See, e.g., MBA Student's Attempt to Deduct Tuition Fails in the Tax Court*, BERGER L., https://www.bergerlaw.net/mba-students-attempt-to-deduct-tuition-fails-in-the-tax-court.html [https://perma.cc/J47E-YV5Y].
71. Treas. Reg. §§ 1.162-5(b)(2) to (3) (as amended in 1967).
72. *See, e.g., Allemeier v. Comm'r*, 90 T.C.M. (CCH) 197 (2005), *supplemented by* 91 T.C.M. (CCH) 758 (2006) (allowing MBA work-related education expense deductions).
73. Drucker & Hakim, *supra* note 27.
74. *See generally* Victor Fleischer, *Two and Twenty: Taxing Partnership Profits in Private Equity Funds*, 83 N. Y. U. L. REV. 1 (2008) (describing in detail).
75. Drucker & Hakim, *supra* note 27.
76. *See generally* Gregg D. Polsky, *Private Equity Management Fee Conversions*, TAX NOTES, Feb. 9, 2009, at 743 (describing in detail).
77. *Id.*
78. For instance, a central issue was whether receiving an additional carried interest in investment partnerships, instead of a management fee waiver, constituted receipt of a profits interest. The taxation of profits interests is notoriously complex and ambiguous and has spawned regulations, proposed regulations, anti-abuse statutory provisions, legislative history, revenue rulings, case law, and more. *See, e.g.*, Laura E. Cunningham, *Taxing Partnership Interests Exchanged for Services*, 47 TAX L. REV. 247 (1991).
79. I.R.C. § 6662(b)(1).
80. Treas. Reg. § 1.6662-3(b)(3) (1991).
81. *Id.* ("[P]osition [must be] reasonably based on one or more of the authorities set forth in § 1.6662-4(d)(3)(iii) ....").
82. *See id.*
83. I.R.C. § 6664(c)(1).
84. *See* Joshua D. Blank & Leigh Osofsky, *Simplexity: Plain Language and the Tax Law*, 66 EMORY L. J. 189, 229–31 (2017).
85. *Bunney v. Comm'r*, 114 T.C. 259, 267 (2000).
86. *Id.*; *see, e.g., Bartlett v. Comm'r*, 104 T.C.M. (CCH) 267 (2012); *Bulakites v. Comm'r*, 113 T.C.M. (CCH) 1384 (2017); *see also* Randy P. Mock & Nancy E. Shurtz, *The TurboTax Defense*, 15 FL. TAX REV. 443 (2014).
87. *See* Treas. Reg. § 1.6664-4(c)(1) (as amended in 2003).
88. *See* Heather M. Field, *Tax Lawyers as Tax Insurance*, 60 WM. & MARY L. REV. 2111, 2121 (2019).
89. *See* Chapter 5, "Agency Interviews."
90. *See id.*
91. *See id.*
92. *See id.*
93. Exec. Order No. 13,891, 84 Fed. Reg. 55235 (Oct. 9, 2019).

94. Exec. Order No. 13,992, 86 Fed. Reg. 7049 (Jan. 20, 2021).
95. U.S. Dep't of Just., Just. Manual § 1-19.000 (2018).
96. *Fact Sheet: FDA Good Guidance Practices*, U.S. FOOD & DRUG ADMIN. (Dec. 4, 2017), https://www.fda.gov/about-fda/transparency-initiative/fact-sheet-fda-good-guidance-practices [https://perma.cc/96BN-DZHS (uploaded archive)].
97. Exec. Order No. 13,891, 84 Fed. Reg. 55235 (Oct. 9, 2019).
98. U.S. Dep't of Just., Just. Manual § 1-19.000 (2018).
99. *See generally* Louis Kaplow, *A Model of the Optimal Complexity of Legal Rules*, 11 J. L. ECON. & ORG. 150 (1995) (exploring the accuracy/complexity tradeoff).
100. *See, e.g.*, Karl Manheim & Lyric Kaplan, *Artificial Intelligence: Risks to Privacy and Democracy*, 21 YALE J. L. & TECH. 106, 111 (2019).

8

The Democracy Deficit

While automated legal guidance offers many benefits to both agencies and members of the public, it also imposes hidden costs, including deviations from formal law, lack of notice to users, and increased unequal access to justice. As discussed in Chapter 7, these costs are especially concerning when the actor that is providing automated legal guidance is the government. To state the obvious, people have different expectations when seeking guidance from the government than they do when asking a Starbucks virtual barista about coffee options. However, what is less obvious, while also involving much higher stakes, is that people also have different expectations when receiving guidance from the IRS than when they get it from TurboTax.

In the end, government communications should, and often do, carry special weight. A central aspect of administrative law is motivated by this very premise. Mindful of this special weight, large swaths of administrative law are designed to regulate, and render legitimate, statements of law that agencies make to the public. These guardrails are supposed to ensure that agencies can advise people without wielding unchecked power. Extensive administrative law doctrine and scholarship is dedicated to policing agency statements to ensure that appropriate guardrails not only apply but are also consistently in use.

Our study of automated legal guidance reveals a hole in this framework. The explanations of the law that we have been examining throughout this book – the types of explanations provided, for instance, by Emma, ITA, or Aidan – are often not subject to key administrative law guardrails. The formal reason for this is that an agency's explanations of law that are delivered by automated legal guidance are not, at least within the administrative law framework, considered to be the type of statements that compel any sort of response from the public. As a result, they are not subject to formal administrative law process on formulation.

This result, however, does not match the reality of how the public uses automated legal guidance. Millions of people turn to Emma, ITA, Aidan, and other types of automated legal guidance precisely because they are seeking information about what they should do. Can they leave the country without negatively affecting their immigration status? Can they take a certain deduction on their tax return? Can they change their job without forfeiting student loan forgiveness? Further, the agencies themselves explicitly encourage people to use the automated legal guidance to get answers to questions like these. As a result, agencies are using statements issued by these tools to affect public behavior, even though there is no place for such statements in the administrative law framework.

This chapter examines how this blind spot in the administrative law framework mirrors a broader democracy deficit in administrative law. Strikingly, this area of law, the purpose of which is to mandate that administrative agencies act in certain ways to protect the public, simply fails to address the pervasive, and impactful, ways that agencies often communicate law to people through the types of informal explanations found in automated legal guidance. This reflects an unfortunate bias toward sophisticated parties, rather than the general public. In Chapter 9, we will address how automated legal guidance should evolve, offering suggestions for policymakers about its future. The concerns addressed in this chapter will help inform that discussion.

GUARDRAILS AROUND GOVERNMENT COMMUNICATIONS

Tension at the Heart of Administrative Law

A central insight of administrative law is that agency statements command attention. When agencies promulgate regulations that create new rights and duties in a procedurally and substantively legitimate fashion, the public is then bound by those regulations.[1] Moreover, even when agencies offer less formal statements about the law, members of the public are likely to listen. This can be true even when the statements only purport to offer internal agency guidance.[2]

This widespread public attention to agency statements emanates from the agency's authority to administer legal regimes. Agencies are typically charged not only with communicating the law but also with administering benefits and enforcing the legal regime through penalties and other mechanisms.[3] As a result, when agencies make statements about the law – even in the form of allegedly nonbinding guidance – members of the public have strong reasons to adhere to them. The result? Agency statements have significant power to affect public behavior.[4]

This power creates a fundamental tension in administrative law. To operate efficiently, agencies must be able to make statements about the law with relative ease. Congress often delegates wide-ranging and significant decisions to administrative agencies.[5] Arguably, this delegation is essential to the functioning of government in an increasingly complex world.[6]

However, despite their critical role in ensuring the government's viability, agencies often operate on limited budgets and without adequate resources.[7] If, given these circumstances, it is too burdensome for agencies to make statements about the law, the legal regime may falter, with attendant, negative consequences for public welfare and, potentially, even for constitutional governance. Even if agencies were always adequately resourced, they would still need the freedom to respond expeditiously to pressing problems and open questions.

That said, it would also be problematic if agencies were able to make statements too freely. For some, concerns of this nature reflect constitutional skepticism about the administrative state. In this line of critique, if agencies were able to both make and enforce the law, this would not only raise the specter of tyranny, but it would also violate constitutional demarcations of power.[8] Others have rejected this sentiment, however, as being out of step with the realities and necessity of administrative bureaucracy for a well-functioning system of modern governance,[9] or even contrary to the history of our system of governance.[10] Regardless, even those who welcome the role of agency bureaucracy in modern American governance believe that the production and publication of agency statements must be inculcated with an appropriate process and procedure.[11] Indeed, this process and procedure does, at least in part, legitimate legal pronouncements made by federal agencies.[12]

The Administrative Procedure Act

The Administrative Procedure Act (APA) is the federal law that governs the operation of agencies in certain key ways. This law can be, and has been, understood as a compromise, in that it is meant to mediate between these tensions regarding agency power.[13]

As Professor George B. Shepherd has described, the APA resulted from a "pitched political battle" over the power of government in the New Deal Era.[14] On the one hand, under the guise of "efficiency," liberals sought to achieve an easy, agency-led implementation of New Deal programs, unhampered by "cumbersome procedural requirements or intrusive judicial review."[15] On the other hand, under the guise of "individual rights," conservatives sought to impose procedural and judicial restraints, with the goal of undermining these New Deal expansions of agency power and programs.[16]

Regarding how the APA addresses agency statements in particular, the law certainly reflects this compromise. In particular, the APA sets forth a framework for agency rulemaking, which is one of the principal forms of agency action this law contemplates.[17] Under this framework, agency rulemaking is generally subject to certain minimal requirements: the agency must provide (1) notice of the proposed rule, (2) an opportunity for the public to comment, and (3) a "concise general statement" of the "basis and purpose" of the rule that the agency adopts after public comment.[18] However, these requirements do not apply to a number of categories of agency statements, or rules, that do not fall under this prescribed category of rulemaking, including "interpretative rules, general statements of policy, or rules of agency organization, procedure, or practice."[19]

Over time, courts and, to a lesser extent, Congress and the executive branch have greatly elaborated on the requirements that apply to what have come to be known as legislative rules, or the rules that are specifically subject to notice-and-comment procedures.[20] As Professor Thomas McGarity explains, a variety of factors, including "hard look" review by courts, have transformed legislative rulemaking into a laborious and costly process.[21] In contrast, what have become known as interpretive rules and policy statements remain much freer of procedural requirements. It is these latter types of rules and policies that some agencies have determined are applicable to guidance documents.[22]

One significant example of this development involves the Office of Management and Budget (OMB), the federal agency that is "responsible both for promoting good management practices and for overseeing and coordinating the Administration's regulatory policy."[23] In 2007, the OMB adopted "good guidance practices" for agencies to use in producing "significant guidance documents."[24] Most notably, "significant guidance documents" include those that "[l]ead to an annual effect on the economy of $100 million or more" or that "[r]aise novel legal or policy issues."[25] The OMB is not the only federal government actor that concerns itself with the procedure that agencies use to develop and explain their policies. For example, the Supreme Court has held that agencies must be cognizant of "serious reliance interests" that their policies may engender, such as, for instance, when considering rescinding a major executive policy, such as Deferred Action for Childhood Arrivals (DACA).[26] However, outside of these exceptional categories, agencies generally remain able to speak relatively freely when issuing interpretive rules or policy statements.

Aside from procedural requirements, there are other distinctions between legislative rules and the categories of statements characterized as "guidance," which includes interpretive rules and policy statements. More stringent procedural requirements apply to legislative rules because these rules bind the agency and the public, whereas less formal guidance is supposed to be more advisory.[27] The binding quality of legislative rules, as well as the procedural requirements, also means that legislative rules are much more likely than guidance to be subject to intensive judicial review.[28]

These distinctions between legislative rules and less formal guidance reflect the tension between promoting and controlling agency power. This framework essentially has a dual function. On the one hand, it is designed to provide agencies space to communicate openly and easily with the public when the agencies are merely offering their own views.[29] On the other hand, and consistent with concerns about agency power, the framework subjects agencies to many more requirements, as well as a much stricter level of review, when agencies create new, binding legal requirements.

DEMOCRACY DEFICIT IN ADMINISTRATIVE LAW

If the administrative law framework provides guardrails around agency statements, what is its impact when agencies attempt to explain the law to the public, as in the case of explanations by automated legal guidance? If these explanations of the law are a widely used form of communication by agencies, shouldn't they fit into this framework? Although one would think so, the administrative law framework neither categorizes nor otherwise accommodates these explanations. This omission reflects a broader bias toward sophisticated parties, rather than the general public, in administrative law.

Agency Explanations to the Public

Notwithstanding the widespread use of agency explanations and the role they play in government service to the public, the administrative law framework fails to capture them. As an initial matter, despite the importance of distinguishing between the different categories of legislative rules, interpretive rules, and policy statements, it is notoriously difficult to do so. As scholars and courts have widely acknowledged, the distinctions between these categories are "baffling," "tenuous," "fuzzy," "blurred," and "enshrouded in considerable smog."[30]

Example of an Agency Explanation

Indeed, in part because of this doctrinal confusion, if one wanted to apply the existing administrative law framework to agency explanations, they may be able to argue that any of the categories applied. To illustrate this point, let's use an example from the IRS's ITA. Imagine a chronically ill taxpayer who is not able to take care of her daily needs, such as bathing, cooking, basic house cleaning (including laundry and dishes), and administering daily medication. She hires a home health aide, who assists with all these needs. To determine whether the expense of hiring the home health aid is tax deductible, the taxpayer turns to ITA and selects the category of questions titled "Can I Deduct My Medical and Dental Expenses?"[31] After asking her a series of introductory questions, ITA prompts the taxpayer to choose from a list of potential expenses. After selecting "Household Help Expenses," ITA responds with the following guidance: "The Household Help Expenses are not a deductible expense. Your Household Help Expenses are not a qualified medical expense."[32]

This answer is a prototypical agency explanation offered through automated legal guidance. The answer is straightforward – the taxpayer received a clear message that the expense is not a qualified medical expense. However, as we have seen with other examples, that answer may be inconsistent with the governing law. It is true that, under the Internal Revenue Code, as a general matter, "no deduction shall be allowed for personal, living, or family expenses."[33] It is also true that, historically, even a taxpayer who was medically incapable of providing for their own basic needs could not deduct the cost of hiring help to provide for such needs.[34]

However, after 1996, the Internal Revenue Code added payments for "qualified long-term care services" to the list of deductible medical care expenses.[35]

Moreover, "qualified long-term care services" is defined as including, among other things, "maintenance or personal care services, which (A) are required by a chronically ill individual, and (B) are provided pursuant to a plan of care prescribed by a licensed health care practitioner."[36] Further, the legislative history for this provision makes clear that "maintenance or personal care services" may include "meal preparation, household cleaning, and other similar services which the chronically ill individual is unable to perform."[37] As a result, the taxpayer may, in fact, be entitled to take the very deduction for "Household Help Expenses" that ITA just told her she was not eligible to take.

It is hard to say why the IRS programmed ITA to give this answer in this scenario. Perhaps the IRS did this because of its duties to explain the law clearly to taxpayers under the Plain Writing Act. Or it is possible that the IRS independently thinks that making the explanation simple and mostly right (but also systematically wrong in some number of cases) is a better way to serve the public. However, this example illustrates the point we have seen time and again with automated legal guidance: In its attempt to present the law in a straightforward manner, agency guidance often deviates materially from the underlying law.

Legislative Rule, Interpretive Rule, or Policy Statement?
In what ways could this agency explanation, and the deviation within it, arguably fit within any of the three categories of agency statements? In other words, is this guidance offered by ITA a legislative rule, an interpretive rule, or a policy statement?

To start, while the definition of a "legislative rule" is highly contested, lower courts have often explained that legislative rules "'create law,' 'prescribe, modify, or abolish duties, rights, or exemptions,' or 'fill' statutory 'gaps.'"[38] We know that Treasury Regulations fall under the legislative rule category; however, the regulations regarding the medical expense deduction have not been amended since 1979.[39] As a result, they do not reflect the addition to the Internal Revenue Code of the available deduction for qualified long-term care services. While, as stated earlier, the statute allows such deductible long-term care services to include "maintenance or personal care services ... required by a chronically ill individual,"[40] it is possible that the IRS is intending to create law by excluding "Household Help Expenses" from the deductible category of expenses.

However, the fact that the legislative history for this statutory amendment explicitly references "meal preparation, household cleaning, and other similar services" for chronically ill individuals as deductible[41] makes it unlikely that the IRS is trying to change the law to exclude such items from deductibility. The source of the conflicting information should also be considered. If the Treasury Department did want to create this legal rule regarding the nondeductibility of these expenses, despite the clear tension with the legislative history on this point, it seems unlikely that it would do so in the online, interactive tax assistant, rather than in a more authoritative source (such as, ideally, a Treasury Regulation).

Indeed, as the Federal Court of Appeals for the D.C. Circuit recognized in a 1993 case, *American Mining Congress v. Mine Safety and Health Administration*, a key marker of a legislative rule is "if Congress has delegated legislative power to the agency and if the agency intended to exercise that power in promulgating the rule."[42] The agency can exhibit its intent to exercise this power in a number of ways, including, for instance, by explicitly invoking its general legislative authority in making the rule.[43] It strains credulity to imagine that the Treasury Department, or the IRS operating on Treasury's behalf, is invoking general legislative authority to make new law in an online tax assistant, without first having promulgated applicable regulations.

If it is problematic to view the "Household Help Expenses" statement as a legislative rule, perhaps, instead, it is an interpretive rule. According to the Attorney General's *Manual on the Administrative Procedure Act*, interpretive rules include "rules or statements issued by an agency to advise the public of an agency's construction of the statutes and rules which it administers."[44] This is distinct from "substantive rules," which the *Manual* describes as "implement[ing] the statute," and which "have the force and effect of law."[45] That said, determining the line between legislative and interpretive rules is often an exercise in hair-splitting. As Professor Ronald Levin explains, "[b]eyond these truisms ... the doctrine runs into trouble," because it is nearly impossible to distinguish between what makes law and what merely interprets it.[46]

Despite the definitional difficulty surrounding interpretive rules, one could at least argue that ITA's "Household Help Expenses" guidance offers the IRS's interpretation, or construction, of the *existing* statutes and regulations. In the end, putting aside the deviation in the IRS's explanation, the interpretive rule category seems to be the best fit for ITA's statement. Here, as is generally the case with ITA, the IRS is taking a body of underlying, formal law, and telling the taxpayer how the IRS thinks it applies, or what the agency's construction is, in a given case.

The trouble, however, comes with what to do with the deviation in the explanation. One argument might be that we should ignore the deviation and treat the IRS's explanation as just an interpretive rule. Or, perhaps, somewhat similarly, we should treat the explanation as an interpretive rule, but just an incorrect one. This approach, however, is problematic, as interpretive rules are not subject to any of the rulemaking procedures of legislative rules: In fact, as far as lawmaking is concerned, interpretive rules are supposed to be a big nothing. They should not change rights or obligations and thus should have no significant impact on public behavior.

If, however, the agency is not accurately representing what the law is, it is not a big nothing. The agency is, in fact, changing legal rights and obligations, at least to the extent that people pay attention to and follow the statement. There is, therefore, an inherent, and problematic, contradiction in characterizing the statement as interpretive, or saying that interpretive, but incorrect, statements are not subject to procedure.

Is it possible, then, to conclude that the deviation itself is the interpretive view of the IRS? Here, the argument might be that, in the absence of any additional governing statutory or regulatory guidance, the IRS is expressing its view that "maintenance or personal care services"[47] does not include household help expenses, such as meal preparation, cleaning, or laundry. Unfortunately, viewing the "Household Help Expenses" statement as interpretive is problematic too. As the Federal Court of Appeals for the Ninth Circuit has explained in its 2001 decision in the case of *Gunderson* v. *Hood*, "[i]f a rule is inconsistent with or amends an existing legislative rule, then it cannot be interpretive. Such a rule would impose new rights or obligations by changing an existing law and must follow the applicable procedures of the APA."[48] Regarding an interpretive rule, the case is even stronger that it cannot be inconsistent with the statute. Such a rule would not be a valid interpretation.

The issue here, of course, is that ITA's "Household Help Expenses" statement seems inconsistent with the statute, at least as applied to "maintenance or personal care services" that "(A) are required by a chronically ill individual, and (B) are provided pursuant to a plan of care prescribed by a licensed health care practitioner."[49] In this regard, the statute itself does not seem to provide room for an interpretation that rejects deductibility, a conclusion made only stronger by the legislative history.[50]

Further, the analysis regarding policy statements is similar. The Attorney General's *Manual* describes policy statements as "statements issued by an agency to advise the public prospectively of the manner in which the agency proposes to exercise a discretionary power."[51] The key inquiry is whether a statement really leaves the matter open for future determination or establishes a "binding norm."[52] While one could argue that the "Household Help Expenses" guidance merely constitutes the IRS's policy with respect to certain types of expenses (such as cleaning and laundry expenses), an agency also cannot legitimately have a policy inconsistent with the statute.[53] As a result, for the same reasons that it is problematic to view the guidance as an interpretive rule, viewing the guidance as a policy statement raises issues as well.

The difficulty fitting the IRS's explanation regarding "Household Help Expenses" into any of the APA's existing categories of agency statements illustrates a striking point: regarding this agency explanation, none of the existing categories really seem to apply. Most likely, when offering the guidance regarding "Household Help Expenses," the IRS simply was not considering the "chronically ill individual" who is paying for "maintenance or personal care services ... pursuant to a plan of care prescribed by a licensed health care practitioner."[54] Instead, the IRS was likely contemplating the vast majority of taxpayers, for whom "Household Help Expenses" are not, in fact, deductible medical expenses. In other words, as to the qualifying chronically ill taxpayer, the IRS does not really mean what it says when offering the guidance through ITA.

In this case, it is unlikely that the IRS is trying to create new law that denies the deduction. Further, it is equally implausible that the IRS's interpretive position is that the statute and legislative history do not, in fact, allow a deduction for the expenses in this situation.[55] Finally, it is highly doubtful that the IRS's policy would be to deny the deduction for such taxpayers, if it examined the issue.[56] Rather, the best explanation is that, with this simplified explanation of complex law, the IRS is knowingly offering an incomplete and, at times, even inaccurate answer. What could the agency's motivation have been for doing this? It is possible that the IRS simply made a calculated judgment and determined that explaining the law in a way that gets it wrong for some number of taxpayers is worth it if that same explanation makes the law comprehensible to many more taxpayers.

None of the existing categories of agency statements appears to capture this situation. Indeed, the strongest conclusion might be that agency explanations may not even qualify as a "rule" that would be subject to the APA's classification framework at all. The APA defines a "rule" as "the whole or a part of an agency statement of general or particular applicability and future effect designed to implement, interpret, or prescribe law or policy or describing the organization, procedure, or practice requirements of an agency."[57] Generally, courts have not been particularly attentive to this definition, ignoring it and applying common-sense understandings when necessary.[58] However, when called upon to consider the definition of a "rule," such as in the context of an agency's informational guide to the public, multiple courts (including the Federal Courts of Appeals for the Fourth Circuit and the D.C. Circuit) have explained that the mere provision of information does not "change any law or official policy presently in effect," and therefore does not constitute an agency "rule," especially since the guide in question was not officially published in the Code of Federal Regulations or the Federal Register.[59]

In the end, careful examination reveals that the most likely treatment, at least under judicial consideration of the matter thus far, might be that these explanations of the law, which are a critical part of agencies' service of the public, may simply have no place at all within the administrative law framework.

Broader Democracy Deficit

We believe that the fact that the administrative law framework fails to categorize and address agencies' explanations of the law is not mere happenstance. Rather, it represents a more general failure of administrative law to ensure that agency communications to the general public occur in ways that are consistent with essential features of democratic governance, such as transparency, public scrutiny, and debate.[60]

The APA and other sources of administrative law attempt to ensure that agencies act transparently and provide affected parties with opportunities to contribute to the development of the guidance. However, "affected parties" under these circumstances are often limited to industry insiders and others with the knowledge and sophistication to understand these legal requirements and be able to hold the agencies to account. Comparable procedures and protections are absent, however, when members of the general public receive explanations of the law from agency officials through channels like automated legal guidance tools. This discrepancy reflects a democracy deficit in administrative law.

Notice and Comment
As an initial matter, if an agency statement is categorized as a legislative rule, the statement must comply with notice-and-comment rulemaking procedures. This process is supposed to inculcate an agency's creation of binding legal rules with transparency and legitimacy, thereby serving as a constraint on agency power. Ideally, notice-and-comment rulemaking is supposed to serve as a pluralistic blend of ideas and divergent interests, producing binding legal rules that yield the greatest collective good.[61] For this reason, Professor Kenneth Culp Davis, in his 1979 treatise on the topic, referred to agency rulemaking as "one of the greatest inventions of modern government."[62] This sentiment has been echoed, albeit in less exclamatory terms, in more recent administrative law scholarship.[63]

However, an extensive literature review shows that the formulation of legislative rules is dominated by industry insiders, with public interest groups having significantly less influence in the process and the general public having almost none.[64] Worse yet, administrative law itself has the perverse impact of encouraging these disparate influences, in particular through its elaboration of the APA's seemingly minimal requirements for the creation of legislative rules, which are merely to provide (1) notice of the proposed rule, (2) an opportunity for the public to comment, and (3) a "concise general statement" of the "basis and purpose" of the rule that the agency adopts after public comment.[65] This section describes each of these requirements in more detail.

First, agencies must provide adequate notice of the proposed rule. Under the APA, this adequate notice must include:

1. A statement of the time, place, and nature of public rulemaking proceedings;
2. Reference to the legal authority under which the rule is proposed; and
3. Either the terms or substance of the proposed rule, or a description of the subjects and issues involved.[66]

Despite the seemingly straightforward nature of this requirement, courts have raised the stakes significantly on what agencies must do when providing a notice of proposed rulemaking. Courts have held that final regulations must be a "logical outgrowth"[67] of the notice of proposed rulemaking, and agencies must provide detailed information about the development of the regulations, such as the data and evidence on which the agency is relying.[68]

Due to this stringent requirement, agencies that, in their notice of proposed rulemaking, fail to provide a detailed basis for and elaborations of their proposed rules risk having their time- and resource-intensive rulemakings overturned as a result of lack of notice.[69] The somewhat perverse outcome is that an agency has a strong incentive to engage in extensive rule development prior to issuing a notice of proposed rulemaking, which leaves little room for contemplation and change during the public rulemaking period.[70] To be able to offer these well-developed rules at the notice stage, an agency may feel it is necessary to engage privately with the sophisticated parties and industry groups who are most likely to challenge the final rules.[71] Because these insiders tend to have contacts with agencies, this interaction provides them with access to and influence over the rule development process prior to public comment. Studies have confirmed this outcome, finding significant prenotice engagement with these insiders.[72]

A related problem is that, even if less informed members of the public wanted to participate in the public comment period of the rulemaking, the level of detail and technicality in the notice of proposed rulemaking is often so high that it makes such engagement difficult.[73] While rulemakings often implicate contested values such as how to weigh the benefits of environmental protection against the cost,[74] by the time the notice of proposed rulemaking is issued, agencies generally have decided on a technical approach that obscures these choices.[75] Indeed, agencies tend to offer a kitchen sink elaboration of technical, detailed rules in the notice of proposed rulemaking, which has the effect of crowding out participation by members of the public who lack sufficient technical expertise to provide meaningful comments.[76]

Next, the APA requires the agency to "give interested persons an opportunity to participate in the rule making through submission of written data, views, or arguments with or without opportunity for oral presentation."[77] Courts have interpreted this requirement in ways that contradict the seemingly low threshold suggested by the requirement, which is merely to provide an "opportunity to participate." Specifically, there is precedent for courts to reject a rulemaking process due to an agency's failure to adequately consider a comment in the notice-and-comment period.[78] The lesson here? Agencies that fail to respond to every comment do so at their peril, because they run the risk of regulations potentially being invalidated, even years after their finalization.[79]

As scholars have identified, this has resulted in notice-and-comment periods that are extraordinarily expensive behemoths, well beyond the basic framework suggested by the APA in scope.[80] Worse yet, scholars have repeatedly observed that sophisticated parties and industry insiders end up dominating this process, crowding out participation by the general public.[81] Indeed, Professor Wendy Wagner has expertly highlighted how well-informed individuals and entities manipulate the notice-and-comment procedures by flooding agencies with information.[82]

Even on the back end, the rulemaking process does not seem to accommodate the general public. The text of the APA seems to provide a simple mechanism for agencies to engage with the public, providing that, when issuing a final regulation, the agency shall "incorporate in the rules adopted a concise general statement of their basis and purpose."[83] However, as administrative law scholar Alec Webley has explained, courts have essentially written the "concise" and "general" aspects out of the requirement for preambles for final rules.[84] Instead, courts have struck down agency regulations that were otherwise backed by extraordinarily voluminous rulemaking records because their preambles failed to mention very specific facts or reasoning contained elsewhere in the records.[85]

Predictably, agencies have responded by producing highly detailed, lengthy, and complex explanations of their final regulations that are far too complicated for any nonexpert to understand.[86] Agencies have also largely eschewed a requirement put into place by the OMB's regulatory oversight authority, the Office of Information and Regulatory Affairs (OIRA), that they provide comprehensible "executive summaries" of the regulations they promulgate.[87] Indeed, a study of these executive summaries found that they are "significantly less readable than the preambles they are supposedly explaining."[88] The result is that agencies leave the general public largely at sea to navigate incomprehensible regulations and preambles. As Professor Lars Noah has pointed out, in one extreme case, the text of an FDA tobacco regulation was only three pages – but the preamble was almost 1,000 pages![89] Tax practitioners have also noted that preambles of tax regulations have grown increasingly lengthy and complex over time.[90]

While many had hoped that the advent of e-rulemaking would have allowed more democratic public participation in the rulemaking process,[91] the reality has been less encouraging. As Professor Cary Coglianese has described, e-rulemaking has been stymied by many of the same dynamics as traditional rulemaking.[92] In particular, agencies seem unwilling or unable to make much use of the types of value considerations that the general public is likely to express.[93]

As a result, the process for generating legislative rules is a far cry from the participatory ideal envisioned by the APA and some of the framers of the administrative law regime. Instead, administrative rulemaking is, at least in some ways, an example of a vision of democratic governance gone awry. The very requirements that are supposed to assure widespread participation and transparency have become weapons that make the process obscure and open only to the sophisticated and resourced few.

Informal Explanation

Even if the general public cannot meaningfully participate in the promulgation of regulations through the notice-and-comment rulemaking procedure, there are other ways to interact with legislation and regulations. One way is to consult the informal guidance that agencies generate at a prolific rate. This guidance ranges from relatively formal rulings that offer an agency's official interpretation of how the law applies in a specific situation, all the way down to very informal social media posts.

Consider the range of guidance produced by the IRS. On the more formal end of the spectrum, this agency provides "revenue rulings," which are "an official interpretation by the IRS of the Internal Revenue Code, related statutes, tax treaties and regulations."[94] They are published to provide the public with the "conclusion of the IRS on how the law is applied to a specific set of facts."[95] Tax practitioners, in particular, place great weight on such guidance.[96] At the other end of the spectrum, the IRS, like many other agencies, also maintains an active social media presence. On X (formerly Twitter), the agency uses 280-character posts to deliver tax law tips, as well as other information, to its more than 130,000 followers.[97] As we have seen in Chapter 2, other agencies engage in similar social media communications, which they are encouraged to do as a way of meeting their service obligations to the public.

For all the reasons that impenetrable, technical agency communications seem problematic, perhaps we should cheer the fact that agencies are willing to engage in informal communications with the general public. This, of course, is the rationale behind much of the development of automated legal guidance. Further, the Administrative Conference of the United States (ACUS) has embraced and even advocated for broader agency use of social media.[98] Informal communications, including the types of explanations provided by automated legal guidance and offered through social media, often use plain language the public can understand, facilitating access to information about the law that may otherwise be lost in the regulatory process.[99] As such, this style of communication seems to promise more democratic, public engagement with the law.[100]

However, as we explored in Chapter 7, informal guidance does not put the general public on equal footing with sophisticated parties and industry insiders. Instead, as we have seen, it creates a two-tiered system of law, with regular folks relegated to the lower tier. Indeed, even informal guidance features multiple categories with, effectively, varying levels of status.

Take, for instance, informal guidance from the IRS, which includes both revenue rulings and social media posts. The fact that the IRS posts tweets may be praiseworthy, because this can increase public awareness of the law. However, these tweets have extremely limited legal value. In contrast, revenue rulings, which are certainly below Treasury Regulations in terms of authoritativeness, nonetheless have legal properties. The Treasury Department authorizes taxpayers not only to rely upon revenue rulings[101] but also to use them to avoid penalties.[102] Further, the IRS carefully and publicly catalogs revenue rulings, indicating when one has been revoked, superseded, or otherwise rendered obsolete.[103] This, of course, is not the case with tweets. Not only can they come and go without a word, but the IRS may, in fact, contradict or reject the information they contain in the future without fanfare, or, indeed, without any notice whatsoever.

To be sure, as Chapter 2 explained, some "low stakes" communications with the public, like tweets, may be a central way that the government can mimic private sector responsiveness. For this reason, it may be reasonable to worry that any attempts to formalize these interactions further would, in fact, be a regression. Not only could doing so hamstring agency attempts to communicate, but it could also limit their capacity to serve the public in the ways that are possible for private industry.

Regarding this line of objection, we agree that very informal agency communications, such as those posted on social media, can have an important role to play in agency engagement with the general public. Acknowledging this role, however, should not cause us to lose sight of the fact that the form of law that the general public is receiving – refracted through these unreliable media and created through a process that is opaque and much less deliberate – offers the general public *inferior* access to law, especially relative to that offered to sophisticated parties and insiders. These communication efforts, therefore, in some ways both accept and entrench the broader hierarchies in agency communications. In the end, the lower legal status of certain types of informal communications that agencies deliver to the general public is another facet of the democracy deficit that arises from the administrative law regime.

Challenge

A final difference in the administrative regime between sophisticated parties and the general public is the ability to challenge agency communications. The general public is systematically disadvantaged in its ability to do this for two reasons. First, agency communications with the general public are less likely to be "final" agency guidance that is "ripe" for review. Second, barriers to challenging agency inaction specifically prevent the general public from raising challenges to harmful deregulation. Put together, these features once again display, in a striking way, how the administrative regime regarding agency communications offers little accommodation for the general public.

The APA dictates that only those agency actions that are "final" and "ripe" for review can be challenged in court: "[a]gency action made reviewable by statute and final agency action for which there is no other adequate remedy in a court are subject to judicial review."[104] Whether a regulation is final in this sense relates to the "ripeness" doctrine in administrative law, which seeks to "prevent the courts, through avoidance of premature adjudication, from entangling themselves in abstract disagreements over administrative policies."[105]

What qualifies as a "final" agency action has, naturally, been subject to judicial disagreement. One line of authority has a "flexible view of finality," in that it inquires whether the agency position (a) was "definitive" and (b) had a "direct and immediate ... effect on the day-to-day business" of the parties bringing the suit.[106] However, another line of authority follows a 1997 decision by the US Supreme Court in the case of *Bennett* v. *Speer*, which provides a more formal inquiry. The *Bennett* test requires that two conditions are met for agency action to be final: (1) "First, the action must mark the 'consummation' of the agency's decisionmaking process," and (2) "second, the action must be one by which 'rights or obligations have been determined,' or from which 'legal consequences will flow.'"[107] While the

Court since *Bennett* has, at times, suggested a blend with a more flexible inquiry,[108] and lower courts have followed suit in some circumstances,[109] the formal inquiry under *Bennett* remains prominent.[110]

The "finality" and "ripeness" inquiries matter because they create the same sort of hierarchy regarding agency communications as that which exists with respect to the reliability of agency statements. Legislative rules represent final agency action; accordingly, they can be challenged.[111] This means that the sophisticated parties and industry insiders are not only much more likely to be able to access legislative rules, but they are also much more likely to be able to challenge them.

Informal guidance, in contrast, is generally more of a muddle.[112] In some cases, courts have concluded that informal guidance represents a final agency action that is subject to judicial challenge.[113] This is akin to the ways that the public can rely on certain types of informal guidance, such as the IRS's revenue rulings, even though it is not as reliable as legislative rules. However, more typically, courts have concluded that "finality" or "ripeness" serve as barriers to judicial review of informal guidance.[114] Moreover, the more agency guidance seems to merely explain the law to the general public, rather than engaging in any form of more sophisticated (and likely complex) lawmaking, the less likely it will be deemed to be final agency action subject to any sort of judicial review.

Take, for example, the 2010 case decided by the Federal Fourth Circuit of Appeals, *Golden & Zimmerman, LLC v. Domenech*.[115] This case was brought in relation to the publication by the Bureau of Alcohol, Tobacco, Firearms, and Explosives (ATF) of its "Firearms Regulations Reference Guide 2005," the stated intent of which was to provide "information designed to help [licensees] comply with all of the laws and regulations governing the manufacture, importation, and distribution of firearms and ammunition."[116] The petitioners sought a judgment declaring that one of the "frequently asked questions" in the guide was inconsistent with the Gun Control Act.[117]

The Fourth Circuit concluded that there was no "agency action" in this case, much less "final agency action," because the role of the Reference Guide "is simply to *inform* licensees of what the law, previously enacted or adopted, is, and its publication did not itself alter the legal landscape."[118] This was true, according to the court, even to the extent that the Reference Guide did something "other than simply restate the requirements of the Gun Control Act," because, even in that case, the Reference Guide would be drawing on a revenue ruling published long ago.[119]

In reaching this conclusion, the court did not think it mattered that the Gun Control Act had changed since the time the purportedly governing revenue ruling had been published, even though this would suggest that the agency had conducted some analysis to determine that the law still stayed the same despite the change to the Gun Control Act.[120] Instead, the simple fact that this was a Reference Guide, meant to inform the public of what the law was, was dispositive.[121] Accordingly, the court held that this type of communication could not be final agency action that was subject to judicial challenge.[122]

Golden & Zimmerman, LLC raises two important issues. First, the case reveals the way that, in the context of finality, as in that of categorizing agency statements, administrative law fails to consider how agency explanations can create subtle deviations from what the underlying law is, and that these deviations are not subject to challenge. Second, the case reveals, strikingly, the way that the general public is systematically disadvantaged in its ability to challenge the law. Explanations of the law like the ATF's Reference Guide, alongside simpler digital communications such as those offered by automated legal guidance, are how the general public is likely to access the law, especially because the more authoritative regulations are inaccessible. Despite this, the finality doctrine dictates, in effect, that people cannot challenge the very form of the law that the agency provides to them as their means of access.

Added to this difficulty is the fact that the general public is often an indirect beneficiary of agency regulation. Professor Nina Mendelson has observed that, "[o]f the countless statutes passed by Congress to serve the 'public interest,' many regulatory statutes, including those aimed at pharmaceutical safety, workplace safety, and protecting the environment," indirectly benefit the public at large, including drug consumers, workers, and people affected by environmental harm.[123]

Further, as indirect beneficiaries of agency action, members of the general public are typically harmed by agency *inaction*,[124] and their ability to challenge this inaction is severely limited by judicial authority.[125] As the Supreme Court explained in its 1985 decision in *Heckler* v. *Chaney*, courts should concern themselves with agency exercises of "*coercive* power over an individual's liberty or property rights," situations that "provide[] a focus for judicial review."[126]

The result is that when an agency issues guidance that is overly favorable to regulated parties, such as those companies that pollute the drinking water supply or fail to ensure that workplaces are safe for their employees, the general public often lacks the ability to challenge such guidance and protect its interests.[127] Making this dynamic even worse is the fact that the costs to agencies for engaging in inaction are relatively low, which may distort their choices and cause them to engage in even less regulatory action.[128] Plus, as Mendelson has pointed out, as difficult as it may be for the general public to influence the formation of regulations in the notice-and-comment process, in some ways the creation of less formal regulatory guidance is not only even more obscure but is also subject to disproportionate insider influence.[129] Altogether, these dynamics systematically make it difficult for the general public to challenge communications of agency inaction.

Putting It All Together
The broad spectrum of administrative law rules regarding agency communications – from the notice-and-comment process, to the rules applicable to informal explanations, to the requirements for raising judicial challenges – are all tilted toward

sophisticated parties and industry insiders, and away from the general public. While the failure of the basic classification of agency statements to incorporate agency explanations makes sense, this broader regime regarding agency communications, in fact, makes its effects even worse. The general public receives its information about the law from communications for which there is, effectively, no space in administrative law.

This would be less problematic, of course, if agency explanations were akin to mere photocopies of the underlying formal law. No one would think that additional administrative process should apply to the act of photocopying.[130] But, as we have shown, both here and in Chapter 3, agency explanations are not mere photocopies of the rest of the regulatory regime. The very process of offering seemingly simple explanations of complex regulatory law involves changing the nature of the legal rules, potentially denying people benefits to which they may be entitled, or putting them at risk for taking positions that may not be supported by the underlying legal regime. Administrative law's failure to classify, or even consider, such explanations exemplifies its general, broad-based inattention to communications with the general public.

A FUNDAMENTAL TENSION

At this point, it is worthwhile to pause and identify a significant tension in the book. On the one hand, as Chapters 1 and 2 illustrated, there are powerful forces, both from the private sector and in the federal government, that are pushing agencies to act more like Stitch Fix, Expedia, Wealthfront, Amazon, Starbucks, and other private companies that use artificial intelligence to innovate their operations. Government, under this model, should work smarter, faster, and more seamlessly. Ideally, it should solve people's problems before people realize they even have them. Further, the government certainly should not subject people to time-consuming, confusing tasks, like having to wonder about the reliability of the information they are receiving, or having to think carefully about ways that the answer they receive does not exactly answer their question. In addition, agency officials charged with explaining complex law to people, through automated legal guidance tools, have been influenced by these views and goals. As a result, these tools tend to provide answers that are as simple as possible, and abstract away from a more complex legal regime. Indeed, this abstraction is so significant that agency officials developing these tools often do not even think of them as providing "law," nor do they believe that people would rely upon them. Agency officials have adopted this view even though millions of people turn to these tools, at the agencies' encouragement, to answer questions about how the law applies to their lives.

On the other hand, easy application, simple answers, few caveats, and abstraction away from the intricacies of a complex legal regime unfortunately is not how the law works. As much as we would like to *imagine* a system in which we have very simple legal rules, this characterization does not, in fact, describe any area of federal law. Further, the administrative law that is designed to empower and control agencies in all these areas is itself extremely involved. While the ins and outs of administrative law provide a plethora of ways to challenge agencies and their decisions, only the most sophisticated actors can do so, because this possibility requires deep engagement with an intricate set of procedures, as well as a capacity to understand extremely complex underlying law.

Sophisticated parties have always had a different relationship to the law than the general public, including in the area of administrative law. But automated legal guidance threatens to widen this disparity. That this form of communication, the primary audience for which is the general public that often lacks resources to access the underlying law, makes the application of the law seem that much easier, may, paradoxically, create a greater chasm between the haves and the have nots.

NOTES

1. *See, e.g.*, Nicholas R. Parrillo, *Federal Agency Guidance and the Power to Bind: An Empirical Study of Agencies and Industries*, 36 YALE J. ON REG. 165, 168 (2019) (describing "[f]ull-blown regulations that officially bind the agency and the public" and the procedures that are required to promulgate them).
2. *See, e.g.*, Kristin E. Hickman, *IRB Guidance: The No Man's Land of Tax Code Interpretation*, 2009 MICH. ST. L. REV. 239–40 (2009) (explaining that "prudent regulated parties take seriously agency guidance in virtually any form").
3. *See, e.g., Our Mission and What We Do*, EPA, https://www.epa.gov/aboutepa/our-mission-and-what-we-do [https://perma.cc/U3S7-ETYT] (last updated May 23, 2023) (explaining that, among other things, the EPA writes environmental regulations, helps companies understand the regulations, and enforces the regulations.).
4. *See, e.g.*, Parrillo, *supra* note 1, at 169–70 (describing this "great fear" in administrative law).
5. *See, e.g., Whitman v. Am. Trucking Associations*, 531 U.S. 457, 474–76 (2001) (upholding Clean Air Act's delegation to the EPA to set national ambient air quality standards at level "requisite to protect public health").
6. See, *e.g.*, Gillian E. Metzger, *The Supreme Court, 2016 Term – Forward: 1930s Redux: The Administrative State Under Siege*, 131 HARV. L. REV. 1, 7 (2017) (arguing both that "the administrative state today is constitutionally obligatory, given the broad delegations of authority to the executive branch that represent the central reality of contemporary national government" and that "[t]hose delegations are necessary given the economic, social, scientific, and technological realities of our day").
7. *See, e.g., Maier v. U.S. EPA*, 114 F.3d 1032, 1045 (10th Cir. 1997) (concluding that EPA's rejection of rulemaking was not arbitrary and capricious, in part because "[p]romulgating revised regulations necessitates a substantial commitment of limited agency resources").
8. *See generally, e.g.*, PHILIP HAMBURGER, IS ADMINISTRATIVE LAW UNLAWFUL (2014); Gary Lawson, *The Rise and Rise of the Administrative State*, 107 HARV. L. REV. 1231 (1994) (for particularly forceful recent, as well as more longstanding, attacks). As many have noted, these attacks are no longer merely academic, but rather have attracted adherence from important members of the judiciary. *See, e.g., West Virginia v. EPA*, 597 U.S. 697, 753 (2022) (Gorsuch, J., concurring) ("In our Republic, '[i]t is

the peculiar province of the legislature to prescribe general rules for the government of society.'" (quoting *Fletcher v. Peck*, 10 U.S. (6 Cranch) 87, 136 (1810))); *Dep't of Transp. v. Ass'n of Am. R.Rs.*, 575 U.S. 43, 86 (2015) (Thomas, J., concurring) ("We should return to the original meaning of the Constitution: The Government may create generally applicable rules of private conduct only through the proper exercise of legislative power."); *City of Arlington v. FCC*, 569 U.S. 290, 313 (2013) (C. J. Roberts, dissenting) ("The Framers could hardly have envisioned today's 'vast and varied federal bureaucracy' and the authority administrative agencies now hold over our economic, social, and political activities" (quoting *Free Enter. Fund v. Pub. Co. Acct. Oversight Bd.*, 561 U.S. 477, 499 (2010))).

9. *See, e.g.*, Metzger, *supra* note 6, at 7 ("In fact, however, the administrative state is essential for actualizing constitutional separation of powers today, serving both to constrain executive power and to mitigate the dangers of presidential unilateralism while also enabling effective governance.").

10. *See, e.g.*, Julian Davis Mortenson & Nicholas Bagley, *Delegation at the Founding*, 121 COLUM. L. REV. 277 (2021) (arguing that there was no nondelegation doctrine at the Founding, undermining the originalist objection to administrative delegations); Nicholas Bagley, *The Procedure Fetish*, 118 MICH. L. REV. 345, 375 (2019) ("To read into the spare text of the Constitution some kind of distaste for federal agencies – because they wield 'too much' power, because they blend functions, or because they're too insulated from the public will – is the sort of constitutional adventurism that principled originalists are supposed to eschew.").

11. *See, e.g.*, Lisa Schultz Bressman, *Beyond Accountability: Arbitrariness and Legitimacy in the Administrative State*, 78 N. Y. U. L. REV. 461, 527–53 (2003) (discussing how "ordinary" administrative law principles and procedures confer legitimacy on the administrative state). *But see, e.g.*, Bagley, *supra* note 10, at 349 ("Proceduralism has a role to play in preserving legitimacy and discouraging capture, but it advances those goals more obliquely than is commonly assumed and may exacerbate the very problems it aims to address.").

12. *See generally, e.g.*, JERRY L. MASHAW, CREATING THE ADMINISTRATIVE CONSTITUTION 285 (2012) (explaining that administrative practice has helped fill in the hole in the text of the US Constitution by asking, "What structures and processes for administrative action satisfy our demands for effective government and the legitimate exercise of governmental authority?").

13. *Wong Yang Sung v. McGrath*, 339 U.S. 33, 40, *modified*, 339 U.S. 908 (1950).

14. George B. Shepherd, *Fierce Compromise: The Administrative Procedure Act Emerges from New Deal Politics*, 90 NW. U. L. REV. 1557, 1560 (1996).

15. *Id.* at 1680.

16. *Id.*

17. The other is agency adjudication. *See* Christopher J. Walker, *Modernizing the Administrative Procedure Act*, 69 ADMIN. L. REV. 629, 633 (2017) ("The APA establishes detailed procedures for the two core means of agency action – rulemaking and adjudication – while recognizing that other statutes may provide for different forms of agency action.").

18. 5 U.S.C. § 553.

19. *Id.* § 553(b)(A).

20. *See, e.g., Lincoln v. Vigil*, 508 U.S. 182, 196 (1993) (distinguishing between "so-called legislative or substantive rules," which are subject to notice-and-comment procedures, and the other categories of rules, which are not).

21. *See* Thomas O. McGarity, *Some Thoughts on "Deossifying" the Rulemaking Process*, 41 DUKE L. J. 1385, 1396–436 (1992) (contrasting the "bare-bones procedure" required by the APA with the many requirements imposed by courts, Congress, and the executive). *But See* Jason Webb Yackee & Susan Webb Yackee, *Testing the Ossification Thesis: An Empirical Examination of Federal Regulatory Volume and Speed, 1950–1990*, 80 GEO. WASH. L. REV. 1414 (2012) (casting doubt on the notion that ossification is a serious problem for agency rulemaking).
22. *See, e.g.*, 21 C.F.R. § 10.115 (2023) (setting forth the FDA's "good guidance practices").
23. Final Bulletin for Agency Good Guidance Practices, 72 Fed. Reg. 3432, 3432 (Jan. 25, 2007).
24. *Id.*
25. *Id.* at 3439.
26. *Dep't of Homeland Sec. v. Regents of the Univ. of Cal.*, 140 S. Ct. 1891, 1913 (2020).
27. *See, e.g.*, Richard J. Pierce, Jr., *Distinguishing Legislative Rules from Interpretative Rules*, 52 ADMIN. L. REV. 547, 552 (2000) (explaining that "[a] legislative rule binds the public and courts in a manner indistinguishable from a statute [whereas] an interpretative rule is only a statement of the agency's present interpretation of the statute," but also indicating some ways courts have blurred the distinction).
28. *Nat'l Min. Ass'n v. McCarthy*, 758 F.3d 243, 251 (D.C. Cir. 2014) ("In terms of reviewability, legislative rules and sometimes even interpretive rules may be subject to pre-enforcement judicial review, but general statements of policy are not.")
29. *See, e.g., Ctr. for Auto Safety v. Nat'l Highway Traffic Safety Admin.*, 452 F.3d 798, 808 (D.C. Cir. 2006) ("[T]he case law is clear that we lack authority to review claims under the APA 'where "an agency merely expresses its view of what the law requires of a party, even if that view is adverse to the party"'" (quoting *Indep. Equip. Dealers Ass'n v. EPA*, 372 F.3d 420, 427 (D.C. Cir. 2004))).
30. *Cmty. Nutrition Inst. v. Young*, 818 F.2d 943, 946 (D.C. Cir. 1987) (citations omitted); KENNETH CULP DAVIS, ADMINISTRATIVE LAW TREATISE 32 (2d ed. 1979).
31. *Can I Deduct My Medical and Dental Expenses?*, IRS, https://www.irs.gov/help/ita/can-i-deduct-my-medical-and-dental-expenses [https://perma.cc/57PG-9Y9C] (last updated Jan. 16, 2024).
32. *Id.* (click "Begin"; then click "Continue"; then select a tax year; then select Yes; then select No; then select Yes; then select No; then select marital status and filing status; then select "H"; then select "Household Help Expenses") [https://perma.cc/LM95-C4RB (uploaded archive)].
33. I.R.C. § 262(a).
34. *See, e.g.*, Rev. Rul. 76-106, 1976-1 C.B. 71 (explaining that a quadriplegic taxpayer who hired an assistant for help with medical and household needs had to apportion the time the assistant spent on the medical and household needs because payments for the latter were nondeductible).
35. I.R.C. § 213(d)(1)(C).
36. I.R.C. § 7702B(c)(1).
37. STAFF OF THE JOINT COMM. ON TAXATION, 104TH CONG., JCS-12-96, GENERAL EXPLANATION OF TAX LEGISLATION ENACTED IN THE 104TH CONGRESS 338 (Comm. Print 1996), [https://perma.cc/7G4R-KB3Y (uploaded archive)]; *see* Ron West, *Diagnose Payments for Bigger Medical Expense Deductions*, 62 PRAC. TAX STRATEGIES 289, 298, 1999 WL 687323, 12 (exploring history and application of these provisions).
38. Kristin E. Hickman, *Unpacking the Force of Law*, 66 VAND. L. REV. 465, 477 (2013) (citing, *e.g., Prof'ls & Patients for Customized Care v. Shalala*, 56 F.3d 592, 602 (5th Cir. 1995); *Indiana v. Sullivan*, 934 F.2d 853, 856 (7th Cir. 1991); *Am. Hosp. Ass'n v. Bowen*,

834 F.2d 1037, 1045 (D.C. Cir. 1987); *Hemp Indus. Ass'n v. DEA*, 333 F.3d 1082, 1087 (9th Cir. 2003); *Splane v. West*, 216 F.3d 1058, 1063 (Fed. Cir. 2000); *United Techs. Corp. v. EPA*, 821 F.2d 714, 719 (D.C. Cir. 1987)).
39. T.D. 7643, 1979-2 C.B. 6.
40. I.R.C. § 7702B(c)(1)(A).
41. STAFF OF THE JOINT COMM. ON TAXATION, 104TH CONG., JCS-12-96, GENERAL EXPLANATION OF TAX LEGISLATION ENACTED IN THE 104TH CONGRESS 338 (Comm. Print 1996), [https://perma.cc/7G4R-KB3Y (uploaded archive)].
42. *Am. Mining Cong. v. Mine Safety & Health Admin.*, 995 F.2d 1106, 1109 (D.C. Cir. 1993).
43. *Id.* at 1112.
44. U.S. DEP'T OF JUST., ATTORNEY GENERAL'S MANUAL ON THE ADMINISTRATIVE PROCEDURE ACT 30 n.3 (1947)
45. *Id.*
46. Ronald M. Levin, *Rulemaking and the Guidance Exemption*, 70 ADMIN. L. REV. 263, 317–19 (2018).
47. I.R.C. § 7702B(c)(1).
48. *Gunderson v. Hood*, 268 F.3d 1149, 1154 (9th Cir. 2001).
49. I.R.C. § 7702B(c)(1).
50. *See infra* notes 55–56.
51. ATTORNEY GENERAL'S MANUAL, *supra* note 44, at 30 n.3.
52. *Pac. Gas & Elec. Co. v. Fed. Power Comm'n*, 506 F.2d 33, 38 (D.C. Cir. 1974).
53. The issue is more complicated with agency nonenforcement, particularly when such nonenforcement is motivated by limited resources. *See, e.g., Heckler* v. *Chaney*, 470 U.S. 821, 831–32 (1985). In any event, such nonenforcement is not at issue in this case.
54. I.R.C. § 7702B(c)(1).
55. *See, e.g.*, STAFF OF JOINT COMM. ON TAXATION, JCX-38-06, TECHNICAL EXPLANATION OF H.R. 4, THE "PENSION PROTECTION ACT OF 2006," AS PASSED BY THE HOUSE ON JULY 28, 2006, AND AS CONSIDERED BY THE SENATE ON AUGUST 3, 2006, at 193 (Comm. Print 2006), [https://perma.cc/U2GT-ES8F (uploaded archive)].
56. *See id.*
57. 5 U.S.C. § 551(4).
58. *See, e.g.*, Antonin Scalia, *Vermont Yankee: The APA, the D.C. Circuit, and the Supreme Court*, 1978 SUP. CT. REV. 345, 383 (explaining that "it is generally acknowledged that the only responsible judicial attitude toward this central APA definition is one of benign disregard").
59. *Indus. Safety Equip. Ass'n, Inc.* v. *EPA*, 837 F.2d 1115, 1120–21 (D.C. Cir. 1988); *see also, e.g., Golden & Zimmerman, LLC v. Domenech*, 599 F.3d 426 (4th Cir. 2010), discussed *infra* at text accompanying notes 116–22.
60. *See, e.g.*, Frederick Schauer, *Transparency in Three Dimensions*, 2011 U. ILL. L. REV. 1339, 1348; Jeremy Waldron, *Accountability: Fundamental to Democracy* 11 (N.Y.U. Sch. of Law, Pub. Law & Legal Theory Research Paper Series, Working Paper No. 14-13, 2014), http://papers.ssrn.com/sol3/papers.cfm?abstract_id=2410812 [https://perma.cc/PAB6-A3CV (uploaded archive)].
61. *See, e.g.*, Robert B. Reich, *Public Administration and Public Deliberation: An Interpretive Essay*, 94 YALE L. J. 1617, 1618–24 (1985) (describing how administrative process became an uneasy way to imagine that agency officials both intermediated between different interests and maximized net benefits for the collective).
62. DAVIS, *supra* note 30, at 30.
63. *See, e.g.*, Bressman, *supra* note 11, at 546 (arguing that allowing agencies to avoid notice-and-comment procedures jeopardizes agency legitimacy).

64. *See, e.g.,* sources cited in *infra* note 72.
65. *See supra* text accompanying note 18.
66. 5 U.S.C. § 553(b)(1)–(3).
67. *See* Phillip M. Kannan, *The Logical Outgrowth Doctrine in Rulemaking*, 48 ADMIN L. REV. 213, 214 (1996) (exploring in detail).
68. *Portland Cement Ass'n v. Ruckelshaus*, 486 F.2d 375, 392–93 (D.C. Cir. 1973) ("It is not consonant with the purpose of a rule-making proceeding to promulgate rules on the basis of inadequate data, or on data that, critical degree, is known only to the agency.").
69. *See, e.g., Int'l Union, United Mine Workers of Am. v. Mine Safety & Health Admin.*, 407 F.3d 1250, 1252 (D.C. Cir. 2005) (overturning Secretary of Labor's final regulations adopting a velocity cap in part because, in the notice of proposed rulemaking, the Secretary suggested that "empirical research indicated a cap would increase safety problems"); *Shell Oil Co. v. EPA*, 950 F.2d 741, 757–63 (D.C. Cir. 1991) (overturning EPA's final regulation when the EPA's approach to an environmental hazard shifted from the approach offered in the notice of proposed rulemaking).
70. E. Donald Elliott, *Re-Inventing Rulemaking*, 41 DUKE L. J. 1490, 1495 (1992).
71. Wendy E. Wagner, *Administrative Law, Filter Failure, and Information Capture*, 59 DUKE L. J. 1321, 1367–68 (2010).
72. For a sample of such studies, see, for example, Kimberly D. Krawiec, *Don't "Screw Joe the Plummer": The Sausage-Making of Financial Reform*, 55 ARIZ. L. REV. 53, 71–83 (2013); Shu-Yi Oei & Leigh Osofsky, *Legislation and Comment: The Making of the § 199A Regulations*, 69 EMORY L. J. 209, 212 (2019); Wendy Wagner et al., *Rulemaking in the Shade: An Empirical Study of EPA's Air Toxic Emission Standards*, 63 ADMIN. L. REV. 99, 110–13 (2011); Susan Webb Yackee, *The Politics of Ex Parte Lobbying: Pre-Proposal Agenda Building and Blocking During Agency Rulemaking*, 22 J. PUB. ADMIN. RES. & THEORY 378–89 (2012).
73. *See, e.g.,* Jack M. Beermann & Gary Lawson, *Reprocessing Vermont Yankee*, 75 GEO. WASH. L. REV. 856, 894 (2007) ("Notices can easily run tens of tiny-typed pages in the Federal Register and incorporate by reference hundreds or thousands of pages of supporting documentation."); Oei & Osofsky, *supra* note 72, at 258 (finding that "Treasury repeatedly referenced pre-notice comments in the proposed regulations and granted many of the requests made").
74. Nina A. Mendelson, *Foreword: Rulemaking, Democracy, and Torrents of E-Mail*, 79 GEO. WASH. L. REV. 1343, 1347–48 (2011) (making plain the significant values questions decided in agency rulemakings).
75. Wagner, *supra* note 71, at 1368 ("If affected parties have been left out of pre-proposed-rule discussions and are faced with the prospect of processing and critiquing a one-hundred-page, opaque explanation and discussion during a short notice-and-comment period, it is at least possible that they will choose to forgo this rather time-intensive exercise.").
76. *See id.* (for general discussion of the issue).
77. 5 U.S.C. § 553(c).
78. *See, e.g., United States v. Nova Scotia Food Prod. Corp.*, 568 F.2d 240, 253 (2d Cir. 1977) (providing an old cautionary tale in the form of a court rejecting FDA rulemaking as a result of failure to consider a comment in the rulemaking).
79. *See, e.g.,* Petition for Writ of Certiorari, *Oakbrook Land Holdings, LLC v. Commissioner*, 28 F.4th 700 (6th Cir. 2022) (No. 22-323) (petitioning for cert in 2022 to determine whether Treasury's failure to respond to a comment made in a 1983 rulemaking proceeding, which had over 700 pages of comments from ninety commenters, should invalidate the regulation).

80. *See generally* McGarity, *supra* note 21, at 1449; Richard J. Pierce, Jr., *Seven Ways to Deossify Agency Rulemaking*, 47 ADMIN. L. REV. 59 (1995) (both of which are foundational explorations of ossification). *But see* Yackee & Yackee, *supra* note 21 (challenging ossification thesis); Connor Raso, *Agency Avoidance of Rulemaking Procedures*, 67 ADMIN. L. REV. 65 (2015) (exploring agency avoiding of rulemaking).
81. *See, e.g.*, Cary Coglianese, *Challenging the Rules: Litigation and Bargaining in the Administrative Process* (1994) (on file with authors) (finding that 60 percent of comments on environmental regulations studied came from industry groups, and only 4 percent came from the environmental community); Wagner et al., *supra* note 72, at 128–31 (also finding that industry groups dominate in the commenting process); Clinton G. Wallace, *Congressional Control of Tax Rulemaking*, 71 TAX L. REV. 179, 216–30 (2017) (finding low participation in many tax notice-and-comment processes and domination by private interests when participation occurred); Jason Webb Yackee & Susan Webb Yackee, *A Bias Towards Business? Assessing Interest Group Influence on the U.S. Bureaucracy*, 68 J. POL. 128 (2006) (concluding that notice and comment have not "succeeded in 'democratizing' the agency policymaking process," based on empirical findings that "business commenters, but not nonbusiness commenters, hold important influence over the final content of the rules").
82. *See generally* Wagner, *supra* note 71 (setting forth in depth the theory of information flooding and agency capture).
83. 5 U.S.C. § 553(c).
84. *See generally* Alec Webley, *Seeing through a Preamble, Darkly: Administrative Verbosity in an Age of Populism and "Fake News,"* 70 ADMIN. L. REV. 1 (2018).
85. *See, e.g.*, Weyerhaeuser Co. v. Costle, 590 F.2d 1011, 1028 (D.C. Cir. 1978) (finding regulatory process invalid as a result of inadequate agency explanation, despite the fact that, according to the court, the agency "appears to have bent over backwards to accommodate public participation in, and understanding of, the promulgation of" the regulations).
86. Webley, *supra* note 84, at 20–21.
87. Cynthia R. Farina et al., *The Problem with Words: Plain Language and Public Participation in Rulemaking*, 83 GEO. WASH. L. REV. 1358, 1379–405 (2015).
88. *Id.* at 1405.
89. Lars Noah, *Divining Regulatory Intent: The Place for a "Legislative History" of Agency Rules*, 51 HASTINGS L. J. 255, 310 (2000).
90. *Preambles to Regulations: More Important than the Regulations?*, J. TAX'N: SHOP TALK, Sept. 2015, at 141, 144, 2015 WL 5343606, 6.
91. *See, e.g.*, Mendelson, *supra* note 74, at 1344–45 (citing enthusiasm for e-rulemaking); Beth Simone Noveck, *The Electronic Revolution in Rulemaking*, 53 EMORY L. J. 433, 462–94 (exploring the promise of e-rulemaking) (2004). Another phenomenon examined by some scholars is "visual rulemaking," which seeks to engage the public with easier-to-understand visual appeals. *See* Elizabeth G. Porter & Kathryn A. Watts, *Visual Rulemaking*, 91 N. Y. U. L. REV. 1183 (2016) (exploring visual rulemaking in depth). Even within this space, there are reasons to be concerned about inequities. As the authors note, agencies may provide the general public an opportunity to participate in online forums (like Facebook) without taking adequate account of such responses as official "comments." *Id.* at 1249–51.
92. Cary Coglianese, *Citizen Participation in Rulemaking: Past, Present, and Future*, 55 DUKE L. J. 943, 949 (2006) ("Will e-rulemaking actually increase thoughtful citizen participation in regulatory policymaking? The answer appears to be, after a

careful consideration of the available evidence, decidedly 'no.'"); *see also* Stuart Minor Benjamin, *Evaluating E-Rulemaking: Public Participation and Political Institutions*, 55 DUKE L. J. 893 (2006) (concluding that there is good reason to think, albeit on a preliminary basis, that the costs of e-rulemaking outweigh its benefits). *But See* Lauren Moxley, *E-Rulemaking and Democracy*, 68 ADMIN. L. REV. 661 (2016) (arguing that e-rulemaking "has democratized the highly technical, highly consequential regulatory process").

93. Mendelson, *supra* note 74, at 1359–71 (finding that agencies tend to be unresponsive to comments that address values); *see also* Mariano-Florentino Cuéllar, *Rethinking Regulatory Democracy*, 57 ADMIN. L. REV. 411, 428–90 (2005) (finding that sophistication of comments is critical to likelihood of influence on agencies); Jim Rossi, *Participation Run Amok: The Costs of Mass Participation for Deliberative Agency Decisionmaking*, 92 NW. U. L. REV. 173, 174 (1997) (arguing that merely increasing participation can paradoxically reduce deliberation in the administrative system).

94. *Understanding IRS Guidance – A Brief Primer*, IRS, https://www.irs.gov/newsroom/understanding-irs-guidance-a-brief-primer [https://perma.cc/W2C7-P8V3] (last updated May 1, 2023).

95. *Id.*

96. *See, e.g.*, Pat Raskob, *Revenue Ruling & Tax: Understanding the Basics*, TAXPROFESSIONALS.COM, https://www.taxprofessionals.com/articles/revenue-ruling-tax-understanding-the-basics [https://perma.cc/8GGX-EYB4] ("Revenue Rulings are important because they provide guidance on how the IRS interprets and applies tax laws. This guidance can be critical for taxpayers and tax professionals trying to understand their tax obligations and ensure that they comply with the law.")

97. *See, e.g.*, @IRSTaxPros, X, https://twitter.com/irstaxpros [https://perma.cc/3C65-6XVV] (providing "IRS news and guidance for tax professionals").

98. Adoption of Recommendations, 77 Fed. Reg. 2257, 2264 (Jan. 17, 2012). For one evaluation of agency use of social media, *see* MICHAEL HERZ, USING SOCIAL MEDIA IN RULEMAKING: POSSIBILITIES AND BARRIERS, FINAL REPORT TO THE ADMINISTRATIVE CONFERENCE OF THE UNITED STATES (2013) (final report to the Administrative Conference of the United States), https://www.acus.gov/sites/default/files/documents/Herz%20Social%20Media%20Final%20Report.pdf [https://perma.cc/7ZYL-JZ4A]. For an interesting article about how agencies need to respond to "fake news" on social media and other places, *see* Kathleen DeLaney Thomas & Erin Scharff, *Fake News and the Tax Law*, 80 WASH. & LEE L. REV. 803 (2023).

99. *See* Plain Writing Act of 2010, Pub. L. No. 111-274, 124 Stat. 2861 (codified at 5 U.S.C. § 301).

100. *Cf.* Ruth Sullivan, *The Promise of Plain Language Drafting*, 47 MCGILL L. J. 97 (2001) (explaining that "The purpose of drafting legislative texts in plain language is to enhance democracy and the rule of law by making legislation accessible to the people whose lives it affects," but also identifying some problems with this approach).

101. Treas. Reg. § 601.601(d)(2)(v)(e) ("Taxpayers generally may rely upon Revenue Rulings published in the Bulletin in determining the tax treatment of their own transactions and need not request specific rulings applying the principles of a published Revenue Ruling to the facts of their particular cases.").

102. Treas. Reg. § 1.6662-3(b)(3); Treas. Reg. § 1.6662-4(d)(3)(iii). Revenue Rulings are published in the Internal Revenue Bulletin.

103. *See, e.g.*, Rev. Rul. 98-37, 1998-2 C.B. 133 (providing list of revenue rulings that have been obsoleted because "(1) the applicable statutory provisions or regulations have been changed or repealed; (2) the ruling position is specifically covered by a statute,

regulation, or subsequent published position; or (3) the facts set forth no longer exist or are not sufficiently described to permit clear application of the current statute and regulations").

104. 5 U.S.C. § 704.
105. *Abbott Lab'ys v. Gardner*, 387 U.S. 136, 148–49, *abrogated by Califano v. Sanders*, 430 U.S. 99 (1977).
106. *FTC v. Standard Oil Co. of Cal.*, 449 U.S. 232, 239–40 (1980) (quoting *Abbott Lab'ys*, 387 U.S. at 151–52); *see also, e.g., Frozen Food Express v. United States*, 351 U.S. 40, 44–45 (1956) (order of the Interstate Commerce Commission, listing which commodities were within the agricultural exemption of the Interstate Commerce Act, was justiciable, in part because it was "the basis for carriers in ordering and arranging their affairs").
107. *Bennett v. Spear*, 520 U.S. 154, 177 (1997) (first quoting *Chi. & S. Air Lines, Inc. v. Waterman S.S. Corp.*, 333 U.S. 103, 113 (1948); and then quoting *Port of Bos. Marine Terminal Assn. v. Rederiaktiebolaget Transatlantic*, 400 U.S. 62, 71 (1970)).
108. *U.S. Army Corps of Eng'rs v. Hawkes Co.*, 578 U.S. 590, 597–600 (2016) (relying both on *Bennett* and the "pragmatic" approach from *Abbott Laboratories* and *Frozen Food* in its analysis).
109. *See, e.g., Friedman v. FAA*, 841 F.3d 537, 541 (D.C. Cir. 2016) (finding that an FAA position was final agency action, despite citation to *Bennett*, because "[c]ase law interpreting this standard is 'hardly crisp,' and it 'lacks many self-implementing, bright-line rules, given the pragmatic and flexible nature of the inquiry as a whole'" (quoting *Rhea Lana, Inc. v. Dep't of Lab.*, 824 F.3d 1023, 1027 (D.C. Cir. 2016))).
110. *See, e.g.*, Recent Case, *Soundboard Ass'n v. FTC*, 888 F.3d 1261 (D.C. Cir. 2018), 132 HARV. L. REV. 1345, 1352 (2019) (worrying that the formalist approach in the recent D.C. Circuit case will undermine the ability to review agency decisions made in guidance).
111. *See, e.g.*, Steven J. Lindsay, *Timing Judicial Review of Agency Interpretations in Chevron's Shadow*, 127 YALE L. J. 2448 (2018) (concluding as much). There are certainly other potential barriers to judicial review that could apply. To name just one example, the Anti-Injunction Act prohibits suit "for the purpose of restraining the assessment or collection of any tax." I.R.C. § 7421(a). This can bar pre-enforcement judicial review in some cases. *But see, e.g., CIC Servs., LLC v. IRS*, 593 U.S. 209, 226 (2021) (finding that the AIA did not enjoin suit to challenge notice requiring taxpayers to engage in information reporting).
112. *See, e.g.*, Lindsay, *supra* note 111, at 2457 (describing judicial "confusion in determining the finality of concededly nonlegislative rules").
113. *See, e.g., Or. Nat. Desert Ass'n v. U.S. Forest Serv.*, 465 F.3d 977, 979 (9th Cir. 2006) (finding that "the United States Forest Service's issuance of annual operating instructions ('AOIs') to permittees who graze livestock on national forest land constitutes final agency action for purposes of judicial review").
114. *See, e.g., Truckers United for Safety v. Fed. Highway Admin.*, 139 F.3d 934, 937–38 (D.C. Cir. 1998) (finding Federal Highway Administration's question-and-answer guidance unripe for review).
115. 599 F.3d 426 (4th Cir. 2010).
116. *Id.* at 428 (alteration in original).
117. *Id.*
118. *Id.* at 433.
119. *Id.* at 432.
120. *Id.* at 429.
121. *Id.* at 432–33.

122. *Id.* at 433.
123. Nina A. Mendelson, *Regulatory Beneficiaries and Informal Agency Policymaking*, 92 CORNELL L. REV. 397, 414–15 (2007).
124. Some exceptions to this orientation apply. For instance, the tax law applies broadly to the general public. Even in this context, however, the inability to challenge deregulation remains an issue. Limitations on taxpayer standing, for instance, limit the ability to challenge regulations or enforcement that is too favorable to others.
125. *Heckler v. Chaney*, 470 U.S. 821, 831–32 (1985).
126. *Id.* at 832.
127. Mendelson, *supra* note 123, at 420–24.
128. *Cf.* Cass R. Sunstein, *Reviewing Agency Inaction after Heckler v. Chaney*, 52 U. CHI. L. REV. 653, 656 (1985) (pointing out that "the availability of review will often serve as an important constraint on regulators during the decisionmaking process long before review actually comes into play").
129. Mendelson, *supra* note 123, at 424–33.
130. *Cf. Indep. Equip. Dealers Ass'n v. EPA*, 372 F.3d 420, 428 (D.C. Cir. 2004) (explaining that "it would be folly to allow parties to challenge a regulation anew each year upon the annual re-publication of the Code of Federal Regulations").

9

How Should Automated Legal Guidance Evolve?

Chapters 3 and 4 have demonstrated how automated legal guidance tools often enable federal agencies to present complex law as though it is simple, without requiring them to engage in the actual simplification of the underlying law. While this approach offers advantages in terms of administrative efficiency and ease of use, it also causes the government to provide the public with imprecise advice and descriptions of potentially inaccurate legal positions. Our interviews with representatives of federal agencies revealed that many government officials are not adequately apprised of these issues, resulting in practices that, in some ways, make the problems worse.[1] Further, agencies design automated legal guidance tools without meaningful input from knowledgeable members of the public regarding the information that these tools provide, including the content of their questions and answers.

As technology continues to evolve, the use of automated legal guidance by government agencies to explain the law is also likely to continue to grow. What steps, if any, can legislators, agency officials, and other policymakers take to address the existing and potential costs of this method of communication?

A single comprehensive reform that would address all potential drawbacks of automated tools, while at the same time not diminishing their potential benefits to agencies and the public, is not likely to appear. Multiple policy interventions, therefore, are necessary. In this chapter, we present practical recommendations for federal agencies that have introduced, or may introduce, chatbots, virtual assistants, and other automated tools to communicate the law to the public. In Chapter 10, we will explore how our policy recommendations relate to the broader democracy deficit in administrative law and a potential future of automated compliance.

AN AGENDA FOR POLICYMAKERS

In this section, we offer multiple, detailed policy recommendations for federal agencies that currently use, or may use in the future, automated legal guidance tools to communicate the law to the public. We present these recommendations regarding the design of automated legal guidance tools in five general categories: (1) transparency; (2) reliance; (3) disclaimers; (4) process; and (5) accessibility, inclusion, and equity.

Transparency

Transparency in government communications exists when agencies are open regarding their rules and policies, interpretations of the law, decision-making processes, and enforcement methods. Transparency is essential in the administrative state for several reasons. Primarily, it allows members of the public to engage in informed discussion and debate regarding the government's policies and actions. It empowers the public, often through legislative oversight committees, to monitor the actions of agency officials and to hold them accountable. Further, it provides members of the public the information they need to make decisions regarding their own legal compliance.

To achieve these benefits, we believe that automated legal guidance tools should have important transparency features in four areas: (1) notice of unsettled formal law, (2) explanations of changes, (3) notifications of effective dates, and (4) descriptions of decision tree structures.

Unsettled Formal Law

Automated legal guidance tools respond to a range of questions regarding legal compliance issues, from the simple to the complex. In many cases, these queries involve issues for which the underlying formal law is not settled because of conflicting judicial decisions in different circuits, recent legislative changes, and the introduction of proposed regulations, among other reasons. This uncertainty applies to several of the scenarios discussed throughout this book, including the answers to questions regarding the tax deductibility of expenses for an MBA degree, or the factors that may permit a green card holder to travel without adversely affecting the US citizenship process.

When agencies use automated legal guidance tools to answer questions on ambiguous legal issues such as these, they often illustrate simplexity in their responses, as detailed in Chapter 4.[2] This feature has a number of effects: It can make the underlying formal law appear more definite than it is, or it can reflect the agency's own gloss on the law. As we have seen, there have even been occasions when these tools have delivered answers that deviate from the underlying formal law.

To increase transparency, agencies should provide users with explicit notice when their automated tools provide answers regarding formal law when the law is unsettled. They should also provide this notice when those answers deviate from the formal law. These notices should include citations or links to conflicting formal law sources, such as judicial decisions with which the agency disagrees. Ideally, the automated tools would present the government-favorable position by default, along with explicit warnings regarding conflicting or unsettled formal law. Indeed, this would not be a new concept for the agencies to implement, since they already do this in other forms of guidance. For example, in 2010, when the IRS issued a revenue ruling regarding deductibility of home equity indebtedness, the IRS specifically noted that its position conflicted with decisions of the US Tax Court.[3]

These notices would allow users to make informed planning decisions that correspond to their risk tolerance levels. For example, someone who wants to adopt the most conservative position possible regarding any issue that could affect their ability to become a naturalized US citizen would likely follow the guidance offered by automated tools such as Emma, even if Emma provides a warning that there are judicial decisions in conflict with its advice. A similar situation could arise regarding advice from the IRS's ITA. If someone who is considering whether to claim a tax deduction receives a warning from ITA about conflicting formal law authorities, that person might investigate the issue further by consulting with an accountant or lawyer.

One concern that this recommendation raises is that the inclusion of warnings regarding formal law could make automated legal guidance *less* useful to members of the public. The whole purpose of these tools, after all, is to help individuals navigate the law quickly, without the need to consult complex statutes and regulations. Rather than include lengthy discussion, however, agencies could present brief, clear warning notices that include citations to specific cases.

Agencies have demonstrated that they can provide such brief notice on their websites and in print publications. In printed IRS publications, for example, the agency uses a caution symbol – an exclamation point inside a triangle – to indicate an instance where the law is unsettled.[4] Agencies could include the same type of symbols, followed by brief citations and hyperlinks, to alert users that they should consider seeking professional third-party guidance regarding certain questions.

Explanation of Changes

During our research, we observed instances in which federal agencies revised or deleted answers that had been provided by their chatbots and other automated tools but did not issue public statements or records regarding these revisions.

As an example, in 2021, we visited Aidan, the FSA chatbot, and asked it questions regarding the effects of bankruptcy proceedings on federal education loans. After we typed, "Can I discharge my student loan in bankruptcy?," Aidan responded as follows:[5]

Question: Can I discharge my student loan in bankruptcy?
Aidan: Here are federal student loan discharge cases:

1. Total and permanent disability
2. Closed school
3. False certification
4. Unpaid refund
5. Discharge due to death
6. Bankruptcy (rare cases)

Several months later, we returned to Aidan and asked it the same question. On that occasion, Aidan did not provide this response, but instead directed us to another section of the FSA website. We then searched for an archive or list of changes that agency officials had made to statements provided by Aidan, but none existed.

The fact that agencies make changes to automated legal guidance without any explanation or notice means that people who relied on agency statements in automated legal guidance in the past may no longer have a record of them. This, of course, weakens any reliance claim they may be able to make. The lack of a record also hampers the public's ability to monitor agency processes. By making archives of changes easily accessible to users, agencies would promote both government transparency and fundamental fairness.

How would this work? To illuminate agencies' revisions to their automated tools' statements, agencies should maintain a publicly accessible record of these changes. Throughout our research, we learned that agencies have different processes for making revisions in response to changes in the formal law, including new legislation, judicial decisions, and changes in agency positions. However, we did not observe any instances where agencies created a mechanism for informing the public of these revisions, or for maintaining a searchable archive on their websites.

Indeed, in 2021, in response to criticism from taxpayers and practitioners, the IRS committed to create an archive of certain frequently asked questions (FAQs) on its website.[6] There is a public need for this type of resource. Therefore, we believe that agencies should adopt this approach regarding statements made by automated legal guidance tools.

Effective Dates

In addition to not providing the public with information about *what* they have changed when revising automated legal guidance tools, agencies have also failed to inform the public about *when* they have made these changes. For instance, in the example we described earlier involving Aidan, FSA officials did not provide any information to users about the timing of the changes they made to the chatbot's responses.[7] Throughout our study, we did not observe an agency's automated tool indicating to users the effective date of the information it provided. This approach stands in stark contrast to the way that legislators, judges, and regulators draft formal law sources – such as statutes, regulations, and rulings – all of which contain effective dates.[8]

How would these notifications appear? A publicly accessible archive of any change made to the information that the tool delivers could, for example, include the effective dates of each change, allowing users to see what information was provided and when. An even more direct approach, however, could be to program the tool to include a brief statement, such as "This information is effective as of [date]," at the end of each user session.

Effective dates serve several important functions. First, they provide information to users about a specific time period.[9] Second, if an agency created a publicly searchable archive of statements made by its automated tools, the effective dates would allow users to review how the agency revised statements over time, particularly in response to legislative, judicial, and other developments. Finally, if users could rely on statements made by automated legal guidance tools to either bind the agency or defend against penalties for noncompliance (issues we discuss in subsequent recommendations), then the inclusion of effective dates of statements made by these tools would be critical information for users, agencies, and, potentially, courts.

Publication of Decision Tree Structures

As we have documented, agencies adopt different approaches to designing automated legal guidance tools.[10] For example, the IRS's ITA reflects a decision tree approach to assisting users, meaning that, for every topic, it provides the same responses to every inquiry, and only varies these answers based upon users' inputs when answering ITA's uniform set of questions.[11] Automated tools that use machine learning, on the other hand, deliver different responses to users' questions over time as they discover patterns.[12]

In the interest of transparency, agencies that adopt decision tree structures when implementing automated legal guidance should publish the entire content of these decision trees. Public disclosure of the decision tree would provide an immediate and comprehensive source of guidance to users who seek to learn the agency's views on legal issues that may vary depending upon the circumstances. The current approach does not offer such a vantage point, as it requires users to provide alternative inputs (*e.g.*, answering "yes" or "no" to specific questions) rather than allowing them to view the full set of possible agency positions at once.[13] Further, disclosing the decision tree would facilitate public scrutiny of the questions and answers provided by agencies' automated tools. Without such disclosure, agency employees could adjust the wording or ordering of the questions without alerting members of the public that they have made revisions.

Reliance

"Reliance" in the automated legal guidance context involves two separate questions:

1. Can users assert the statements of an agency's automated tool to prevent that agency from applying contrary rules or interpretations of the law?
2. Can users offer these automated statements as defenses against penalties for legal noncompliance?

As we argue here, when policymakers address these two questions, they should adopt reforms that consider differences between two types of automated legal guidance:

- "Unilateral" guidance, in which an agency uses language that is fixed and intended for all users, and
- "Bilateral" guidance, in which an agency tailors its statements to individual users based on information they enter.

Binding Agencies

Unlike formal law, such as statutes and regulations, statements provided by automated legal guidance tools do not currently bind agencies. If an agency makes a statement through automated legal guidance but later applies a different interpretation of the law, an affected user cannot point to these statements to estop the agency.

Some of the agencies' automated legal guidance tools that we reviewed provide information to users who inquire about specific topics without asking the users any follow-up questions. These automated tools present unilateral guidance to all users, which is comprised of identical information that does not factor in any user's specific circumstances.

For example, during our research, we asked USCIS's Emma the following question: "If I am a lawful permanent resident, may I travel?" Emma provided this answer in response:[14]

> Question: If I am a lawful permanent resident, may I travel?
> Emma: Permanent residents are free to travel outside the United States, and temporary or brief travel (less than 1 year) usually does not affect your permanent resident status.

This answer also included a link to other sections of the USCIS website. Emma did not ask for additional information or vary the response depending on the user's response to questions.[15] This statement is an example of what we describe as unilateral guidance because the agency is the only actor providing information.

There are compelling reasons to change the status quo regarding whether a user can rely on unilateral guidance provided by automated tools to bind agencies. If agency officials are bound by the statements made by the agency's automated tool, those officials may exercise greater caution when programming the responses from that tool. This change would support procedural fairness, create more equal reliance opportunities for users with different economic resources, and potentially enhance agencies' perceived legitimacy.[16] This approach could also result in statements that are more consistent with the formal law. This effect would benefit users by making agency contradictions less likely during subsequent enforcement actions.

As we discuss further at the end of this chapter, where agencies offer unilateral statements through their automated legal guidance tools, they should allow users to reasonably rely on such statements to bind the agencies.

For several reasons, however, we do not propose that this recommendation should extend to bilateral administrative guidance. When the guidance changes depending on what the user enters, there are different considerations. Chief among these is that the quality of the bilateral guidance that automated tools deliver is only as good as the users' inputs. For example, because tools such as ITA often do not ask the taxpayer follow-up questions, they may generate incorrect answers because of limited information supplied by taxpayers. Additionally, bilateral guidance might vary between users, depending on the extent to which each user accurately entered the requested information. Allowing people to assert statements from bilateral automated legal guidance to bind agencies could result in unequal treatment of those that are otherwise under similar circumstances. In either of these situations, it would be unfair to bind the agency to its responses.

Finally, allowing users to rely on bilateral automated legal guidance could be subject to abuse. For example, knowing that they could use ITA's statements to bind the IRS, a user could input information regarding a purchase of equipment into ITA but ignore the legal requirement that the equipment be related to medical care. This could prompt ITA to indicate that the equipment is tax deductible, when it is not. Users should not be permitted to use statements made in bilateral automated legal guidance to estop the agency from taking a contrary position when the agency has a legitimate reason for doing so.

Defenses against Penalties for Noncompliance

Currently, people who rely on unilateral guidance offered by agencies' automated tools may not be able to use certain statutory and regulatory defenses against penalties for legal noncompliance.

Consider some examples involving the use of certain defenses in tax noncompliance cases. If, for example, the IRS offers unilateral guidance regarding a tax compliance issue in an informal statement on its website (rather than in a formal announcement or press release), taxpayers would have difficulty using this statement to assert a "reasonable basis" defense. This is a specific tax penalty defense, defined in Treasury Regulations, that taxpayers can use to defend against "accuracy-related" tax penalties.[17] Under this penalty defense, individuals must show that they reasonably relied upon a specific, formal tax law source, such as the Internal Revenue Code, Treasury Regulations, IRS revenue rulings, judicial decisions, and announcements published by the IRS in the Internal Revenue Bulletin.[18] However, because the IRS has not published many informal statements on its website in the Internal Revenue Bulletin, taxpayers have not been able to use them to present a reasonable basis defense.[19] Other potential tax penalty defenses, such as the statutory "reasonable cause and good faith" defense, could also be challenging. This defense focuses on several subjective factors, including the knowledge and sophistication of the individual taxpayer, rather than automatically finding reliance if the user can point to specific types of tax law sources.[20]

By contrast, individuals who can afford to hire lawyers and accountants have greater opportunities to defend against penalties for noncompliance than those who must turn to sources like ITA for assistance. For instance, if the IRS asserts an accuracy-related tax penalty against a taxpayer, that taxpayer may defend against this tax penalty by showing that they acted with reasonable cause and good faith.[21] This requirement can often be satisfied by presenting the IRS with a written tax opinion from legal counsel upon which the taxpayer relied.[22]

As a matter of equity, agencies should allow users to reasonably rely on statements made by agencies' automated legal guidance tools to defend against penalties for noncompliance. Further, this rule should apply in situations regardless of the type of automated guidance reasonably relied upon: *either* unilateral *or* bilateral guidance.

In situations involving bilateral administrative guidance, users should be able to show reasonable reliance to assert defenses against penalties for noncompliance. While we have not recommended that bilateral administrative guidance should be internally binding upon agencies, we do not believe that allowing individuals to rely on such statements to defend against penalties would present the same opportunities for manipulation and abuse. Primarily, this is because individuals must still show reasonable reliance when claiming legal positions. The reasonableness requirement would enable agencies and courts to reject penalty defenses where individuals inputted misleading or false information to generate a response that could be used as a penalty defense.[23] It is also the case that, under the law applicable to certain agencies, such as the IRS, individuals must inform the agency that they relied on a specific source if they hope to later use this reliance to claim a penalty defense.[24] This disclosure requirement should deter abusive use of bilateral statements by automated tools for the purpose of penalty defenses.

Record of Correspondence

One common aspect of agencies' automated legal guidance tools that we observed during our research is that it was difficult to obtain a record of interactions between the tools and users. For instance, when we interacted with chatbots such as USCIS's Emma and FSA's Aidan, we attempted to keep records of our questions and each chatbot's responses. We did this by cutting and pasting our interactions into a document or taking screen shots of our computer screens.

As academic researchers, we knew that we needed to record our interactions with the tools so that we could refer to them as we wrote articles and reports on this new type of administrative guidance. Members of the public, however, may not have the foresight, or desire, to engage in this type of time-consuming and manual process simply to keep a record for the future. This is especially likely to be the case when people reasonably, but incorrectly, assume that the guidance they are getting is accurate.

Obtaining a record of interactions with automated legal guidance tools could be important for many reasons. At the most practical level, individuals could later refer to this record when deciding to take a specific action. In addition, if the other reforms we recommend are adopted, they could also use this record when responding to agency challenges to their actions in the future, including as support for their defense against penalties for noncompliance. If policymakers adopt our proposal regarding the binding nature of unilateral automated legal guidance, people may need to be able to present this record to agency officials and, potentially, to judges.

Because records of agency communications may be both practically and legally significant, agency officials should design their automated tools to allow users to easily reproduce an electronic written record of every input by the user and output by the automated tool. In most cases of automated legal guidance that we studied, we did not see an option for creating such a record. This absence may become even more significant if agencies eventually adopt technology in their automated legal guidance tools that is more seamless and does not display every input and output in the correspondence between the user and the automated system. Government chatbots could one day use technology like that of Snapchat, a messaging app that automatically deletes "Snaps" after recipients view them.[25] Our recommendation, thus, addresses the current and potential future limited ability of users to preserve records of their interactions with agencies' automated tools.

Following recommendations that we made to ACUS in 2022, which subsequently adopted many of these recommendations in June 2022,[26] at least one agency has started to take steps to offer users the ability to retain a record of interactions with an automated legal guidance tool. In 2024, when ITA provided a user with an answer to their tax law inquiry, the IRS included an option to download a record of the exchange. This first step, however, is not enough. Every agency should provide users with the ability to obtain these records, including all questions asked, all answers submitted, and the date and time of each interaction.

Disclaimers

During our agency interviews, which are described in Chapter 5, officials often told us that they believed that their automated legal guidance tools did not issue legally binding information. Instead, these officials stated, the tools simply provided access to information that was already publicly accessible in other places, including on their agency websites.

Despite this belief, the tools we studied rarely included explicit disclaimers that notified users of the agency's understanding of this. Due to this absence of disclaimers, these tools can mislead users. This is the case when the tools address legal issues that are ambiguous or uncertain, especially when the tools claim to provide "answers" to users' legal questions. To better inform users, we recommend that agency officials configure automated legal guidance tools to include explicit warnings indicating that the information they provide may not conform to sources of formal law.

Limited Ability to Bind Government

While some agencies have provided limited disclaimers, none of the tools provided a clear statement indicating whether the agency was bound, or not, by the information provided. Especially in the case of chatbots, such as Emma and Aidan, the tools tended to pop up on the screen quickly and offer to help users, but did not preface their guidance with warnings. Instead, the agency websites often included statements regarding how these tools were "here to help you find an answer."[27]

In addition to salutations and greetings to users, agencies should also include explicit disclaimers in their automated tools that explain that, under current law, the information given by the tools cannot legally bind the agency, nor can it be used to estop the agency from adopting contrary positions in the event of an agency challenge. If agencies adopt our recommendations on this point, these disclaimers should be amended to clearly inform users what types of statements by automated tools are binding on agencies.

One potential objection to this recommendation is that automated tools are designed to offer concise and simple explanations, and such disclaimers would add a significant amount of text that may clutter the screen or confuse users. We believe this argument is unpersuasive: disclaimers like this can be clear and brief, without referring extensively to legal authorities. These disclaimers could be as simple as "The information presented by [name of tool] does not bind the agency. We may adopt alternative interpretations of the law in the event of future disputes or challenges."

Limited Noncompliance Penalty Defenses

Penalty relief was another area in which we did not observe the widespread use of disclaimers, although there were limited exceptions. For example, the IRS included a statement on ITA's final answer screen that described the limited ability of taxpayers to use ITA statements to assert protections against erroneous agency statements under Section 6404(f) of the Internal Revenue Code. However, the IRS's statement did not include disclaimers regarding the use of defenses against civil or criminal tax penalties, including, notably, the reasonable cause and reasonable basis defenses.[28]

These tools should include disclaimers that address whether users can rely upon these statements to defend against penalties for noncompliance. If our prior recommendation is adopted, tools should notify users that they may use their reliance on the information provided by the tools to defend against specific penalties for noncompliance.

Speaker Not Human

Like private sector businesses, agencies have attempted to anthropomorphize automated legal guidance tools, such as chatbots and virtual assistants, to make them appear friendly and welcoming. This strategy is not new, as users of early versions of

Microsoft Word may remember Clippit (more commonly known as Clippy), an animated paperclip with eyebrows and warm smile, who offered to provide help to users to perform routine tasks like writing letters.[29]

In the present day, USCIS's chatbot, Emma, appears to be an animated version of a human being. Emma has brown hair and speaks to users in the first person, starting interactions by typing "Hi, I'm Emma."[30] When combined with a lack of disclaimers and warnings, the human-like appearance of these automated tools may only further induce users to accept what they say, without skepticism, even if the content of the information provided is of limited legal value.

When agencies use automated tools that have human appearance and employ natural language processing, they should inform users that the source of the responses is not, in fact, a human being. While USCIS does explain to visitors that Emma is a "computer-generated virtual assistant who can answer your questions,"[31] this statement is insufficient. The agency should provide further disclaimers by programming Emma to state explicitly that a human being (such as an agency employee) is not providing the responses to users' questions in real time.

Without this type of disclosure, automated legal guidance tools may cause some users to place too much confidence in their guidance. This is especially problematic regarding guidance that is not consistent with the formal law, or that users cannot rely on to bind the agency or defend against penalties.

Process

In embracing the use of automated legal guidance tools to respond to questions from the public, agencies have adopted different processes and decision-making structures to implement and evaluate this new technology. During our research, we quickly learned that agency officials' knowledge of these processes varied from agency to agency. Some high-level officials we interviewed had a detailed understanding of their agency's approach to reviewing the content of tools' questions and answers. Others were not certain which officials or offices in their agency were responsible for overseeing the development of the tools.

Without internal and external awareness of an agency's processes, agency officials will have difficulty meeting some of the transparency and equity objectives we have discussed in this section. Three aspects of the development and delivery process for these tools require specific attention from agency officials: the chains of command, evaluation by independent experts, and the use of outside vendors.

Chains of Command

Agency officials should develop clear chains of command regarding the creation, review, and maintenance of the information offered by automated legal guidance tools. This action should occur regardless of the development model that agencies adopt.

As we learned, some agencies use a "top-down" approach to develop and manage these tools. This is where the agency's general counsel's office directs members of a technology team to program the tool to address substantive legal issues and questions. Other agencies use more of a "bottom-up" approach. Here, product developers have autonomy not only to create the tool but also to program and update its content.

Irrespective of the development model, we observed that, in several agencies, many employees who are intricately involved in or responsible for creating automated legal guidance did not know the internal process for doing so. For example, in some agencies, individuals responsible for computer programming were not aware of who made final decisions on the substantive legal rules that should be conveyed, nor did they know who was responsible for reviewing legislative and judicial developments.

To enhance accountability and transparency, agencies should adopt clear chains of command regarding automated legal guidance, with detailed responsibilities of the actors in each of the units involved, including the general counsel's office, the policy group, the communications group, and the technology group. In addition, this command structure should be publicly accessible on each agency's website. This will ensure that the chain of command is known by everyone in the agency involved in the creation and maintenance of the tool and can also be reviewed by oversight institutions and representatives of the public.

Independent Expert Evaluation

Agencies should include external expert review and analysis as part of the formal process of developing and maintaining automated legal guidance. During our interviews with agency officials, we learned that many different people are involved in the creation and maintenance of automated legal guidance at agencies.[32] Among others, they included the product owner and members of the technology group, members of the policy team, members of the content team, members of senior leadership, content specialists, general counsel representatives, and members of the communications department.

We were frequently told that the automated tools offered by agencies were highly effective for two reasons. One was that they provided answers that were consistent with the agency's own summaries of the law, either through the general counsel's office or other agency publications. The second reason was that users reported high rates of satisfaction with the tools.[33]

To our surprise, however, we did not hear much about the participation of outside experts in the creation and maintenance of these tools. Technology experts should regularly review the automated tools used by federal agencies, and such reviews should evaluate whether the agency's automated tools are user-friendly and consistent with relevant industry standards. Legal practitioners with expertise in the regulatory field should also be involved throughout the process of developing and updating automated tools to ensure that they deliver information that is not only as consistent as possible with the formal law but is also unlikely to confuse users.

Evaluation of Use of Outside Vendors

The federal government should also evaluate the costs and benefits of relying on outside vendors for the development of automated tools. Our interviews revealed that most agencies that offer automated legal guidance tools purchased them, at least in part, from outside vendors.[34] After purchase, the agency and the vendor typically work together to design questions and answers that the automated tool provides to users. There is a significant benefit to this approach. Agencies that have gone down this path have been able to introduce automated tools, such as Emma and Aidan, relatively quickly. The tools also appear and operate in a manner that is consistent with the types of services that private sector banks, airlines, and media companies offer to consumers.[35]

This reliance on outside vendors, however, has its drawbacks. Tools developed in this way may be significantly different from agency to agency. This can make it difficult for all federal agencies to adopt consistent standards. In addition, vendors that primarily serve private sector businesses often seek to create the most personable and user-friendly automated tools. These vendors may not be attuned to concerns that are unique to government agencies. For instance, they may not consider or want to accommodate the need to include disclaimers into the basic design of their automated platforms.[36]

Federal agencies, possibly following an executive order or even legislation, should regularly evaluate the costs and benefits of contracting with outside vendors for the development and maintenance of automated tools. We also recommend that the federal government consider developing templates for automated legal guidance tools that agencies could adopt. These templates would provide needed government-wide consistency and prevent agencies from having to purchase platforms from multiple external vendors.

Accessibility, Inclusion, and Equity

When explaining why their agencies have adopted automated legal guidance tools, agency officials have repeatedly described the objective of fostering the public's understanding of and compliance with the law. This is a laudable goal, and it should be encouraged. However, it is also important to evaluate whether this is taking place, especially with respect to those for whom access to the law is not otherwise easy, or even possible. Later, we offer several recommendations for how agency officials could achieve this goal in ways that are inclusive, equitable, and effective.

Study of User Characteristics

Throughout our interviews, officials across federal agencies told us that they do not collect or study demographic information about the users of their automated tools,[37] and explained that they do not collect information regarding users' race, income, education, marital status, gender, or disability.

The absence of this data and apparent lack of interest in collecting it raise several concerns. Without knowing who is using the tools to obtain information, agency officials may be designing automated legal guidance to provide responses that are incomplete, inapplicable, or both. If these tools provide misleading or inaccurate information, this could have a significant negative and disproportionate impact on certain groups of users. Further, if agency officials do not know who is using specific features or asking certain questions, the tools may be failing to offer these users meaningful support by providing information in ways that are either too vague or, alternatively, too detailed.

Agencies should consider the demographic data of the people who access and rely upon their automated legal guidance tools and incorporate that information into their design and functionality. Indeed, the federal government has recently shown a targeted interest in this area. As a result of the "cascading effects" of lack of data, in 2021, President Biden issued an executive order that established an "Interagency Working Group on Equitable Data," which must offer recommendations on best practices for studying the effects of legal rules and policies on different individuals based on race, ethnicity, gender, disability, and other characteristics.[38] Consistent with this initiative, agencies should research the types of users who rely on automated legal guidance to comply with the law to better "measure and advance equity."[39]

That said, any plan by federal agencies to gather data on the characteristics of the users of automated legal guidance would likely, and justifiably, raise several concerns. If the tools requested even more personal information from users, by asking questions regarding gender or income, users might not respond to them, especially if they are optional. These types of questions could also discourage users from engaging with the tools at all, particularly if they believed doing so would put their personal privacy at risk.

Certain data could raise additional concerns, such as that related to race. If, for example, an agency that conducts enforcement activities, such as the IRS, were to ask for information regarding taxpayers' race, these questions could, as Professor Jeremy Bearer-Friend has suggested, create the appearance that the agency discriminates against certain groups.[40] And the introduction of questions regarding users' characteristics, including race, could cause agencies to become the focus of scrutiny and debate by legislators, which may hamper their ability to seek increased budgetary resources in the future.

Yet there are many ways in which agencies could design their studies of the personal characteristics of users. Based on what we learned in our interviews, many agencies conduct extensive advance testing before they make these tools publicly accessible. They also track the annual usage of these tools.[41] These data collection opportunities could be expanded to gather helpful user demographic information.

Your privacy concerns

We use your confidential survey answers to create statistics like those in the results below and in the full tables that contain all the data—no one is able to figure out your survey answers from the statistics we produce. The Census Bureau is legally bound to strict confidentiality requirements. Individual records are not shared with anyone, including federal agencies and law enforcement entities. By law, the Census Bureau cannot share respondents' answers with anyone—not the IRS, not the FBI, not the CIA, and not with any other government agency.

FIGURE 9.1 US Census Bureau: Why We Ask Questions about Race – Your Privacy Concerns (www.census.gov/acs/www/about/why-we-ask-each-question/race/)

Another option for collecting demographic data could be to include user surveys, which could have questions about, for example, income, marital status, and race. Private sector businesses use these types of surveys regularly, especially when potential consumers access websites and other online services.[42]

Agencies that decide to collect demographic data on their users would benefit from taking a page out of the US Census Bureau's playbook. When that agency requests personal information from people, it ameliorates the potential appearance of discrimination by providing brief explanations of the reasons for the questions.[43] As Figure 9.1 above illustrates, the agency also assures users that the data collected will be kept confidential and not be misused.

Finally, such information requests can, and should, include brief explanations of the legal rules that prevent agency officials involved in enforcement from engaging in discrimination or otherwise abusing their discretion.

Human Customer Service Backup

As anyone who has used an automated system, whether online or on the phone, knows, finding a way to reach a human being who can help quickly becomes a frustrating search. This is especially true where the question involves any unique circumstances.

In general, the automated legal guidance tools that we studied did not, during their interactions with users, provide information about how to contact a human customer service agent. For example, ITA's answer screen did not include references to IRS help lines or live customer service.[44] Similarly, Emma did not automatically offer this information during chat sessions, although it was available elsewhere on the USCIS website.[45] This, however, was not ideal: to find information regarding human customer service, users had to leave the chat session and hunt through multiple pages on the website.

When an automated tool cannot answer a question, it should automatically tell the user how to reach human customer service representatives. Without addressing this omission, automated legal guidance may disproportionately disadvantage those who lack experience with online platforms, those who have disabilities that affect their ability to access such information, and those who are unfamiliar with the formal law in the specific area they are asking about.

Supplemental Support
While automated legal guidance offers agencies an efficient and immediate way to provide information about the law, agency officials should view it as just a single component of a greater effort to assist the public. Automated tools cannot address every user and answer every possible legal question. Therefore, agencies must continue to pursue other ways to inform the public, especially low-income users and those who lack access to lawyers and other expert advisors.

This approach can be accomplished through multiple avenues. For example, agencies that adopt automated legal guidance should also continue to allocate resources for human customer service representatives who can help in person, by phone, or electronically. In addition, agencies should continue to support pro bono legal advisors who offer services to low-income people. They should also provide access to free online filing platforms, such as the IRS Free File program.[46]

Other government actors can also provide supplemental support to foster accessibility, inclusion, and equity. For example, to reduce the gap between formal and informal law, policymakers should explore reforms regarding how they draft legislation to make it less susceptible to ambiguity and error. Approaches could include the use of rule-based, rather than standards-based, statutory provisions and formalization of statutory language.[47]

DIFFERENCES FROM ACUS RECOMMENDATIONS

On June 16, 2022, at its annual meeting, the Administrative Conference of the United States (ACUS) Assembly adopted twenty policy recommendations based on our 2022 report on automated legal guidance at federal agencies.[48] Following the meeting, ACUS notified agencies of these adopted recommendations by publishing them in the Federal Register.[49] To be clear, ACUS only provides recommendations, rather than binding rules, to federal agencies. Agency officials may view them as "best practices" and revise their agency's policies in response, or they may decide not to follow them at all.

In many cases, the formal ACUS recommendations reflect our proposals. For example, they include, among other things, a call for agencies to consider when and if a user's good faith reliance on guidance from automated legal guidance tools should serve as a defense against penalties for noncompliance.[50] They encourage agencies to allow users to obtain a written record of their communication with automated legal guidance tools, including date and time stamps.[51] In addition, they state that agencies should explain the limitations of the advice that users receive when the underlying law is unclear or unsettled.[52] They also provide that, "[t]o the extent practicable," agencies should offer access, through the tools themselves, to the legal materials underlying the tools, including relevant statutes, rules, and judicial or adjudicative decisions.[53] We hope that agencies will follow ACUS's recommendations to follow many of our policy reforms.

Agency-Binding Statements: A Key Difference

While ACUS adopted twenty recommendations based on our report, it did not adopt one proposal that we felt was especially important: our call to require federal agencies to be bound by certain statements that agencies make through automated legal guidance to users.[54] We had proposed that if an automated legal guidance tool, such as a chatbot, provides unilateral guidance (that is, the tool is the only actor providing information), agencies should allow users to reasonably rely on such statements to bind the agency.[55] Unlike formal regulations, automated explanations do not allow individuals who relied upon them to estop agencies during subsequent enforcement actions.[56]

We understand agencies' reticence to be bound to statements they make. As a general matter, bindingness reduces an agency's flexibility and raises the stakes on what the agency says. However, this issue has wider implications. An agency's committed adherence to its own public statements of law is critical in a society that values the rule of law.[57]

If agencies considered themselves bound to follow automated explanations, these explanations would be far more reliable than they are under current law. This would be particularly valuable for individuals who lack access to formal law. Policymakers could also encourage individuals to consider automated explanations of the law fully and in the appropriate contexts by establishing the requirement that reliance on this guidance is only valid if it is reasonable. Further, by committing themselves to being bound by their own explanations of the law, agencies could enhance their perceived legitimacy by the public.

We recognize, however, that our proposal raises several concerns. For example, it may not be possible for agencies to be bound by statements that conflict with the underlying law. Among other things, this could raise separation-of-powers concerns.[58]

However, there are ways in which agencies could effectively "self-bind" themselves to the statements offered by their automated legal guidance tools. For instance, agencies could follow the model offered by the IRS's treatment of statements published in the Internal Revenue Bulletin.[59] The IRS has adopted the position that whenever it publishes statements in the Internal Revenue Bulletin, a weekly government publication, IRS employees must apply the law in a manner consistent with these statements, and taxpayers may rely on them when fulfilling their tax compliance obligations.[60] This example illustrates a mechanism for converting automated explanations into internally binding rules. Other agencies that have, or will have, similar publications as the IRB could use these publications to commit to following unilateral automated explanations.

Another potential objection to our proposal is that its breadth may introduce administrative challenges. Specifically, agency officials may not be able to keep track of all the explanations offered by automated tools. Such administrability concerns could be addressed, however, in a number of ways, such as by establishing online archives of statements and dates on automated explanations. Again, in limited circumstances, some agencies, such as the IRS, have already begun implementing such features in the case of certain online FAQs.[61]

Another potential objection to binding agencies to their unilateral guidance is that it may disincentivize agencies from offering this guidance to the public. After all, agencies' views of the law may reasonably change over time, and binding them to their prior explanations could undermine their ability to reflect such changes. However, this proposal does not require agencies to adhere to the same explanations of the law forever. Rather, agencies would be bound only on a retroactive basis and only regarding parties who had relied on such statements. Agencies may prospectively change their explanations of the law to conform to their views over time. This approach would balance the rule-of-law benefits of binding agencies to their statements with the flexibility that agencies need to administer the law most effectively.

We acknowledge that democratic values such as transparency, participation, and reliability can increase the burdens of governance. However, we do not believe that we should only be willing to bear these costs for sophisticated parties and industry insiders. We believe that adopting our proposed reform regarding bindingness may improve agency communication norms over time, resulting in a more democratic system of agency communications with the public.

NOTES

1. *See* Chapter 5, "Agency Interviews."
2. *See* Chapter 4, "Emma (USCIS)" and "Interactive Tax Assistant (IRS)."
3. *See* Rev. Rul. 2010-25, 2010-2 C.B. 571.
4. *See* IRS, PUB. 17, YOUR FEDERAL INCOME TAX (2020), 4, https://www.irs.gov/pub/irs-prior/p17–2020.pdf [https://perma.cc/X8LD-N5DR].
5. *Meet Aidan (Beta)*, FED. STUDENT AID, https://studentaid.gov/h/aidan (Type: "Can I discharge my student loan in bankruptcy?"; then click send) (last visited Jan. 20, 2022).
6. *See* IRS News Release IR-2021-202 (Oct. 15, 2021), https://www.irs.gov/newsroom/irs-updates-process-for-frequently-asked-questions-on-new-tax-legislation-and-addresses-reliance-concerns [https://perma.cc/K4FF-ZXRE].
7. *See supra* note 5.
8. *See, e.g.*, IRM 32.1.1.2.5 (Aug. 2, 2018).
9. For example, some users who visit ITA may submit inquiries about prior years, not just the current year. *See Interactive Tax Assistant (ITA)*, IRS, https://www.irs.gov/help/ita [https://perma.cc/SNS7-KPEV] (last updated Jan. 16, 2024).
10. *See* Chapter 4, "Emma (USCIS)," "Interactive Tax Assistant (IRS)."
11. *See Interactive Tax Assistant (ITA), supra* note 9.
12. *Meet Emma, Our Virtual Assistant*, U.S. CITIZENSHIP & IMMIGR. SERVS., https://www.uscis.gov/tools/meet-emma-our-virtual-assistant [https://perma.cc/QM9K-UAYV] (last updated Apr. 13, 2018).
13. *See Interactive Tax Assistant (ITA), supra* note 9.

14. *See* Chapter 4, "Emma (USCIS)."
15. *See id.*
16. *See, e.g.*, Karyl A. Kinsey, *Deterrence and Alienation Effects of IRS Enforcement: An Analysis of Survey Data*, *in* WHY PEOPLE PAY TAXES: TAX COMPLIANCE AND ENFORCEMENT 259 (Joel Slemrod ed., 1992); John T. Scholz & Mark Lubell, *Trust and Taxpaying: Testing the Heuristic Approach to Collective Action*, 42 AM. J. POL. SCI. 398, 408 (1998).
17. Treas. Reg. § 1.6662-3(b)(3) (as amended in 2003).
18. Treas. Reg. § 1.6662-4(d)(3)(iii) (as amended in 2003).
19. *Id.*
20. *See* Treas. Reg. § 1.6664-4(c)(1) (as amended in 2003).
21. I.R.C. § 6664(c)(1); Treas. Reg. § 1.6664-4 (as amended in 2003).
22. *See* Treas. Reg. § 1.6664-4(c)(1) (as amended in 2003).
23. *See id.*
24. *See* Treas. Reg. § 1.6662-4(f) (as amended in 2003).
25. *See How to Use Snapchat*, https://help.snapchat.com/hc/en-us/articles/7012332815508-How-to-Use-Snapchat (last updated June 6, 2024).
26. *See* Adoption of Recommendations, 87 Fed. Reg. 39798, 39802 (July 5, 2022) (Recommendation 18).
27. *See, e.g., Meet Aidan*, FED. STUDENT AID, https://studentaid.gov/h/aidan [https://perma.cc/N69U-3X8B (uploaded archive)].
28. *See, e.g., Can I Deduct My Medical and Dental Expenses?*, IRS, https://www.irs.gov/help/ita/can-i-deduct-my-medical-and-dental-expenses [https://perma.cc/VK54-YLTX] (last updated Jan. 16, 2024).
29. For history, *see* Benjamin Cassidy, *The Twisted Life of Clippy*, SEATTLE MET (Aug. 23, 2022), https://www.seattlemet.com/news-and-city-life/2022/08/origin-story-of-clippy-the-microsoft-office-assistant [https://perma.cc/RBC4-558D].
30. *Meet Emma, Our Virtual Assistant*, *supra* note 12 (click "Need help? Ask Emma") [https://perma.cc/3N67-X2BM (uploaded archive)].
31. *Meet Emma, Our Virtual Assistant*, *supra* note 12.
32. *See* Chapter 5, "Agency Interviews."
33. *See id.*; *cf.* Prentiss Cox & Kathleen Engel, *Student Loan Reform: Rights Under the Law, Incentives Under Contract, and Mission Failure Under ED*, 58 HARV. J. ON LEGIS. 357, 398 (2021).
34. *See* Chapter 5, "Agency Interviews."
35. *See, e.g., Erica, Your Guide by Your Side*, BANK OF AM., https://promo.bankofamerica.com/erica [https://perma.cc/VHJ8-4J2M]; *Azure Health Bot*, MICROSOFT, https://www.microsoft.com/en-us/research/project/health-bot [https://perma.cc/WW86-X3JP].
36. *See* Chapter 5, "Agency Interviews."
37. *See id.*
38. Exec. Order No. 13,985, 86 Fed. Reg. 7009, 7011 (Jan. 20, 2021).
39. *Id.*; *see also* Jeremy Bearer-Friend, *Should the IRS Know Your Race? The Challenge of Colorblind Tax Data*, 73 TAX L. REV. 1, 2 (2019); Dorothy Brown, *Race and Tax: Colorblind No More*, JOTWELL (Feb. 25, 2021), https://tax.jotwell.com/race-and-tax-colorblind-no-more [https://perma.cc/GN3K-Y8K9].
40. Bearer-Friend, *supra* note 39, at 55–56.
41. *See* Chapter 5, "Agency Interviews."
42. *See* Eugene Berko, *3 Reasons Why AI-Powered Customer Service Is the Next Big Thing*, ELEKS, https://eleks.com/blog/artificial-intelligence-customer-service-next-big-thing [https://

perma.cc/V5LD-QS3G] (last updated Apr. 3, 2023); Aakrit Vaish, *Five Reasons Why Chatbots Are the Future of Customer Service*, ENTREPRENEUR (Jan. 5, 2019), https://www.entrepreneur.com/article/325830 [https://perma.cc/6TZV-WFCV].
43. *See American Community Survey (ACS): Why We Ask Questions About ... Race*, U.S. CENSUS BUREAU, https://www.census.gov/acs/www/about/why-we-ask-each-question/race/ [https://perma.cc/87K9-4YW7].
44. *See Interactive Tax Assistant (ITA)*, *supra* note 9.
45. *See Meet Emma, Our Virtual Assistant*, *supra* note 12.
46. *See File Your Taxes for Free*, IRS, https://www.irs.gov/filing/free-file-do-your-federal-taxes-for-free [https://perma.cc/RUY9-NQYD] (last updated Mar. 25, 2024).
47. For further discussion *See* Joshua D. Blank & Leigh Osofsky, *The Inequity of Informal Guidance*, 75 VAND. L. REV. 1093, 1098–99 (2022).
48. Adoption of Recommendations, 87 Fed. Reg. 39798, 39802 (July 5, 2022).
49. *See id.*
50. *See id.* (Recommendation 19).
51. *See id.* (Recommendation 18).
52. *See id.* (Recommendation 11).
53. *See id.*
54. *See id.*; JOSHUA D. BLANK & LEIGH OSOFSKY, AUTOMATED LEGAL GUIDANCE AT FEDERAL AGENCIES (2022) (report to the Administrative Conference of the United States) [hereinafter BLANK & OSOFSKY, GUIDANCE AT FEDERAL AGENCIES], https://www.acus.gov/projects/automated-legal-guidance-federal-agencies [https://perma.cc/4FQF-TKFK]; Joshua D. Blank & Leigh Osofsky, *Automated Legal Guidance*, 106 CORNELL L. REV. 179, 236–37 (2020) [hereinafter Blank & Osofsky, *Automated Legal Guidance*].
55. *See* Blank & Osofsky, *Automated Legal Guidance*, *supra* note 54, at 236–37.
56. *See, e.g., Miller v. Comm'r*, 114 T.C. 184, 194–95 (2000); *United States v. Josephberg*, 562 F.3d 478, 498–500 (2d Cir. 2009); *Carpenter v. United States*, 495 F.2d 175, 184 (5th Cir. 1974); *Adler v. Comm'r*, 330 F.2d 91, 93 (9th Cir. 1964); *Zimmerman v. Comm'r*, 71 T.C. 367, 371 (1978), *aff'd*, 614 F.2d 1294 (2d Cir. 1979) (unpublished table decision); *Johnson v. Comm'r*, 620 F.2d 153, 154–55 (7th Cir. 1980) (per curiam).
57. *Cf., e.g., Michigan v. Bay Mills Indian Cmty.*, 572 U.S. 782, 798 (2014).
58. *See, e.g.*, Fred Ansell, *Unauthorized Conduct of Government Agents*, 53 U. CHI. L. REV. 1026, 1027 (1986); Stephanie Hoffer, *Hobgoblin of Little Minds No More*, 2006 UTAH L. REV. 317, 333 (2006).
59. IRM 4.10.7.2.4 (Jan. 10, 2018).
60. *See id.*
61. *See* IRS News Release IR-2021-202 (Oct. 15, 2021), https://www.irs.gov/newsroom/irs-updates-process-for-frequently-asked-questions-on-new-tax-legislation-and-addresses-reliance-concerns [https://perma.cc/64YP-NE5S].

10

The Future of Agency Communications

Our study of automated legal guidance yields more than just important insights regarding the tools themselves. As highlighted in Chapter 8, many statements regarding the law provided by these tools do not fit neatly within the administrative law framework. This mismatch reflects and contributes to the democracy deficit in administrative law. Thus, our study has broader lessons for how our legal system should conceive of agency interactions with the public going forward. This chapter roots our insights about automated legal guidance in a broader examination of why and how to address the democracy deficit in administrative law.

As this chapter contemplates the future of agency communications, it also explores in greater detail the possibility that technological developments may allow government agencies not only to explain the law to the public using automated tools but also to automate the legal compliance obligations of individuals. While automated legal compliance raises serious concerns, recent examples reveal that it may soon become a powerful tool that agencies can apply broadly under the justifications of administrative efficiency. As we argue, the lessons learned from our study of automated legal guidance are critical to maintaining values such as transparency and legitimacy, as automated compliance expands as a result of perceived benefits like efficiency.

HOW TO ADDRESS THE DEMOCRACY DEFICIT

Automated legal guidance highlights the need to reorient our thinking about how agencies communicate to the public about the law. It is possible to understand how administrative law scholars and agency officials might shrug off problems with automated explanations. It is also possible to understand how the notice-and-comment process has become dominated by interested industry groups,[1] and how explanations that precede and succeed such engagement are tailored to these groups.[2] Further, it is possible to understand how agencies are reticent to be bound by informal statements that they make through automated tools in an attempt to help the public comply with the law,[3] and how courts are reluctant to expand bindingness and penalty protections to informal guidance.[4] Finally, it is also possible to understand how certain parties that are directly targeted by regulations can more easily challenge agency communications than the general public can.[5] However, altogether, this regime is extremely difficult to justify.

Therefore, we offer a new agency communication framework for policymakers. This framework is designed to address the broader democracy deficit that we have observed in relation to automated legal guidance. It is not, however, an attempt to:

- apply the same rules to informal agency engagement as those that apply in formal engagement;
- require notice-and-comment at every turn;[6]
- take the hyper-legalized norms that have, in some ways, perverted the administrative process and expand them to all engagement; or
- expand judicial review.[7]

Instead, the goal of this proposed framework is to infuse agency interactions with the public through automated legal guidance, as well as through other forms of informal guidance, with the sorts of values that were at the heart of the APA prior to hyper-legalization. These values included, among other things, a commitment to transparency, inclusion, and fairness.[8]

As scholars have emphasized, administrative law can and should embrace these values through norms and practices, not just through hyper-legalized, judicially enforceable rules. For instance, Professors Gillian Metzger and Kevin Stack have explored how "internal directives, guidance, and organizational forms ... [are] critical means for ... ensuring accountability within agencies"[9] and how this conception was important when the APA was created.[10] Likewise, Professor Chris Walker has emphasized that many important agency functions operate outside of judicial review, and that it is a mistake to focus myopically on a "court-centric theory of administrative law."[11] Instead, Walker advises that we must find safeguards in agency practices and procedures that lie beyond judicial review.[12]

Agencies should provide more participatory formulations of automated legal guidance, irrespective of how this guidance is characterized under the administrative law framework. For instance, when an agency is creating centralized explanations of the law that it will offer broadly to the public, these explanations should be created through careful involvement of counsel. When a rule does require notice-and-comment procedures, the agency should structure the process to engage broadly with the public prior to getting bogged down in industry concerns.[13] To do so, the agency should make clear the underlying values at stake with the rule formulation and how particular decisions may affect the public interest.[14]

Even with informal interactions with the public, such as through websites, tweets, and automated explanations, there should be an internal review process within the agency to decide when statements should be modified or amended, and legal counsel should be involved in this review. This is especially important as these forms of communication become more common.

Further, agencies and courts alike should be more open to arguments regarding reasonable reliance on agency statements in automated legal guidance, as well as in other informal communications. These approaches, and others like them, should recognize that administration of the law affects the public at large, not just sophisticated parties. Agencies should articulate and follow a clear set of norms and practices that suggest as much.

In embracing this framework, we are aware of and sympathetic to concerns that this process can be used as a stealth way to weaken agencies. For instance, Professor Nicholas Bagley has forcefully argued against excessive procedural requirements in administrative law, since "proceduralism drains agency resources, introduces delay, and thwarts agency action. To that extent, it puts a thumb on the scale in favor of the status quo; by itself, that's enough to give administrative law a libertarian, anti-statist cast."[15] Likewise, tax law scholars have recently considered how applying administrative proceduralism to tax administration can have pernicious effects on the IRS's ability to administer the tax law and raise revenue.[16]

In some ways, this concern – and the broader fight over administrative doctrines as a political tool for dismantling the administrative state[17] – is a mere continuation of the focus in the New Deal era on proceduralism as a proxy for a deeper fight over the role of the administrative state. The worry, and it is not unfounded, is that pushing additional proceduralism is really a way to bury agencies by making them ineffectual. The worry is reasonably heightened in an era in which there is a very real and ongoing threat to the administrative state that exists at the highest levels of government.[18]

While we are sympathetic to such concerns, we believe that a response that demands uncritical acceptance of all aspects of the current administrative state is the wrong one. We believe that the administrative state plays an essential role in US governance – one that should be protected. But we also believe that the administrative law framework, as it has evolved over time, does not make sufficient space for administrative communications with the general public.

Why Focus on Automated Legal Guidance?

Agency communications with the general public, including explanations of the law, appear in a variety of different resources, media, and platforms. These formats range from oral communication by agency officials to static, printed publications, and from FAQs appearing on agency websites to interactive automated legal guidance tools. Policymakers must devote their immediate attention to the types of automated explanations that are most likely to lead to use and reliance by parties who lack access to resources such as legal counsel.

Policymakers should first address statements from automated legal guidance and other online tools on agency websites. Specifically, they should begin by applying our reforms to chatbots, virtual assistants, and other online tools offered and maintained by agencies for use by the public.

As we have shown, members of the public access these tools due to the speed and efficiency with which they can provide information.[19] In 2020, USCIS, for instance, reported that its chatbot Emma successfully responded to more than thirty-five million inquiries from more than eleven million users.[20] USCIS also described Emma as a "very useful tool for many of [its] applicants and the general public" because of its ability to provide responses to users' inquiries.[21] In contrast, the agency's printed publications about immigration rules often include dozens of pages of dense text that people must read and interpret to find relevant information.[22]

To strengthen the administrative state, policymakers should reorient administrative law in two ways: (1) embrace agency engagement with the general public more robustly and (2) provide norms and practices around it. Indeed, such a reorientation may be critical in shoring up support for the administrative state.[23] Below we illustrate core features of our proposed framework for addressing the democracy deficit. The chief elements of this framework are (1) public participation in the development of agency communications and (2) the opportunity for the public to use these communications to challenge agency action.

Public Participation

To address the democracy deficit, agency officials should introduce procedures that would allow members of the public to participate in the issuance of agency communications, including automated explanations of the law. Two primary aspects of these new procedures are highlighted in this section: (1) the opportunity for public comment and (2) the implementation of external advisory councils.

The goal of these recommendations is to provide members of the public with the ability to contribute to the development of automated explanations. This would yield greater parity with the participatory opportunities that are currently available to sophisticated parties and industry insiders.

Opportunity for Public Comment

Agency officials should offer members of the public opportunities to comment on agencies' automated legal guidance and other informal explanations of the law, especially if they expect people to reasonably rely on automated explanations when attempting to comply with legal obligations. This could be implemented by requiring agencies to (1) post automated explanations with a "draft" label on their websites and (2) offer the public an opportunity to submit comments on these drafts.

The Food and Drug Administration (FDA), in its "good guidance practices," offers a model for this type of procedure. It invites members of the public to submit comments on its "draft Level 1 guidances," which serve one or more of the following purposes:

- They set forth initial interpretations of significant regulatory requirements,
- They describe substantial changes to earlier FDA interpretations, or
- They address complex or controversial issues.[24]

An agency can also solicit feedback from the public on its automated explanations. Then, it can issue revised versions of those explanations that address inaccurate or misleading statements. Some agencies already do this. For example, the IRS hosts a website with an online form that members of the public can use to submit comments on published tax forms, instructions, and publications.[25] Similarly, the FDA allows members of the public to submit comments on any guidance documents and states that FDA officials review all comments and revise the documents if necessary.[26] Each of these models would increase the public's ability to contribute to the development, publication, and revision of automated explanations of the law.

One reaction to our proposal is that members of the public may not be equipped to identify inaccuracies and deviations in automated explanations, which may make it unlikely that they can offer meaningful feedback to agency officials. This response, however, overlooks the possibility that, by offering the opportunity for public comment on automated explanations, agencies may encourage participation not only from the public at large but also from representatives of public interest organizations, experts, and other intermediaries.

For instance, in 2020, at the onset of the COVID-19 pandemic, Congress enacted the CARES Act, which provided "economic impact" payments to joint-filing married taxpayers, as long as their adjusted gross income did not exceed certain thresholds.[27] At the time of enactment, many taxpayers, including individuals whose spouses had died that year, questioned whether they were eligible to receive the payments.[28]

In response to this confusion, the IRS posted an FAQ on its website that included the following question: "**Q10: Does someone who has died qualify for the Payment?**"[29] The IRS responded to this question with the following answer: "**A10: No. A Payment made to someone who died before receipt of the Payment should be returned to the IRS by following the instructions in the Q&A about repayments.**"[30] Even though the IRS's FAQ lacked the force of formal law, within six months of it appearing on the IRS website in May 2020, taxpayers returned nearly 60,000 economic impact payments, totaling more than $72 million that the agency had distributed to deceased taxpayers.[31]

Despite the IRS's strong public statement on this issue, former government officials and other commentators questioned the agency's interpretation of this provision of the CARES Act.[32] Nina Olson, former National Taxpayer Advocate, analyzed the requirements of the newly enacted statute and the IRS FAQ.[33] Olson published detailed criticism of the IRS's claim that individuals were ineligible to receive this payment if they were deceased in 2020, even though they had been eligible individuals in 2018 or 2019.³⁴ She also commented that, in 2008, when Congress enacted stimulus legislation during the financial crisis and used the same statutory language as in the CARES Act, the IRS adopted a contrary position in its FAQs regarding payments of stimulus checks to deceased taxpayers.³⁵ Following Olson's criticism, several tax practitioners agreed that, according to the statutory language, as long as taxpayers were "eligible individuals" in 2018 or 2019, they should be entitled to the payments in 2020, even if they had died that year.³⁶

If agencies routinely offered opportunities for public comment on automated explanations prior to their distribution, representatives of public interest organizations, including experts in the relevant legal areas, could offer similar evaluation and criticism of them, which could lead to significant improvements to guidance for the public.

External Advisory Councils

Agency officials should also solicit participation from external advisory councils and other groups in developing automated explanations of the law and should not expect internal review alone to identify discrepancies between these explanations and the formal law. During our research, we found that many agencies evaluate the efficacy of these tools by measuring the "I don't know rate" – the frequency with which the tools cannot answer user inquiries.³⁷ This information alone cannot identify situations where an automated legal guidance tool provides users with an answer that deviates, sometimes significantly, from the underlying statutes, regulations, and judicial decisions.

Many federal agencies receive advice from external advisory groups, such as the Department of Education's National Board for Education Sciences,³⁸ the IRS's Internal Revenue Service Advisory Council,³⁹ and the FDA's multiple advisory committees.⁴⁰ Each of these groups consists of experts, third-party advisors, and members of the public. Some agencies, such as the IRS, appear to include these external institutions in discussion of certain forms of automated explanations, such as IRS publications and forms,⁴¹ while others do not. Providing external advisory councils with a role in issuing automated explanations allows their members to voice concerns, questions, and criticism on behalf of individual users and their advisors.

A likely objection to an increased role of the public in drafting and reviewing automated explanations of the law is that it could prevent agencies from providing this guidance quickly and efficiently. There are, however, several responses to this criticism.

If agency officials expect members of the public to reasonably rely on these informal agency explanations to comply with their legal obligations, they should increase opportunities for the public to evaluate them. The types of explanations that could merit this treatment can include those that appear in FAQs that appear on agency websites, automated legal guidance tools, and printed publications.

The agency can introduce reasonable limits to public input. For example, it does not need to be duplicative: if members of the public participate in the drafting of a new explanation that will appear in automated legal guidance, there is no need for their input if the identical information will be posted on the agency's Facebook or other social media accounts. Further, in situations where immediate guidance is necessary, such as to address the enactment of new legislation, agency officials can always include a warning and note that the guidance may be subject to future revision when it posts the guidance online.

Finally, and perhaps most importantly, while greater public participation could result in processes that delay issuing automated explanations, it could also improve the accuracy and usability of this guidance. Indeed, a delay due to careful deliberation of the content of the guidance is warranted when the public is likely to rely on it.

Public Challenge

Another opportunity for narrowing the democracy deficit in administrative law is to ensure that, *after* agencies' automated tools have provided explanations of the law, challenges to those explanations may occur on the public's behalf, and agencies will have an obligation to respond to them. Without the potential for *ex post* challenge by an individual or entity acting on behalf of the public, agencies will have little incentive to adjust explanations of the law that deviate from the underlying formal law.[42] If these explanations do not face challenges, most people will simply follow them, whether they are beneficial or adverse to individuals' interests. All of that said, these challenges do not necessarily have to come from outside the agency. Indeed, one of the most effective ways to increase scrutiny of automated explanations is to delegate this task to ombuds offices within agencies, which can act on the public's behalf.

There are currently limited opportunities for parties to raise formal challenges to automated explanations that are inconsistent with the formal law. When the formal law is ambiguous, automated explanations may resolve the ambiguity in ways that are detrimental to the interests of members of the public and may, as a practical matter, serve as binding law. Where an automated explanation deviates from the formal law in ways that are adverse to individuals' interests, in most cases, individuals cannot pursue formal challenges until an enforcement action by the agency occurs.[43] Additionally, when agencies issue explanations that are unfavorable to members of the public, those who are impacted are generally unable to participate in class action lawsuits against the agency because their factual or legal circumstances are too divergent from one another.[44] Further, sometimes automated explanations deviate from the formal law in ways that are favorable to individuals. Not only do the impacted parties not have an incentive to question the agency, but others also lack standing to pursue legal action to ensure that agencies follow the underlying formal law.[45]

To address this deficiency, Congress could mandate that federal agency ombuds offices review agencies' automated explanations and issue regular reports that note inconsistencies with the formal law and require agencies to respond to any challenges included in these reports. These ombuds offices are designed "to foster government as accessible and responsive to the needs and concerns of both external and internal stakeholders" and "serve as a 'voice' to and within government institutions."[46] As a 2016 study by ACUS has noted, ombuds offices that "assist people in 'navigating through the agency, fellow employees, industry, and the public'" have proliferated in recent years.[47] "Advocate [o]mbuds offices," as ACUS has described them, are both externally and internally facing entities that survey constituents and assess timeliness and cost of resolving constituent concerns.[48] One of the primary impacts of these offices is to foster better communication and compliance with laws and regulations by agencies.[49]

Some of the federal agency ombuds offices use an "advocate" model.[50] One prominent example of this is the IRS's National Taxpayer Advocate, which "looks at patterns in taxpayer issues to determine if an IRS process or procedure is causing a problem, and if so, to recommend steps to resolve the problem."[51] Another example is the Small Business Administration National Ombudsman, which rates federal agencies on their dealings with small businesses.[52] In addition, the US Securities and Exchange Commission's Office of Investor Advocate "analyze[s] the potential impact on investors of proposed regulatory changes, identif[ies] problems that investors have with investment products and financial service providers, and recommend[s] changes to statutes and regulations for the benefit of investors."[53] As an ACUS study on this topic noted, in most cases, Congress has delegated specific tasks to these internal agency ombuds offices that prompt them to advocate for systemic change within agencies on the public's behalf.[54]

Several attributes of advocate ombuds offices illustrate why this model would be an effective means of ensuring review of automated explanations of the law. First, Congress can require these offices to review specific agency activities. Second, because these offices are external-facing, they can solicit concerns and questions from members of the public regarding automated explanations.[55] Third, because they are also internal-facing entities, they can investigate the reasoning behind automated explanations of the law by questioning agency officials involved in drafting them.[56] Fourth, Congress can also require the following: (1) that these offices report to Congress regularly, (2) that these reports document concerns regarding automated explanations, and (3) that agencies respond in writing to concerns raised by these reports.

Unlike other forms of internal review and investigation, this entire reporting and responding sequence would occur in public view, thereby enhancing agency transparency with regards to automated explanations. Indeed, if Congress were to require federal agency ombuds offices to review automated explanations of the law as part of their regular duties, it could transform many of these offices into advocate ombuds offices, ensuring that they truly represent the public interest.

But aren't there other federal offices with investigative powers that could review automated explanations of the law? There are, for example, more than seventy federal inspectors general who operate within federal agencies that could review automated explanations to determine whether they describe the formal law accurately and objectively.[57] Such a task, however, may not necessarily be within the purview of these inspectors general: While they provide valuable oversight of agency conduct, they primarily focus on waste, fraud, and abuse within agencies.[58] The substance of agency communications with the public, therefore, would not be suitable for them to oversee. In addition, compared to advocate ombuds offices, inspectors general are internal-facing. They do not investigate user experience, customer service, and similar types of issues that affect routine interactions between members of the public and agencies.

Another possible entity that could review automated explanations is the US Government Accountability Office (GAO), a nonpartisan agency that provides Congress with "fact-based information to help the government save money and work more efficiently."[59] However, there is an important limitation to the GAO's ability to do this effectively: specifically, officials in this office lack expertise and familiarity regarding the formal law that applies to specific agencies. When the GAO has reviewed agency publications in the past, its results have been incomplete. For example, in the early 1990s, the GAO reviewed IRS publications and failed to identify the need for any substantive changes.[60] However, the GAO methodology in this review was quite limited in that it reviewed only four IRS publications.[61] We believe, therefore, that advocate ombuds offices are the best suited to perform this important work.

FROM AUTOMATED LEGAL GUIDANCE TO AUTOMATED COMPLIANCE

As we consider lessons from automated legal guidance to think about the future of agency communications, it is important as well to focus on a new transformation on the horizon: automated compliance. As we mentioned in Chapter 6, through this emerging development, the government can use automation technology to apply the law directly to, and on behalf of, the public, without needing to explain the law to the public. For instance, it is certainly possible to integrate collecting information from taxpayers with filling out their tax returns for them. TurboTax and other private sector firms already do this. Through the IRS Free File program, the IRS provides the same services to eligible, qualifying taxpayers through a "public-private partnership between the IRS and many tax preparation and filing software industry companies who provide their online tax preparation and filing for free."[62] It is possible to imagine automated legal guidance becoming even more sophisticated. In the tax context, for instance, one could imagine a scenario in which taxpayers do not even have to answer questions to have tax software fill out their tax returns. Rather, artificial intelligence could examine taxpayers' financial and other tax-relevant transactions (including, for instance, business trips and medical events) by monitoring email, bank records, and physical locations to seamlessly fill out the person's tax return.[63]

There are many other potential applications of automated legal compliance. Consider, for example, the Free Application for Federal Student Aid (FAFSA), which most colleges and universities in the US use to award financial aid to students.[64] As applicants and their parents and guardians are aware, the FAFSA has historically required detailed information about families' assets and finances, including tax returns and other personal information. To lessen this burden on students and their families, Congress enacted two major pieces of legislation in 2019 and 2021. Under the Fostering Undergraduate Talent by Unlocking Resources for Education Act (FUTURE Act), Congress amended the federal tax privacy rules to allow the IRS to provide information from the tax returns of FAFSA applicants and their families directly to the Department of Education.[65] This was followed by the FAFSA Simplification Act, which introduced significant changes to the formulas that Federal Student Aid was required to apply to determine the "Student Aid Index" (formerly the "Expected Family Contribution") of each FAFSA applicant.[66] As a result of this legislation, the Department of Education spent the next few years revamping the FAFSA online form, finally releasing it to the public in January 2024.[67] After applicants entered some personal information and then clicked a button to provide their consent, the IRS shared tax return information with the Department of Education quickly and automatically. According to the Department of Education, instead of the days and even weeks that it took to fill out the prior version of the FAFSA form, most applicants could now complete the new FAFSA in "less than an hour."[68]

The new automated FAFSA appeared to ease a major legal compliance headache for tens of millions of students and their families – but not for long. Under the FAFSA Simplification Act, every year the Department of Education is required to adjust for inflation certain amounts that are relevant to the Student Aid Index. This includes the "income protection allowance," which is the amount of income that is not counted in determining students' ability to pay for college.[69] In the Fall of 2023, however, Department of Education officials commented that they would not be able to introduce the required inflation adjustments in time for the new 2024–2025 FAFSA form, even though Congress had included this requirement in the FAFSA Simplification Act.[70] This failure by the Department of Education to make the inflation adjustments resulted in some concern that many students would receive lower financial aid awards from colleges and universities. Despite criticism from university financial aid offices and trade organizations, however, the Department of Education went ahead and launched the new FAFSA form in January 2024 – without the required inflation adjustments.[71]

This, however, was not the end of the story. After several weeks of media reports, the Department of Education eventually announced that it would revise the online form. In late January 2024, agency officials announced that they would make updates to the new FAFSA, which many families had already completed, to include the required inflation adjustments.[72] According to government officials, the original 2024–2025 FAFSA form, which did not include the inflation adjustments, would have resulted in an aggregate loss of $1.8 billion in student financial aid.[73] The time delay resulting from the Department of Education's decision to deviate from the FAFSA Simplification Act's requirements, and then to follow the law eventually, caused many colleges and universities to announce that their financial aid awards might not be ready at the time of admission decisions. During this time, millions of students faced uncertainty regarding whether and how much financial aid they would receive and, in some cases, whether they would be able to afford to enroll.[74]

The saga of the 2024–2025 FAFSA form illustrates how automation can result in even less transparency regarding agency decisions than in the case of chatbots, virtual assistants, and other automated tools. When the Department of Education automated the process of transferring applicants' tax and financial information from the IRS directly to the Department of Education, it essentially transformed the FAFSA form into a black box. Individual applicants no longer entered their personal tax information manually and, as a result, could not view as many of the steps that the website would take to calculate each family's expected contribution to college costs. Against this backdrop of automation and opacity, the Department of Education deviated from the formal law regarding key steps in the process. It automatically used tax return information to calculate the key figure, the Student Aid Index, without showing the internal workings of the website and without acknowledging that it was not applying the required inflation adjustments. The decision to ignore the required inflation adjustments in the automated FAFSA became public only after agency officials provided responses to questions about these adjustments in an online webinar.

Especially in the case of automated systems, agency officials should be required to provide the public with clear advance notice of instances in which they deviate from the formal law, apply their own interpretations of unsettled or ambiguous law, or revise their prior interpretations and methodologies. Legislators and other policymakers should also introduce requirements for agencies to offer representatives of the public opportunities to participate in agencies' development of automated systems and to submit formal challenges of their outputs.

Without reform measures focused on transparency, public participation, and public challenge, automation could further exacerbate the democracy deficit in the administrative state. If agencies no longer explain legal rules and requirements, but rather just introduce systems that implement them in an automated fashion, members of the public will become even further detached from the underlying formal law. At the same time, government agencies may increasingly apply their own interpretations of the law through automated processes and systems, such as the Department of Education's initial decision in 2024 to ignore statutory requirements.

Automation will prevent most individuals from noticing situations where agencies deviate from the underlying statutes and regulations and will discourage members of the public from challenging the government's application of the law to their specific circumstances. The recommendations in this chapter are thus relevant to both the present use of automated legal guidance to explain complex law to the public and a future of automated compliance, in which agencies simply apply complex law to the public without explanation.

NOTES

1. *See, e.g.,* Wendy E. Wagner, *Administrative Law, Filter Failure, and Information Capture*, 59 DUKE L. J. 1321, 1400 (2010).
2. *See* Alec Webley, *Seeing Through a Preamble, Darkly: Administrative Verbosity in an Age of Populism and "Fake News*," 70 ADMIN. L. REV. 1 (2018).
3. *See generally* Emily Cauble, *Detrimental Reliance on IRS Guidance*, 2015 WIS. L. REV. 421 (2015).
4. *See, e.g., Miller v. Comm'r*, 114 T.C. 184, 194–95 (2000).
5. *See, e.g.,* Nina A. Mendelson, *Regulatory Beneficiaries and Informal Agency Policymaking*, 92 CORNELL L. REV. 397, 414–15 (2007).
6. *Cf., e.g.,* David A. Weisbach, *Against Anti-Tax Exceptionalism*, 4 (University of Chicago Coase-Sandor Institute for Law and Economics, Working Paper No. 967, 2023), https://ssrn.com/abstract=4328821 [https://perma.cc/HD52-9W2N (uploaded archive)].
7. *Cf., e.g.,* Brian Galle & Stephen Shay, *Admin Law and the Crisis of Tax Administration*, 101 N. C. L. REV. 1645, 1654 (2023); Weisbach, *supra* note 6; *see also* Susan C. Morse, *Old Regs: The Default Six-Year Time Bar for Administrative Procedure Claims*, 31 GEO. MASON L. REV. 191, 192 (2023). For scholarship that helped set the stage for these concerns, see, for example, Stephanie Hunter McMahon, *The Perfect Process Is the Enemy of the Good Tax: Tax's Exceptional Regulatory Process*, 35 VA. TAX. REV. 553 (2015); Lawrence Zelenak, *Maybe Just a Little Special, After All?*, 63 DUKE L. J. 1897 (2014).
8. *See, e.g.,* Kathryn E. Kovacs, *From Presidential Administration to Bureaucratic Dictatorship*, 135 HARV. L. REV. F. 104, 107 (2021).
9. Gillian E. Metzger & Kevin M. Stack, *Internal Administrative Law*, 115 MICH. L. REV. 1239 (2017).
10. *Id.* at 1266–78.
11. Christopher J. Walker, *Administrative Law without Courts*, 65 UCLA L. REV. 1620, 1639 (2018); *see also* Weisbach, *supra* note 6, at 62.
12. Walker, *supra* note 11, at 1639–40.
13. *See, e.g.,* Robert B. Reich, *Public Administration and Public Deliberation: An Interpretive Essay*, 94 YALE L. J. 1617, 1632 (1985). For a more recent suggestion that agencies are still capable of broad-based pre-notice-and-comment engagement, see, for example, Press Release, US Department of the Treasury, Treasury Seeks Public Input on Additional Clean Energy Tax Provisions of the Inflation Reduction Act, (Nov. 3, 2022), https://home.treasury.gov/news/press-releases/jy1077 [https://perma.cc/6HEU-DFEF]; *see also* Michael Sant'Ambrogio & Glen Staszewski, *Democratizing Rule Development*, 98 WASH. U. L. REV. 793, 816–31 (2021).
14. *See* Wagner, *supra* note 1, at 1417–18.
15. Nicholas Bagley, *The Procedure Fetish*, 118 MICH. L. REV. 345, 363 (2019).

16. *See, e.g.*, Galle & Shay, *supra* note 7; Weisbach, *supra* note 6.
17. *See, e.g.*, Lisa Heinzerling, *How Government Ends*, BOS. REV. (Sept. 28, 2022), https://www.bostonreview.net/articles/how-government-ends [https://perma.cc/BW5B-REG9].
18. *Id.*
19. JOSHUA D. BLANK & LEIGH OSOFSKY, AUTOMATED LEGAL GUIDANCE AT FEDERAL AGENCIES 30 (2022) (report to the Admin. Conf. of the US) [hereinafter BLANK & OSOFSKY, GUIDANCE AT FEDERAL AGENCIES], https://www.acus.gov/projects/automated-legal-guidance-federal-agencies [https://perma.cc/4FQF-TKFK].
20. Kathleen Walch & Ronald Schmelzer, AI Today Podcast, #125: *Emma – Immigration Chatbot: Interview with Courtney Winship, US Citizenship and Immigration Services (USCIS)*, COGNILYTICA, at 02:26 (Jan. 22, 2020), https://www.cognilytica.com/2020/01/22/ai-today-podcast-125-emma-immigration-chatbot-interview-with-courtney-winship-us-citizenship-and-immigration-service-uscis.
21. *Id.* at 03:01.
22. *See, e.g.*, U.S. CITIZENSHIP & IMMIGR. SERVS., POLICY MANUAL (2023), https://www.uscis.gov/book/export/html/68600 [https://perma.cc/E9KQ-BF5S].
23. *See, e.g.*, Jody Freeman & Sharon Jacobs, *Structural Deregulation*, 135 HARV. L. REV. 585, 664 (2021).
24. *Fact Sheet: FDA Good Guidance Practices*, U.S. FOOD & DRUG ADMIN. (Dec. 4, 2017), https://www.fda.gov/about-fda/transparency-initiative/fact-sheet-fda-good-guidance-practices [https://perma.cc/E6RP-VRAK (uploaded archive)].
25. *Comment on Tax Forms and Publications*, IRS, https://www.irs.gov/forms-pubs/comment-on-tax-forms-and-publications [https://perma.cc/R843-KPLY] (last updated Jan. 31, 2024).
26. *See Fact Sheet: FDA Good Guidance Practices, supra* note 24.
27. Coronavirus Aid, Relief, and Economic Security (CARES) Act, Pub. L. No. 116-136, § 2201, 134 Stat. 281, 335 (2020) (codified at I.R.C. § 6428).
28. *See* Kate Davidson & Richard Rubin, *Stimulus Checks Sent to Dead Relatives Should Be Returned, Mnuchin Says*, WALL ST. J. (Apr. 28, 2020, 3:48 PM), https://www.wsj.com/articles/stimulus-checks-sent-to-dead-relatives-should-be-returned-mnuchin-says-11588103323 [https://perma.cc/7WCS-P287 (private, uploaded archive)]; William Cummings, *'You're Not Supposed to Keep That Payment': Mnuchin Wants Stimulus Money Given to Dead Taxpayers Returned*, USA TODAY, https://www.usatoday.com/story/news/politics/2020/04/29/steve-mnuchin-wants-stimulus-given-dead-people-returned/3046434001 [https://perma.cc/J3TP-UCH3] (last updated Apr. 29, 2020, 4:33 PM).
29. *See* Nina E. Olson, *The Uncertainty of Death and Taxes: Economic Stimulus Payments to Deceased Individuals*, TAX NOTES: PROCEDURALLY TAXING (May 11, 2020), https://procedurallytaxing.com/the-uncertainty-of-death-and-taxes-economic-stimulus-payments-to-deceased-individuals/ [https://perma.cc/HEM3-9JYG].
30. *See id.* (emphasis omitted).
31. TREASURY INSPECTOR GEN. FOR TAX ADMIN., 2021-46-034, IMPLEMENTATION OF ECONOMIC IMPACT PAYMENTS 6 (May 24, 2021), https://www.oversight.gov/sites/default/files/oig-reports/TIGTA/202146034fr.pdf [https://perma.cc/SAQ9-6WVZ].
32. *See, e.g.*, Olson, *supra* note 29; David M. Fogel, *Must Economic Impact Payments to Deceased Individuals Be Returned?*, 167 TAX NOTES FED. 1719, 1721 (2020); Patrick W. Thomas, *Analyzing the IRS FAQs on Incarcerated and Non-Resident Taxpayers*, TAX NOTES: PROCEDURALLY TAXING (May 12, 2020), https://procedurallytaxing.com/analyzing-the-irs-faqs-on-incarcerated-and-non-resident-taxpayers/ [https://perma.cc/7DXE-T842].
33. Olson, *supra* note 29.

34. *Id.*
35. *Id.*
36. *See* Fogel, *supra* note 32; Thomas, *supra* note 32.
37. *See* BLANK & OSOFSKY, GUIDANCE AT FEDERAL AGENCIES, *supra* note 19, at 27.
38. *See National Board. for Education Sciences*, INST. OF EDUC. SCI., https://ies.ed.gov/director/board/ [https://perma.cc/EU94-75W8].
39. *See Internal Revenue Service Advisory Council (IRSAC)*, IRS, https://www.irs.gov/tax-professionals/internal-revenue-service-advisory-council-irsac [https://perma.cc/LZ96-DCK5] (last updated Jan. 26, 2024).
40. *See Advisory Committees*, U.S. FOOD & DRUG ADMIN., https://www.fda.gov/advisory-committees [https://perma.cc/YZ74-LBS2 (uploaded archive)].
41. *See* IRM 1.1.13.6.4 (Jan. 24, 2023).
42. *Cf., e.g.*, Galle & Shay, *supra* note 7, at 37.
43. *See, e.g., Scholl v. Mnuchin*, 494 F. Supp. 3d 661, 670–71, 692 (N.D. Cal. 2020).
44. *See id.* at 670, 679 (addressing characteristics of class members).
45. *See* Lawrence Zelenak, *Custom and the Rule of Law in the Administration of the Income Tax*, 62 DUKE L. J. 829, 847 (2012).
46. *See* CAROLE S. HOUK, ET AL., A REAPPRAISAL – THE NATURE AND VALUE OF OMBUDSMEN IN FEDERAL AGENCIES: PART 1: EXECUTIVE SUMMARY 23 (2016) (report to the Admin. Conf. of the US), https://www.acus.gov/sites/default/files/documents/PART%201_Executive%20Summary%20%28ACUS%29%2011.16.16_0.pdf [https://perma.cc/7LPU-YPR2].
47. *Id.* at 26.
48. *See id.* at 70.
49. *Id.*
50. *Id.* at 70–71.
51. *Who We Are*, TAXPAYER ADVOC. SERV., https://www.taxpayeradvocate.irs.gov/about-us/ [https://perma.cc/XNR5-2RRW].
52. *Office of the National Ombudsman*, U.S. SMALL BUS. ADMIN., https://www.sba.gov/about-sba/oversight-advocacy/office-national-ombudsman [https://perma.cc/B36J-8LRT] (last updated Mar. 18, 2024).
53. *Office of the Investor Advocate*, U.S. SEC. & EXCH. COMM'N, https://www.sec.gov/advocate [https://perma.cc/RX78-6KA8] (last updated Feb. 8, 2017).
54. *See* Houk et al., *supra* note 46, at 6, 11.
55. *See id.* at 73.
56. *See id.* at 49–50.
57. COUNCIL OF THE INSPECTORS GEN. ON INTEGRITY & EFFICIENCY, THE INSPECTORS GENERAL 1, 11 (2014), https://www.ignet.gov/sites/default/files/files/IG_Authorities_Paper_-_Final_6-11-14.pdf [https://perma.cc/3NED-EV6C].
58. *See id.* at 1.
59. *About*, GAO: U.S. GOV'T ACCOUNTABILITY OFF., https://www.gao.gov/about [https://perma.cc/Y5NH-CCYT].
60. *See* U.S. GEN. ACCT. OFF., GAO/GGD-93-72, TAX ADMINISTRATION: SELECTED IRS FORMS, PUBLICATIONS, AND NOTICES COULD BE IMPROVED 1, 4 (1993), https://www.gao.gov/assets/ggd-93-72.pdf [https://perma.cc/25W8-ZYXC].
61. *See id.* at 4.
62. *File Your Taxes for Free*, IRS, https://www.irs.gov/filing/free-file-do-your-federal-taxes-for-free [https://perma.cc/RUY9-NQYD] (last updated Mar. 25, 2024); *Free File Alliance: Partnered with the IRS to Help Taxpayers E-file*, FREE FILE, https://freefilealliance.org/ [https://perma.cc/RR6S-N3QC].

63. *See, e.g.*, Michael Hatfield, *Taxation and Surveillance: An Agenda*, 17 YALE J. L. & TECH. 319, 340–50 (2015).
64. *FAFSA Form*, FED. STUDENT AID, https://studentaid.gov/h/apply-for-aid/fafsa [https://perma.cc/YW5B-WAP4 (uploaded archive)].
65. Fostering Undergraduate Talent by Unlocking Resources for Education (FUTURE) Act, Pub. L. No. 116-91, 133 Stat. 1189 (2019) (codified at I.R.C. § 6103; 20 U.S.C. § 1098h).
66. FAFSA Simplification Act, Pub. L. No. 116-260, §§ 701–702, 134 Stat. 1182, 3137–91 (2021); FAFSA Simplification Act Technical Corrections Act, Pub. L. No. 117-203, §§ 101–104, 136 Stat. 49, 819–21 (2022).
67. *FAFSA Form, supra* note 64; Press Release, US Department of Education, US Department of Education Announces Over 1 Million 2024–2025 FAFSA Forms Successfully Submitted and Form Now Available 24/7 for Students and Families (Jan. 8, 2024), https://www.ed.gov/news/press-releases/us-department-education-announces-over-1-million-2024-2025-fafsa-forms-successfully-submitted-and-form-now-available-247-students-and-families [https://perma.cc/3VKW-BW9Y].
68. *How Long Will It Take to Fill Out the FAFSA® Form?*, FED. STUDENT AID, https://studentaid.gov/help/how-long [https://perma.cc/2WG3-DB7R (uploaded archive)].
69. FAFSA Simplification Act, Pub. L. No. 116-260, § 702, 134 Stat. 1182, 3138–91 (2021); *See* BENJAMIN COLLINS & CASSANDRA DORTCH, CONGR. RSCH. SERV., R46909, THE FAFSA SIMPLIFICATION ACT 6–7 (2022), https://crsreports.congress.gov/product/pdf/R/R46909 [https://perma.cc/YFP5-YNSA].
70. *See* Danielle Douglas-Gabriel, *An Error in the FAFSA Could Lower Financial Aid for College Students*, WASH. POST (Dec. 1, 2023, 11:17 AM), https://www.washingtonpost.com/education/2023/12/01/fafsa-income-allowance-protection-calculation-error/ [https://perma.cc/C8TP-QQLQ (private archive)].
71. *See* Nat'l Ass'n of Student Fin. Aid Adm'rs, Comment Letter on proposed 2024–2025 Free Application for Federal Student Aid (FAFSA®) (Oct. 16, 2023), https://www.nasfaa.org/uploads/documents/2024-25DraftFAFSAcomments_30day-2.pdf [https://perma.cc/72F8-FMKN]; Cory Turner, *The FAFSA Rollout Has Been Rough on Students: The Biggest Problem Is Yet to Come*, NPR (Jan. 9, 2024, 5:00 AM), https://www.npr.org/2024/01/09/1222664638/fafsa-student-financial-aid-college [https://perma.cc/2PBR-NU9S].
72. *See* Cory Turner, *Exclusive: The Education Department Says It Will Fix Its $1.8 Billion FAFSA Mistake*, NPR (Jan. 23, 2024, 5:25 AM), https://www.npr.org/2024/01/23/1226406495/families-colleges-remain-limbo-education-department-promises-fix-fafsa-mistake [https://perma.cc/SBL4-XVFZ].
73. *See id.*
74. *See* Jessica Dickler, *FAFSA Inflation Fix May Delay Financial Aid Letters, Education Department Says*, CNBC, https://www.cnbc.com/2024/01/30/fafsa-inflation-fix-may-delay-financial-aid-letters-education-dept.html [https://perma.cc/SBW4-CVTV] (last updated Jan. 30, 2024, 1:41PM); Erica L. Green and Zach Montague, *Inside the Blunders That Plunged the College Admission Season into Disarray*, N.Y. TIMES (Mar. 13, 2024), https://www.nytimes.com/2024/03/13/us/politics/fafsa-college-admissions.html [https://perma.cc/9T6Y-4488 (private, uploaded archive)].

Conclusion

We closed Chapter 10 by describing a startling vision of the future of governance. Technological change may soon increase the likelihood that federal agencies will not only provide automated explanations of the law but will also begin to automate the application of the law itself. This possibility raises the prospect of agency officials making significant decisions about how the law applies to each of us in ways that are difficult for us to observe, let alone challenge.

This vision threatens our conceptions of the transparency and legitimacy of governance while also requiring us to think carefully about how, if at all, our system of administrative law protects the public in a world in which automation becomes the norm. As we have shown, at present, administrative law fails to adequately contemplate or consider agency explanations of the law to the public. This lack of attention creates a democracy deficit in administrative law, which threatens to widen the more that agencies use technology to automate legal compliance.

This development originates from a phenomenon that is already occurring, and which is the principal subject of this book – automated legal guidance. As we describe, administrative agencies are using chatbots, virtual assistants, and other automated tools to explain how federal law applies to the public. The result is that, with a few clicks of buttons, you can receive an "answer" from the IRS about whether you can claim a certain tax deduction or whether you must include an item in gross income. With similar ease and rapidity, you can receive information from USCIS about how the immigration law applies to your particularized circumstances. Indeed, a friendly virtual assistant, "Emma," will present you with this information in response to your natural language questions. Many other federal agencies, such as FSA, respond in a similar way to your inquiries, or are in the process of developing and improving technology to do so soon.

This transformation brings some important benefits. Before technological innovation and automation, the public had far fewer opportunities to learn about how the federal law applied to their individual circumstances. Getting this information may have required a trip to a lawyer's office, or at least a phone consultation with a lawyer. But not everyone has the ability, or resources, to meet with a lawyer to request information about how the complex federal legal system applies to their circumstances. In this way, agencies' automation of legal guidance helps to broaden access to the federal legal system. Automation also allows agencies to save money – now, they can offer information about the law online, rather than relying solely on expensive human customer service representatives. Further, automated legal guidance can even help agencies provide more uniform guidance to the public than human representatives in federal agencies would provide.

But automating legal guidance to the public also imposes significant costs. Federal law is extremely complicated for a reason. There are many nuances and exceptions, ambiguities, open questions, and conflicts that exist in governing legal sources. As our research over several years and across several different areas of law has revealed, automated legal guidance inherently involves flattening out some of this complexity. By attempting to present complex law as if it is simple, the federal government has to offer representations of it that deviate from the underlying formal law itself (a phenomenon we have termed "simplexity").

While this is true for many types of explanations of the law, simplexity can be particularly acute for automated legal guidance. As agency officials recognize, when members of the public turn to their computers, phones, and other devices to obtain automated guidance from agencies about the law, they expect this guidance to be quick and concise. With other rapid-fire interactions on the internet as their baseline, users are not interested in or, often, even capable of, absorbing intricate legal exceptions or nuances. Rather, they expect straightforward answers to even the most complicated legal questions. When agencies oblige by providing these seemingly straightforward answers, even when the underlying formal law is, in fact, murkier, the agency guidance may lead people to forego benefits to which they are entitled. Conversely, members of the public may take positions that are too advantageous to them, relative to the underlying federal law.

Worsening some of these outcomes is the fact that automated legal guidance is not subject to many of the procedures and protections that apply to the underlying federal statutes, regulations, and case law. A robust system of administrative law governs the ways that agencies make legal pronouncements. Administrative law does so because of the realization that members of the public will obey what agencies say. Consequently, governmental legitimacy requires agencies to use appropriate, transparent, inclusive, and challengeable procedures to make statements that will substantially impact public rights and responsibilities.

Automated legal guidance, however, is not subject to this procedural framework. This dearth of procedural protections reflects a broader lack of attention in administrative law to the ways that federal agencies influence public perceptions of the law. Administrative law focuses, instead, on the relationship between administrative agencies and sophisticated insiders.

Beyond these procedural differences, automated legal guidance lacks the reliability and penalty protection applicable to and inherent in more formal sources of law, such as statutes, regulations, and case law. As a result, if, for instance, a taxpayer relies on the IRS's own statements in its automated legal guidance tool, the Interactive Tax Assistant, to the taxpayer's detriment, the taxpayer would not be able to hold the IRS to that automated information. As a result, the taxpayer would have a hard time being able use that information to avoid many civil tax penalties. In this way, the federal government's own automated statements about the law are less reliable even than the Air Canada chatbot's erroneous statement about the airline's flight policies, which we discussed in the introduction to this book.[1]

Federal agencies' development and promotion of automated legal guidance, combined with the lack of legal protections surrounding such guidance, reflects an uneasy desire to have it both ways. At present, federal agencies are attempting to meet their duty to educate the public about the law by embracing technology and automation. But, at the same time, our system of federal law disclaims automated legal guidance as a legitimate source of law. The result is that, paradoxically, automated legal guidance may be exacerbating an access to justice gap. Members of the public who have the fewest resources are increasingly receiving the least reliable form of law. People who never would have been able to afford to sit in a lawyer's office to discuss how federal law applies to their day-to-day life may thus have greater apparent access to the law. However, the version of the law they are receiving is a far cry from the nuances, and potential advantages, that exist in the actual, governing statutes, regulations, and judicial decisions.

As federal agencies increase their automation of legal guidance in the future, the potential benefits, as well as pitfalls, of this new form of guidance become even more important. While, on an annual basis, millions of users are already using each of the major forms of automated legal guidance we have studied in this book, there is much more potential transformation that may occur ahead. For example, at present, agencies have not yet embraced automation technology that produces its own content in response to users' inquiries. The possibility that agencies may do this, which could result in users receiving "hallucinated" answers or other deviations from the underlying law, makes questions of reliability and procedural protections only more pressing. The possibility of further technological change, rooted in the same benefits and concerns that we identify, makes it even more important that we think carefully now about what is gained, and what is lost, when agencies automate their legal guidance.

This book has explored the benefits and costs of automated legal guidance and situated this discussion in a broader examination of what our legal system treats as law, who receives the benefits of what kinds of law, and why. We have offered several prescriptions for the future automation of legal guidance. We have outlined detailed policy proposals regarding agencies' use of chatbots, virtual assistants, and other automated tools to explain the law to the public. In addition, we have described how agency officials should invite participation from the public in their design and delivery of these tools. We have also proposed that policymakers should create formal opportunities for members of the public, and representatives acting on their behalf, to assert formal challenges against agencies when their automated tools make statements that are inconsistent with the underlying formal law. These prescriptions offer both concrete ways to improve existing forms of automated legal guidance and broader frameworks to guide the evolution of automated legal guidance that we may see in the future. Our prescriptions also call for administrative law to take more seriously the ways that agencies influence public perceptions of law.

Automating legal guidance can be a useful tool to make the law that applies to many aspects of daily life accessible to those who are living it. In many ways, automated legal guidance can be viewed as part of the story of how technology can democratize access to resources that were previously out of reach to many individuals. But this is only true if we are also cognizant of how automation can facilitate deviations from the law, in ways that the public may not see or understand. Our hope is that this book will help ensure that legislators, agency officials, other policymakers, and legal scholars consider not only efficiency but also accuracy, transparency, equity, and accountability when evaluating automation of the government's interactions with the public, both now and in the future.

NOTE

1. *Moffatt v. Air Canada*, 2024 BCCRT 149 (Can.).

Index

18F team (GSA), 33
21st Century Integrated Digital Experience Act (21st Century IDEA), 31, 107

access to justice, unequal, 127–35
Administrative Conference of the United States (ACUS)
    agency official interviews, facilitation of, 95
    Assembly of the Conference, 97
    broader agency use of social media, encouragement of, 156
    charges for this study, 96–97
    description of, 8
    ombuds offices study (2016), 197
    plain language in regulatory drafting, 2017 report on, 60
    policy recommendations (June 2023), 185–87
administrative guidance. *See* agency guidance
administrative law, 5
    ACUS, advisory role of, 8, 71, 97
    Administrative Procedure Act (APA), 131, 146–47, 152
        adequate notice requirement, 153
        finality and ripeness requirements (for agency actions), 157
        original values of, commitment to transparency, inclusion, and fairness, 191
    agency guidance, uncategorized in, 148–52
    categories of agency statements
        interpretive rules, 147, 150–51
        legislative rules (also called substantive rules), 124–25, 147, 149–50, 153–55, 158
        policy statements, 147, 151
    complexity of, 161
    democracy deficit in, 187–201
    distinctions between agency statement categories (confusion regarding), 148
    e-rulemaking, 155
    guardrails for agency statements, providing, 145–47
    influence over, by industry insiders, 153
    notice-and-comment rulemaking, 5, 125, 147, 153–55
        democratization of, call for, 191
        domination of, by industry groups, 190
        executive summary requirement, 155
        sophisticated parties, 9, 145, 148, 154, 156–58, 160, 187, 192
Administrative Procedure Act (APA). *See* administrative law
administrative rulemaking. *See* administrative law
Affordable Care Act. *See* Patient Protection and Affordable Care Act of 2010
agencies (federal)
    applicability of Plain Writing Act to, 67
    automated legal guidance, use of, 97
    calls to digitize, initial responses to, 31–33
    as customer service providers, 27–29
    customer service standards, 2014 GAO audit of, 30
    digitization of services, 29–34
    duty to explain the law to the public, 4, 160
    external advisory groups
        Internal Revenue Service Advisory Council, 195
        National Board for Education Sciences, 195
    inadequate funding for, 30
    missions, 31, 35
    plain writing requirement, oversight of, 59
    pro bono legal advising services, need for ongoing support of, 185
    understandable explanations of law, expectation to provide, 5, 102–3, 111
agency actions
    finality and ripeness of (APA requirements to challenge them), 157

agency communications
  challenging, 157–59, 196–98
  formats of, 192
  future of, proposals for, 187–201
  plain writing approaches, 61
  public evaluation of, call for, 195
agency explanations (of the law). *See* agency guidance
agency guidance, 34–39, 155–57. *See also* automated legal guidance
  administrative law, uncategorized in, 148–52
  challenging, 157–59
  definition of (as a legal term of art), 34
  format formality, range of, 155
  influence on the public, 5
  nonbinding nature of, 4, 34, 186, 191
  notice-and-comment rulemaking requirements, non-applicability to, 146–47
  printed publications and notices, 5, 41, 111
  proposal to make binding on agencies, drawbacks of, 186–87, 191
  public trust of (compared to information from third parties), 123
  quasi-binding function of, 5
  regulated parties, overly favorable to (difficult to challenge), 159
  significant guidance documents, definition of, 147
agency officials. *See also* interviews (for this study)
  automated legal guidance, beliefs about, 8, 89–108, 135–36, 160, 178
  automated legal guidance, endorsement of, 112
  automated legal guidance system oversight, lack of knowledge about, 180
  budgetary considerations of, 112
  challenges facing automated legal guidance, citing, 106
  generative AI, reasons for not using in automated legal guidance, 103
  interviews of, 3, 8, 89–108
  Plain Writing Act, implementing, 60–61
  private sector analogue, attention paid to, 107, 160
  selection process for study interviews, 97
agency ombuds offices
  description of, 197
agency regulations
  attempts to decrease volume of, 128
  binding nature of, 145
  definitions of vague statutory terms, providing, 64
  length and complexity of, 37
  Medicare, 40
  promulgation of, 5
  TSA, 40
  USDA, 40
agency rulemaking, framework for. *See* administrative law
Aidan (FSA virtual assistant), 2
  agency communications with students, modernizing, 43
  comparison to ITA, 47
  disclaimers, lack of, 127
  explanations of changes made over time, lack of, 172–73
  functionality limits of, 48
  generally, 42–43
  nature of inquiries answered, 42
  technological features, 47
  testing of, over time (by authors), 173
  use of natural language sorting model, 45
Air Canada, 1–2
Akram v. Holder (Seventh Circuit Court of Appeals case), 73
algorithms, use of, 18, 20
Amazon, 16–17, 27, 34, 48, 100, 160
ambiguity. *See* formal law, ambiguity in
American Mining Congress v. Mine Safety and Health Administration (Federal Court of Appeals for the D.C. Circuit case), 150
American Rescue Plan of 2021, 33, 41
artificial intelligence (AI). *See also* generative AI; machine learning; natural language processing
  biases in data, reflecting, 19
  continued evolution of, possibilities created by, 117
  customer service industry, adoption by, 15, 18, 160
  definition of, 14
  DoNotPay.com, use of, 122
  future potential future use of to automatically complete tax returns, 198
  hallucinations. *See* hallucinations (AI)
  human customer service agents, replacing, 15
  large language models, built on, 5
  use of, by Aidan, 42, 47
  use of, by Emma, 45
  VA chatbot, use of, 33
Artificial Intelligence Center of Excellence (GSA), 33
Assembly of the Conference. *See* Administrative Conference of the United States (ACUS)
attention limitations, 37, 41
attorneys. *See* lawyers
automated customer service tools, 11–20
  banking industry, 14, 20

Index

companies, benefits for, 19
competitive advantage of, 15
customers, benefits for, 18
human interaction, impact on, 13
rapid responses, value of (to consumers), 88
travel industry, 15
automated legal guidance
  administration of
    advance testing (prior to release), 183
    challenges (per agency officials), 106
    development process and personnel, 100–2, 180–82
    effectiveness of, per agency officials, 106, 181
    evaluation methods, 106
    measuring performance, 106
    success, measuring (by agency officials), 100, 106
    supervisory role, 101, 108
    technology acquisition process, 101, 182
    usability, focus on (by agency officials), 99, 102–3
  agency officials' beliefs about, 8, 89–108, 135–36, 178
  answers provided by
    consistent with law, example of, 78–79
    failure to consider exercises of discretion, example of, 77
    lacking context and nuance, example of, 73
    non-incorporation of discretionary guidance, example of, 76
    simplifying law to user's benefit, examples of, 79–82
    simplifying law to user's detriment, examples of, 82–85, 131, 148–49
    too narrow, example of, 74
  archiving, public need for, 173
  benefits, 8
    24/7 availability, 112
    administrative efficiency, 89, 110–13
    communication of law to the public, 89, 108–18
    conciseness of information given, 103
    consistency of information given, 110, 116
    cost savings, 110, 112
    democracy, positive impact on, 156
    double-edged nature of, 135
    facilitiation of wide access to legal information, 156
    immediacy of responses, 88
    speed of (compared to other information sources), 111, 193
  concierge role of Emma (USCIS virtual assistant), 45

  content
    agency control over, 103–4
    development and updating, process for, 100–2
    vetting of, 104–5
  customer feedback, nature of, 99, 181
  distributive costs in using, 8
  drawbacks, 9
    archiving of information, lack of, 99, 105–6, 136, 172–73
    categorizing questions, issues with, 76
    decreasing agency accountability, 124
    democracy, negative impact on, 138–61
    deviation from underlying law, 85, 89, 121, 123–25, 130, 135
    ease of use, risks of, 108
    effective dates of information provided, lack of, 173
    evaluation methods, lack of, 136
    formal procedure, lack of, 125
    human-like appearance of (when not actually human), 180
    inaccurate guidance, providing, 6–8, 72–85, 87–88, 121, 130–31, 135, 152, 196
    inequities, perpetuating, 9, 127–35, 138, 177
    legal defenses, ineligiblity to support, 9, 121
    nonbinding nature of, 3, 9, 105, 121, 132, 136, 175, 179
    nonofficial nature of, 133
    notices of changes over time, lack of, 172–73
    omissions of important information, 125–27, 135
    personalized answers, impact of, 86–87, 112, 121, 135
    simplexity, reliance on, 5, 67–89
    user interaction records, lack of, 177–78
    warnings and disclaimers, lack of, 178–80
  evolution of, proposals for, 161–87
  generally, 20–48
  government as author, importance of, 122–23
  human customer service agents, no direct contact to, 184
  natural language sorting models, 45
  plain language, use of in, 156
  print guidance, comparisons to, 86
  reliance on (by users)
    for penalty defenses, 174, 176–77
  second-person pronouns, use of, 86
  two model types, comparison of, 72
  unilateral vs. bilateral guidance
    bilateral, making binding on agencies, reasons against, 176
    definitions, 174
    unilateral, as provided by Emma, 175
    unilateral, making binding on agencies, reasons for, 175

automated legal guidance (cont.)
  user interaction records, lack of, 136
  user surveys, proposed addition of, 184
  user-friendliness, as a fundamental goal, 96, 182
  warnings about conflicting formal law, need for, 171
automatic teller machines (ATMs), 13
automation
  access-to-justice gap, increasing, 129
  risks of, 19–20

Bagley, Nicholas, 192
Bearer-Friend, Jeremy, 183
Bennett v. Speer (US Supreme Court case), 157
Berthoz, Alain, 63
bias
  in administrative law, toward sophisticated parties, 145, 148, 154, 156–58, 160, 187, 192
  in data, based on personal demographics, 19
Biden, Joe, 29, 31, 107, 136, 183
Bing, 72
biometrics, 14
border security, 43
Bowker, Aaron, 77
Braley, Bruce, 59
British Columbia Civil Resolution Tribunal, 1
Bureau of Alcohol, Tobacco, Firearms, and Explosives (ATF)
  Firearms Regulations Reference Guide 2005, challenge to, 158

Cardozo, Benjamin, 65
CARES Act, 194–95
carried interest (in income tax law), 133
case law. *See* formal law
Census Bureau, 184
Centers for Disease Control (CDC), 60
chatbots, 16–17, 33
  Air Canada, 1
  increased government use of, 41
  IRS use of, 32
  VA use of, 32
ChatGPT, 5, 17–18, 116
Child Tax Credit, 33
Children's Health Insurance Program (CHIP), 28
CIC Services, LLC v. IRS (US Supreme Court case), 131
class action lawsuits, 196
Clinton, Bill, 29, 107
Code of Federal Regulations, 152
coercive power (of the government), 27, 159
Coglianese, Cary, 155
Congress, 29, 31, 36, 67, 115, 118
  agency funding, allocating, 112

comparative print (of bills that amend a law), requirement of, 126
  dynamics of, 36
  embrace of agencies' customer services role, 28
  legislation enacted to serve the public interest, 159
  political polarization of, 128
Congressional Joint Committee on Taxation, 126
Constitution, 40
consumer expectations (as influenced by automation), 20
Court of Appeals for the District of Columbia Circuit, 37
Court of Appeals for the Second Circuit, 36
courts
  non-applicability of Plain Writing Act to, 67
covered documents (under the Plain Writing Act of 2010), 59
COVID-19 pandemic, 17, 27, 30, 47, 76, 79, 112–13, 194
COVID-19 vaccines. *See* vaccine finder tool (for COVID-19 vaccines)
customer
  government definition of, 28
customer expectations (as influenced by automation), 5, 102–3
customer experience
  government definition of, 28
customer service agents (human)
  AI, replacing, 15–16
  availability barriers, 26, 34, 112
  availability of through automated legal guidance, lack of, 184
  IRS, 30, 111
  limited customer engagement capacity, 42
  limits of, 38–39, 111
  ongoing need for agencies to provide, 185
  USCIS case workers, 45
Customs and Border Protection (CBP), 43, 77
  customer service standards, 30

DALL-E 2, 17
data
  automated systems, use of, 14–16
  from automated legal guidance users, agency collection of, 182–84
data privacy, 19, 183
Davis, Kenneth Culp, 153
decision tree answer model, 47, 72, 100, 104, 138, 174
decision-making. *See* human decision-making abilities
deep learning (element of machine learning), 14

Index

Defense of Marriage Act (DOMA), 126
Deferred Action for Childhood Arrivals (DACA), 147
democracy
    automated legal guidance, impact on, 138–61
    threats to, from generative AI, 19
Department of Agriculture (USDA)
    AskUSDA, 39–40
Department of Defense (DOD)
    plain writing training, 60
Department of Education, 37, 200
    2024–25 FAFSA form automation, 199–200
    FSA office, 28, 42
Department of Health and Human Services' (HHS), 28
Department of Homeland Security (DHS), 43
Department of Justice (DOJ)
    guidance policy, 136–37
    power of, 27
Department of Labor (DOL), 35
    power of, 27
Department of Veterans Affairs (VA), 28, 32–33
development (of automated legal guidance tools). *See* automated legal guidance
DeVos, Betsy, 43
digital media, 38
Digital.gov (website), 31
digitized consumer experience, 15
disability benefits, 130
discrimination
    generative AI, perpetuating, 19
DoNotPay.com, 122

Earned Income Tax Credit, 33
eighth-grade reading level, 41
Emma (USCIS virtual assistant), 2
    ability to learn over time, 45
    comparison to ITA, 47
    generally, 43–46
    input/output model used, 104
    K visa question (testing example), 72–74
    launch of, 44
    law as unambiguous, notable portrayal of, 125
    locating, 44
    permanent resident questions (testing examples), 74–78
    simplexity, use of (test results), 72–78
    statistics on questions answered, 45, 193
    tasks performed, 116
    unilateral guidance, providing, example of, 175
    unmet agency goals, 45
    use of natural language sorting model, 45
    warning to users of conflicting formal law (proposed), example of, 172

environmental law, 4, 36
e-rulemaking. *See* administrative law
exceptions, deemphasizing (in agency publications), 61
Executive Order 12862, 29, 107
Executive Order 13571, 29, 31
Executive Order 13891, 136
Executive Order 14058, 29, 31
Expedia, 15, 18, 160
expenses, deductibility of
    artificial teeth, 80, 87
    charitable contributions, 84
    cosmetic surgery, 79–80, 87
    household help, 8, 148
    lead-based paint removal, 80
    medical, 8, 46, 78, 80, 83, 87, 124, 148
    ordinary business expenses, 64–67, 81
    qualified long-term care services (as medical expenses), 148
    trade or business, 7
    university tuition, 6, 132
    work clothing, 81
explanations of the law (by agencies). *See* agency guidance

Facebook, 39, 44, 196
Facebook Messenger, 39
facial scanning, 14
FAFSA Simplification Act, 199
Family and Medical Leave Act, 35
FAQs (on government websites), 128, 173, 187
federal agencies. *See* agencies (federal)
Federal Aviation Agency (FAA), 60
federal inspectors general (operating within federal agencies)
    review of agency guidance, potential to provide, 198
Federal Register, 152, 185
Federal Student Aid (FSA) office. *See also* Aidan (FSA virtual assistant)
    Aidan (virtual assistant), 2
    automated legal guidance tools, 97
    customer service standards, 30
    digitization of services, 27
    guidance, nature of, 42
    services, description of, 28
Food and Drug Administration (FDA)
    good guidance practices, 136, 193
    public comments on guidance documents, solicitation of, 194
    regulatory practice, 155
Forest Service
    customer service standards, 30

Index

formal law
  agency interpretation of (through guidance), 9
  ambiguity in, 5, 9, 36, 57, 64–65, 114, 124, 134, 171, 178, 185, 196, 206
  binding nature of, 128
  case law
    circuit splits, 171
  complexity of, 3–5, 7, 35–38, 41, 57–58, 64, 89, 100, 107, 134, 161, 185
  components of (legislation, case law, and regulations), 4, 57, 113, 128, 207
  deviations from in agency guidance, impact of, 10, 58, 67, 123–25
  informal law, compared to, 127–35
  meaningful access to, lack of (by the general public), 127, 161
  public engagement with, through automated legal guidance, 108–18
  unsettled nature of, 171–72
Fostering Undergraduate Talent by Unlocking Resources for Education Act (FUTURE Act), 199
Free Application for Federal Student Aid (FAFSA), 42, 199–200

general public
  access to lawyers, lack of, 9, 58, 108, 110, 113, 121, 127–35, 138, 185, 206
  administrative rulemaking process, participating in, 154
  administrative state transparency, benefits to, 171
  agencies, interactions with, 198
  attention limitations of, 37
  automated legal guidance, expectations of, 5, 102–3, 206
  automated legal guidance, trust in, 122–23
  benefitting through plain writing, 61
  disparate impact of automated legal guidance on, 10, 124, 130
  relationship with the law, 5, 36, 161, 192, 200
  reliance on agency guidance, risks of, 5, 107, 206
  sharing information with (by agencies), 39
  simplicity
    detrimental impact on, 48, 58, 67, 72, 138
    treatment of by agencies, 9
  understanding the law, difficulty in, 4, 107
General Services Administration (GSA), 33, 97
generative AI, 14, 17–18
  automated legal guidance, not currently used in, 103–4
  customer service, suited to revolutionize, 17

Golden & Zimmerman, LLC v. Domenech (Fourth Circuit Court of Appeals case), 158
Google, 17, 27, 72
Government Accountability Office (GAO), 27
  government customer service standards, 2014 review of, 30
  review of agency guidance, potential to provide, 198
government guidance. See agency guidance
Government Performance and Results Act of 1993, 29
Government watchdog organizations
  Plain Writing Act, praise for, 60
GPRA Modernization Act of 2010, 29
Green Card (immigration), 45
Greene, Sara Sternberg, 130
guidance. See agency guidance
Gun Control Act, 158
Gunderson v. Hood (Federal Court of Appeals for the Ninth Circuit case), 151

hallucinations (AI), 1, 19, 207
HealthCare.gov (website), 33
Heckler v. Chaney (US Supeme Court case), 159
HHS Centers for Medicare and Medicaid Services (CMS), 28
human decision-making abilities
  threats to (from automation), 19, 37
human in the loop practice (in AI), 45
human-centered design, 31, 107

image recognition (element of deep learning), 14
Immigration and Customs Enforcement (ICE), 43
immigration law, 36, 38, 75
  widespread applicability of, 37
inequities (inherent in the legal system)
  automated legal guidance, use of, perpetuating, 9, 127–35, 138, 177
Inflation Reduction Act, 46
informal guidance. See agency guidance
informal law, 155–57
  components of (automated legal guidance, form instructions, and website FAQs), 128
  democracy deficit, representing (by perpetuating agency communication hierarchies), 157
Interactive Tax Assistant (ITA) (IRS virtual assistant)
  advisory statement (that answers are not "written advice"), 127
  agency explanation, example of, 148
  answers provided by (during testing), categories of, 78

Index

availability through IRS website, 2
basic tax compliance issues, correct handling of, 79
binary approach to answering questions, drawbacks of, 87
decision-tree model, use of, 174
development of, 46–47
fast and seemingly clear guidance, providing, 7
guidance topics, examples of, 47
input/output model used, 104
interaction example (tuition deductibility questions), 6
record of exchange, providing to users, 178
simplexity, use of (test results), 78–85
simplification of tax law, taxpayer-favorable examples, 79–82
speed of (compared to other information sources), 111
user trust in, 123
warnings to users of conflicting formal law (proposed), example of, 172
Interactive Tax Law Assistant (ITLA)
as precursor to ITA (IRS's current virtual assistant), 46
Interagency Working Group on Equitable Data, 183
Internal Revenue Code (IRC), 4, 59, 66, 80, 114, 134, 148, 176
revenue rulings, as official interpretations of, 156
Internal Revenue Service (IRS). *See also* Interactive Tax Assistant (ITA) (IRS virtual assistant)
2023 report on automated taxpayer support, 32
automated legal guidance tools, comparatively well-developed, 97
budget cuts, impact of on customer service, 46
CARES Act payments to deceased individuals, guidance about (on website FAQ), 194
customer service agents, 39
customer service mandate, 35
customer service volume, 28
digitization of services, 27
duties, nature of, 4
duty to assist the public, 58
Form 1040, 65, 79, 112
Free File program, 185, 198
guidance, range of, 155
historical development of automated tools, 46–47, 115
informal guidance, nature of, 156
insufficient funding of, 30
internal memoranda, 66
Internal Revenue Bulletin (IRB), official publication of, 133–34, 176, 186

ITA, description of, 78
listed transactions, designation of, 131
making ITA statements binding on the agency, reasons against, 176
mission statement, 35, 59
online filing options, expanded, 32
online form for public comments, 194
phone assistors, 39
plain writing requirement, implementation of, 60
printed publications, 46, 88
printed publications, use of caution symbol, 172
public information, duty to provide, 35
publications, audience-based tailoring, 61
records of ITA exchanges, providing to taxpayers, 178
revenue rulings, 80, 83, 134, 155, 158, 172, 176
revenue rulings, IRS-authorized reliance on, 156
revenue rulings, public cataloging of, 156
seeking automated assistance from, process, 6
simplexity, use of, 64–67
statements in the IRB, considered bound to (self-binding model), 186
Taxpayer Bill of Rights, duties under, 35
telephone hotlines, 41
website, 35
website FAQs, commitment to archiving, 173
Internal Revenue Service Restructuring and Reform Act of 1998, 35, 59
International Travel as a Permanent Resident (website guidance), 74, 77
interpretive rules (issued by agencies). *See* administrative law
interviews (for this study), 178
format of, 98–99
interviewees, selection process for, 97
outcomes, contextualized, 106–8
outcomes, summary of, 99–106
questions asked, 98
Intuit, 65, 112, 123, 134
IRS assistors, 46
IRS Publication 502 (Medical Expenses), 87
IRS Publication 526 (Charitable Contributions), 84
IRS Publication 535 (Business Expenses), 65

Judicial Conference of the United States
ACUS charge to inform, 96
judicial decisions
precedential value of, 37
judicial deference (to agency interpretations of statutes), 37
judicial review (of agency actions)
expansion of, not included in this proposal, 191
finality requirement, 157

judicial review (of legislative rules issued by agencies), 147, 150, 153, 155

K Visa (Fiance Visa) (immigration), 45
Khanna, Ro, 31

labor law, 4, 35
  widespread applicability of, 37
language
  English proficiency, 41
  government speak, 2, 44–45, 185
  incorrect simplification of (in automated legal guidance), 82
  legalese, 61
  plain (mandatory use of by government agencies), 48–62
  Spanish, 41, 44–45
laptops, 27, 32
law, formal. *See* formal law
law, formal vs. informal
  unequal access to justice, creating, 127–35
law, understandable explanations of
  in automated legal guidance, 41, 67–89
  by lawyers, 38
law, unsettled, 7
lawyers
  access to, benefits of, 38
  access to, class-based differences, 9, 58, 108, 110, 113, 121, 124, 127–35, 138, 185, 206
Lazarus, Emma, 44
legal counsel. *See* lawyers
legal drafting, 128
legal frameworks, 34, 40–41
legal guidance (issued by agencies). *See* agency guidance
legal regimes, 34, 37, 40–41
Legal Services Corporation, 129
legislation. *See* formal law
legislation, "unorthodox" (used to accomplish Congressional objectives), 128
Levin, Ronald, 150
Link v. *Commissioner* (U.S. Tax Court case), 7
literacy proficiency
  rates of, in American adults, 37
litigation, 9
loneliness epidemic (impacted by automation), 20

machine learning, 14, 16, 20
Manual on the Administrative Procedure Act, 150–51
McGarity, Thomas, 147
McKinsey & Company, 17–18
Medicaid, 28
Medicare, 28, 37
  What's Covered app, 39–40

Medicare Act, 40
Mendelson, Nina, 159
Metzger, Gillian, 191
Microsoft, 17
  Clippy (early example of virtual assistant), 180
Miller v. *Commissioner* (US Tax Court case), 132
Moffatt, Jake, 1–2
my Social Security portal, 32

National Park Service (NPS)
  customer service standards, 30
national parks, 28
National Taxpayer Advocate, 30, 32, 194, 197
natural language processing, 14, 16
  use of, by Aidan, 42, 47
  use of, by Emma, 104
  use of (to interpret questions) in automated legal guidance, 104
natural language sorting model, 45, 72, 100
Netflix, 16, 48
New Deal, 146, 192
New York Times, 133
Noah, Lars, 155
notice-and-comment rulemaking. *See* administrative law

Obama, Barack, 29, 31, 33
Obamacare. *See* Patient Protection and Affordable Care Act of 2010
Office of Information and Regulatory Affairs (OIRA) (OMB), 60–61, 155
Office of Investor Education and Advocacy (SEC), 35
Office of Management and Budget (OMB), 29, 31, 60, 107
  embrace of agencies' customer services role, 29
  good guidance practices (for agencies), adoption of, 147
Olson, Nina, 194
ombuds. *See* agency ombuds offices
outside experts, 181
outside vendors, 182

partisanship (political), 36
passports, 30, 74
Patient Protection and Affordable Care Act of 2010, 36
people with disabilities, 130
personalized communications, impact of, 86
Pevsner v. *Commissioner* (Fifth Circuit Court of Appeals case), 81
Physical Presence Requirements for Naturalization (website guidance), 75
plain language
  agencies, mandatory use of, 48–62

Index

ambiguities and complexities in law, failure to capture, 67
Plain Language Action and Information Network (PLAIN), 60
  digital content, recommendations for, 62
Plain Language Guidelines, 61–62
plain writing
  definition of (Plain Writing Act of 2010), 59
  widely-adopted approaches, 61
Plain Writing Act of 2010, 59, 63, 149
  covered documents, 59
  paper and electronic documents, applicability to, 59
policy statements (issued by administrative agencies). See administrative law
President
  ACUS charge to inform, 96
presidential administrations. See *specific names of President*
Presidential Innovation Fellows (GSA), 33
private sector customer service model
  as a benchmark for government agencies, 29, 31–32, 40–41, 88, 160
promulgation (of regulations). See administrative law

readability
  of legislation, 37
refugee applications, 44
regulations. See formal law
ripeness doctrine (administrative law). See agency actions
robotics, 32
rurality, 130

scholarships
  taxability of, 82, 131
second-person pronouns
  use of, by automated legal guidance, 86–87
Secretary of Education, 43
Secretary of Health and Human Services, 40
Securities and Exchange Commission (SEC), 35
Shepherd, George B., 146
significant guidance documents. See agency guidance
simplicity
  automated legal guidance, use of in, 67–89, 171
  characterization of (by Alain Berthoz), 63
  description of, 5, 57, 62
  general public
    detrimental impact on, 67, 124
  generally, 48–67
  need for, in automated legal guidance, 135
  nonqualified information provided, impact of, 87–88

  use of, in IRS publications, 64–67
  use of, in law (generally), 64
simplexity vs. simplicity, 57, 62–64
simplicity
  description of (by Cass Sunstein), 63
  tax reform, use in, 63
  use of, in law (generally), 63
Small Business Administration National Ombudsman, 197
smartphones, 27
social justice, as undermined by legal system inequities, 128
social media, 38–39, 44
  ACUS position of agency use of, 156
  agency use of, importance for public engagement, 157
  IRS use of, 156
Social Security, 4
Social Security Act, 40
Social Security Administration (SSA), 32
  digitization of services, 27
  workload of, as impacting customer service, 30
speech recognition, 17
Stable Diffusion, 17
Stack, Kevin, 191
Starbucks, 16, 27, 96, 144, 160
State Department, 30
Statue of Liberty, 44
statutes. See formal law
statutory interpretation (by the courts), 37
Stitch Fix, 15, 18–19, 48, 160
Student Aid Index, 199
student loans, 26, 28, 42, 57
substantive rules (issued by agencies). See administrative law
Sunstein, Cass, 60, 62–63

tax audits, 4, 7, 9, 81–82
  advice of tax lawyers, benefits of, 133
  fear of, generational, 122
Tax Cuts and Jobs Act of 2017, 36, 63
tax deductions, 6, 8
tax fraud, 27
tax law. See *also* expenses, deductibility of
  authoritative sources of, 132
  challenges to, 36
  changes to, as explained by Joint Committee on Taxation, 126
  communication of by IRS publications, 64
  complexity and unsettled nature of, 7
  excessive administrative proceduralism, arguments against, 192
  IRS duty to explain to taxpayers, 58
  ITA, as explanatory resource, 78

tax law (cont.)
  ITA answers, consistent with, 78–79
  meaning of (not alterable by administrative guidance), 132
  penalty defenses, raising, 134
  personal and business transactions, application of, 4
  private equity industry, influence over, 133–34
  reliance on, showing of (in reasonable basis penalty defense), 134, 176
  reliance on, showing of (in reasonable cause and good faith tax penalty defense), 176–77
  simplification of, in ITA answers, 79–85
  taxpayer understanding of, eroded by tax preparation software, 118
  transaction of interest, as a reportable transaction, 131
  widespread applicability of, 37
tax penalties, 7
tax practitioners
  IRS revenue rulings, reliance on, 156
taxable income
  academic scholarships, fellowships, and grants, 82, 131
Taxpayer Advocate Service, 32
Taxpayer Bill of Rights, 35, 59
Technology Transformation Services (TTS) (GSA), 33
texting, 38
transparency in government communications
  benefits of, 171
Transportation Security Administration (TSA), 39–40
  AskTSA messaging tool, 39
Treasury Decisions, 133
Treasury Regulations, 4, 127, 133–34, 156, 176
  as legislative rules in administrative law, 149
Trump, Donald, 29, 136–37
TurboTax, 65, 112, 123, 134, 144, 198
tweets. *See* X (formerly Twitter)
Twitter. *See* X (formerly Twitter)
two-tiered legal system, 127–35, 156

United States Citizenship and Immigration Services (USCIS). *See also* Emma (USCIS virtual assistant)
  2019–2021 strategic plan, 44
  2023–2026 strategic plan, 44
  automated legal guidance tools, comparatively well-developed, 97
  Emma (virtal assistant), 2
  Emma, heavy reliance on, 45, 193
  monthly call center volume, 44
  service mission, 44
  workload statistics (2022), 43
United States Code, 37
United States Digital Service (USDS), 33, 41
United States Postal Service (USPS), 30
United States v. *Windsor* (US Supreme Court case), 126
user experience (UX)
  success of automated legal guidance, variable indicating, 100
  user surveys, conducted by agencies, 106

vaccine finder tool (for COVID-19 vaccines), 33
veterans, 28, 33, 130
Veterans Benefits Administration (VBA)
  customer service standards, 30
Veterans Health Administration
  services, description of, 28
Veterans' Group Life Insurance (VGLI)
  customer service standards, 30
video games, 38
virtual assistants, 16
  increased government use of, 41
virtual barista (Starbucks), 16, 27, 96, 144
visas (immigration), 45, 73
visitor traffic
  success of automated legal guidance, variable indicating, 100
voice bots
  IRS use of, 32

Wagner, Wendy, 154
Walker, Chris, 191
Wealthfront, 16, 18, 160
Webley, Alec, 155
websites (government)
  agency use of, 39
  American Rescue Plan of 2021 benefits, 33, 41
  automated legal guidance command structure notification, suggestion for, 181
  Department of Education, 200
  descriptions of automated guidance tools, 179
  DOL, 35
  drafts of automated explanations, posting on (with public opportunities to comment), 193
  FAQs, non-binding nature of, 128
  FSA, 42, 173
  information available on, 178
  IRS, 2, 6, 35, 46, 64, 176, 194
  lack of searchable archives on, 173
  legislative mandate to modernize, 31
  Plain Language Action and Information Network (PLAIN), 60

Index

plain writing, use of, 59, 62
review process of content, suggestion for, 191
SEC, 35
USCIS, 44–45, 72, 116
VA, 33
warnings, display of, 172
websites (private industry)
  Air Canada, 1
  Amazon, 27
  customer surveys, use of, 184
Welch v. Helvering (US Supreme Court case), 65

Whisper, 17
worker displacement (from automation), 19

X (formerly Twitter), 39, 44
  IRS use of, 47, 156
  tweets, limited legal value of, 156
  tweets, review process of content, suggestion for, 191

Yahoo!, 72
YouTube, 38

Printed by Integrated Books International,
United States of America